Buddha and Buddhism
A Collection

Selected by
Vladimir Orel

THE LIFE OF BUDDHA
A. Ferdinand Herold

—

THE DHAMMAPADA

—

THE SUTTA-NIPÂTA

From the editor

This volume introduces the reader to the life of Buddha and to two important religious writings in the domain of Buddhism. The first of them is *Dhammapada* ("The Path of Dharma"), a collection of mostly ethical sayings traditionally ascribed to Buddha and written in Pali. It constitutes a part of the Buddhist canon in the Theravada tradition. The second text, also belonging to the same tradition, is *Sutta-Nipata*, probably the oldest or one of the oldest Buddhist scriptures reflecting – we can believe – the most conservative form of Buddhism.

THE LIFE OF BUDDHA
A. Ferdinand Herold

—

THE DHAMMAPADA

—

THE SUTTA-NIPÂTA

THE LIFE OF BUDDHA
A. Ferdinand Herold

FOREWORD

This Life of Buddha is not a work of fiction, and I think it would be well to mention the books, both ancient and modern, which I have most frequently consulted.

I have, for the most part, relied upon the LALITAVISTARA. This book is a jumbled collection of legends and scholastic dissertations, and yet in these pages are preserved many precious traditions regarding the Buddha's origin, his childhood and his youth, and here, likewise, we are told of his early education and of his first deeds.

I have also made great use of an excellent poem, the BUDDHACARITA of Asvaghosa. In a few of the chapters I have repeated the lines almost word for word. The text of the BUDDHACARITA was edited by E. B. Cowell.

In the Life, I have interpolated several JATAKAS. These are stories in which the Buddha recalls his former lives. Some of them will be found in a vast collection, the AVADANASATAKA.

Two modern books: LE BOUDDHA, by H. Oldenberg, translated by A. Foucher, and the HISTOIRE DU BOUDDHISME DANS L'INDE, by

H. Kern, translated by Gédéon Huet, have also been very useful to me; as well as other works that have appeared in scientific reviews. Thus, for the touching story of Visvantara, I am indebted to a Sogdian version published by R. Gauthiot in the JOURNAL ASIATIQUE.

Finally, I would be guilty of the deepest ingratitude if I did not publicly thank my old friend Sylvain Lévi for his generous and kindly advice.

And may the reader find of interest this marvelous story of Prince Siddhartha who, through meditation, was able to attain supreme wisdom.

A. F. HEROLD

PART ONE
I. King Suddhodana And Queen Maya

SERENE and magnificent was this city where once had dwelt the great hermit Kapila. It seemed to be built out of some fragment of the sky: the walls were like clouds of light, and the houses and gardens radiated a divine splendor. Precious stones glistened everywhere. Within its gates darkness was as little known as poverty. At night, when silver moonbeams fingered each turret, the city was like a pond of lilies; by day, when the terraces were bathed in golden sunshine, the city was like a river of lotuses.

King Suddhodana reigned in Kapilavastu; he was its brightest ornament. He was kindly and generous, modest and just. He pursued his bravest enemies, and they fell before him in battle like elephants struck down by Indra; and as darkness is dissipated by the sharp rays of the sun, even so were the wicked vanquished by his radiant glory. He brought light into the world, and he pointed out the true path to those who were close to him. His great wisdom gained for him many friends, many courageous, discerning friends, and as starlight intensifies the brightness of the moon, so did their brilliance enhance his splendor.

Suddhodana, king of the Sakya race, had wed many queens. His favorite among these was Maya.

She was very beautiful. It was as if the Goddess Lakshmi herself had strayed into the world. When she spoke, it was like the song of birds in the spring, and her words were sweet and pleasant. Her hair was the color of the black bee; her forehead was as chaste as a diamond; her eyes as cool as a young blue-lotus leaf; and no frown ever marred the exquisite curve of her brows.

She was virtuous. She desired the happiness of her subjects; she was attentive to the pious precepts of her teachers.

She was truthful, and her conduct was exemplary.

King Suddhodana and Queen Maya lived quietly and happily in Kapilavastu.

One day, the queen bathed and perfumed her body, then attired herself in a delicate, colorful robe and covered her arms with jewels. Golden bangles tinkled about her ankles, and her face was radiant with happiness as she sought the king's presence.

Suddhodana was seated in a great hall. Sweet music was lulling his tranquil reverie. Maya took the seat on his right, and she said to him:

"Deign to listen, my lord. Deign to grant the favor I have to ask of you, O protector of the earth."

"Speak, my queen," replied Suddhodana. "What is this favor?"

"My lord, there is great suffering in the world, and I look with compassion on all who suffer. I would be helpful to my fellow-creatures; I would close my mind to evil thoughts. And since I shall forbear doing and thinking evil, since I am thus kind to myself, I would be helpful, I would be kind to others, too. I will put aside pride, O king, and I will not listen to the voice of evil desire. I will never utter a vain or dishonorable word. My lord, henceforth I will lead a life of austerity; I will fast; and I will never bear ill will or commit wickedness, suffer anxiety or hatred, know anger or covetousness. I will be satisfied with my lot; I will forswear deceit and envy; I will be pure; I will walk in the straight path; and I will practice virtue. And because of these things my eyes are now smiling, because of these things my lips are now joyous."

She paused a moment. The king gazed at her in tender admiration. She continued:

"My lord, I ask you to respect my austere life. Do not enter the dim forest of desire; allow me to observe the holy law of abstinence. I shall repair to those apartments that are in the lofty reached of the palace, and there, where the swans build their nests, have prepared for me a couch strewn with flowers, a soft, perfumed couch. My maidens shall attend to my wants, and you may dismiss the eunuchs, the guards and all vulgar servants. I would be spared the sight of ugliness, the sound of revelry and the odor of things unpleasant."

She said no more. The king replied:

"So let it be! The favor you ask, I grant." And he commanded:

"Up there, in the lofty reaches of the palace, where the air throbs with the song of the swans, let the queen, resplendent in gold and precious stones, rest on a couch of rare flowers; and let there be music. And to her maidens, gathered about her, she will be like a daughter of the Gods in some celestial garden!"

The queen rose.

"It is well, my lord," said she. "But hear me further. Free your prisoners. Give generously to the poor. Let men and women and children be happy! Be merciful, O king, and, that the world may be joyous, be a father to all living creatures!"

She then left the hall and went to the top of the royal palace.

It was the advent of spring. Birds darted and wheeled above the terraces; birds sang in the trees. The gardens were in flower; on the surface of the ponds, the lotus buds were unfolding. And, as the queen sought her bower, the piping note of flutes and the deeper harmony of strings resounded of their own accord, and a refulgent glory appeared over the palace, a glory so perfect that the sunlight turned to shadow.

2. Maya's Dream

THE same hour that spring was born, a dream came to Maya as she slept. She saw a young elephant descending from the sky. It had six great tusks; it was as white as the snow on mountain-tops. Maya saw it enter her womb, and thousands of Gods suddenly appeared before her. They praised her with immortal songs, and Maya understood that nevermore would she know disquietude or hatred or anger.

Then she awoke. She was happy; it was a happiness she had never felt before. Arising, she arrayed herself in bright colors, and, followed by her most beautiful maidens, she passed through the palace-gates. She walked in the gardens until she came to a little wood, where she found a shaded seat. Then she sent two of her maidens to King Suddhodana with this message: "That the king should come to the wood; Queen Maya wishes to see him and will await him there."

The king promptly complied. He left the hall where, with the help of his counselors, he had been administering justice to the inhabitants of the city. He walked toward the wood, but, as he was about to enter, a strange feeling came over him. His limbs faltered, his hands trembled and tears welled from his eyes. And he thought:

"Never, not even in the heat of battle when fighting my bravest enemies, have I felt as profoundly disturbed as at this moment. Why is it I can not enter the wood where the queen awaits me? Can anyone explain my agitation?"

Whereupon a great voice thundered in the sky:

"Be happy, King Suddhodana, worthiest of the Sakyas! He who seeks supreme knowledge is about to come into the world. He has chosen your family to be his family because of its fame, good fortune and virtue, and for mother he has chosen the noblest of all women, your wife, Queen Maya. Be happy, King

Suddhodana! He who seeks supreme knowledge would fain be your son!"

The king knew that the Gods were speaking, and he rejoiced. Regaining his serenity, he entered the wood where Maya awaited him.

He saw her; quietly, without arrogance, he asked:

"Why did you send for me? What do you wish?" The queen told him of the dream she had had; then added:

"My lord, there are brahmans who are clever at interpreting dreams. Send for them. They will know if the palace has been visited by good or evil, and if we should rejoice or mourn."

The king agreed, and brahmans familiar with the mystery of dreams were summoned to the palace. When they had heard Maya's story they spoke in this manner:

"A great joy is to be yours, O king, O queen. A son will be born to you, distinguished by the favor of the Gods. If, one day, he should renounce royalty, leave the palace, cast love aside; if, seized with compassion for the worlds, he should live the wandering life of a monk, he will deserve marvelous praise, he will richly deserve magnificent gifts. He will be adored by the worlds, for he will give them that which they hunger after. O master, O mistress, your son will be a Buddha!"

The brahmans withdrew. The king and queen looked at each other, and their faces were radiant with happiness and peace. Suddhodana then ordered that alms be distributed to the poor in Kapilavastu; and food was given to the hungry, drink to the thirsty, and the women received flowers and perfume. Maya became the object of their veneration; the sick crowded her path, and when she extended her right hand they were cured. The blind saw, the deaf heard, the dumb spoke, and when the dying touched a blade of grass she had gathered they recovered at once their health and their

strength. And above the city a ceaseless melody was borne on the wind, exquisite flowers rained from the sky, and songs of gratitude rose on the air around the palace walls.

3. The Birth of Siddhartha

MONTHS passed. Then, one day, the queen knew that the time was approaching for her son to be born. She went to King Suddhodana, and she said to him:

"My lord, I would wander through the happy gardens. Birds are singing in the trees, and the air is bright with flower-dust. I would wander through the happy gardens."

"But it will weary you, O queen," replied Suddhodana. "Are you not afraid?"

"The innocent being that I carry in my womb must be born amid the innocence of budding flowers. No, I will go, O master, I will go into the flower-gardens."

The king yielded to Maya's wish. He said to his servants:

"Go into the gardens and deck them out in silver and in gold. Drape the trees with precious hangings. Let everything be magnificent, for the queen will pass."

Then he addressed Maya:

"Array yourself, to-day, in great splendor, O Maya. Ride in a gorgeous palanquin; let your most beautiful maidens carry you. Order your servants to use rare perfumes; have them wear ropes of pearls and bracelets of precious stones; have them carry lutes and drums and flutes, and sing sweet songs that would delight the Gods themselves."

Suddhodana was obeyed, and when the queen reached the palace-gates the guards greeted her with joyous cries. Bells peeled gaily, peacocks spread their gorgeous tail-feathers, and the song of swans throbbed in the air.

They came to a wood where the trees were in bloom, and Maya ordered them to set down the palanquin. She stepped out and began wandering about, aimlessly. She was happy. And behold! she found a rare tree, the branches drooping under their burden of blossoms. She went up to it; gracefully extending her hand, she drew down a branch. Suddenly, she stood very still. She smiled, and the maidens who were near her received a lovely child into their arms.

At that same moment all that was alive in the world trembled with joy. The earth quivered. Songs and the patter of dancing feet echoed in the sky. Trees of all seasons burst into flower, and ripe fruit hung from the branches. A pure, serene light appeared in the sky. The sick were rid of their suffering. The hungry were satisfied. Those to whom wine had played false became sober. Madmen recovered their reason, the weak their strength, the poor their wealth. Prisons opened their gates. The wicked were cleansed of all evil.

One of Maya's maidens hastened to King Suddhodana and joyously exclaimed:

"My lord, my lord, a son is born to you, a son who will bring great glory to your house!"

He was speechless. But his face was radiant with joy, and he knew great happiness.

Presently he summoned all the Sakyas, and he commanded them to accompany him into the garden where the child had been born. They obeyed, and, with a host of brahmans in attendance, they formed a noble retinue as they gravely followed the king.

When he came near the child, the king made a deep obeisance, and he said:

"Do you bow as I bow before the prince, to whom I give the name Siddhartha."

They all bowed, and the brahmans, inspired by the Gods, then sang:

"All creatures are happy, and they are no longer rough, those roads traveled by men, for he is born, he who gives happiness: he will bring happiness into the world. In the darkness a great light has dawned, the sun and the moon are like dying embers, for he is born, he who gives light: he will bring light into the world. The blind see, the deaf hear, the foolish have recovered their reason, for he is born, he who restores sight, and restores hearing, and restores the mind: he will bring sight, he will bring hearing, he will bring reason into the world. Perfumed zephyrs ease the suffering of mankind, for he is born, he who heals: he will bring health into the world. Flames are no longer pitiless, the flow of rivers has been stayed, the earth has trembled gently: he will be the one to see the truth."

4. Asita's Prediction

THE great hermit Asita, whose austerities were pleasing to the Gods, heard of the birth of him who was to save mankind from the torment of rebirth. In his thirst for the true law, he came to the palace of King Suddhodana and gravely approached the women's quarters. His years and his learning lent him great dignity.

The king showed him the courtesies that custom prescribed and addressed him in a seemly manner:

"Happy, indeed, am I! Truly, this child of mine will enjoy distinguished favor, for the venerable Asita has come purposely to see me. Command me. What must I do? I am your disciple, your servant."

The hermit, his eyes shining with the light of joy, gravely spoke these words:

"This has happened to you, O noble, generous and hospitable king, because you love duty and because you are ever kind to those who are wise and to those who are full of years. This has happened to you because your ancestors, though rich in land and rich in gold, were above all rich in virtue. Know the reason for my coming, O king, and rejoice. In the air I heard a divine voice speaking and it said: 'A son has been born to the king of the Sakyas, a son who will have the true knowledge.' I heard these words, and I came, and my eyes shall now behold the glory of the Sakyas."

Overwhelmed with joy, the king went to fetch the child. Taking him from his nurse's breast, he showed him to the aged Asita.

The hermit noticed that the king's son bore the marks of omnipotence. His gaze hovered over the child, and presently his lashes were wet with tears. Then he sighed and turned his eyes to the sky.

The king saw that Asita was weeping, and he began to fear for his son. He questioned the old man:

"You say, O venerable roan, that my son's body differs little from that of a God. You say that his birth was a wondrous thing, that in the future his glory will be supreme, yet you look at him with eyes that are filled with tears. Is his life, then, to be a fragile thing? Was he born only to bring me sorrow? Must this new branch wither before it has burst into flower? Speak, O saintly man, speak quickly; you know the great love a father bears his son."

"Be not distressed, O king," replied the hermit. "What I have told you is true: this child will know great glory. If I weep, it is for myself. My life draws to a close and he is born, he who will destroy the evil of rebirth. He will surrender sovereign power, he will master his passions, he will understand truth, and error will disappear in the world before the light of his knowledge, even as night flees before the spears of the sun. From the sea of evil, from the stinging spray of sickness, from the surge and swell of old age, from the angry waves of death, from these will he rescue the suffering world, and together they will sail away in the great ship of knowledge. He will know where it takes its rise, that swift, wonderful, beneficent river, the river of duty; he will reveal its course, and those who are tortured by thirst will come and drink of its waters. To those tormented by sorrow, to those enslaved by the senses, to those wandering in the forest of existences like travelers who have lost their way, he will point out the road to salvation. To those burning with the fire of passion, he will be the cloud that brings refreshing rain; armed with the true law, he will go to the prison of desires where all creatures languish, and he will break down the evil gates. For he who will have perfect understanding will set the world free. Therefore do not grieve, O king. He alone is to be pitied who will not hear the voice of your son, and that is why I weep, I who, in spite of my austerities, in spite of my meditations, will never know his message and his law. Yes, even he is to be pitied who ascends to the loftiest gardens of the sky."

5. Siddhartha at the Temple

THEY pleased Suddhodana at first, these words of Asita's, and he pondered them. "So my son will live, and live gloriously," he thought, but then he became anxious. For it had been said that the prince would renounce royalty, that he would lead the life of a hermit, and did that not mean that at his death Suddhodana's family would cease?

But his anxiety was short-lived, for since the birth of Siddhartha the king could undertake nothing that did not prosper. Like a great river whose waters are swollen by many tributaries, each day new riches poured into his treasury; the stables were too small to hold the horses and elephants that were presented to him, and he was constantly surrounded by a host of loyal friends. The kingdom was rich in fertile lands, and sleek, fatted cattle grazed in the meadows. Women bore their children without suffering; men lived at peace with their neighbors, and happiness and tranquility reigned in the land of Kapilavastu.

But the joy that had come to Maya proved too sweet. It soon became unbearable. The earth knew her as a mother but seven days; then she died and ascended to the sky, to be received among the Gods.

Maya had a sister, Mahaprajapati, who in beauty and virtue was almost her equal. The prince was given into Mahaprajapati's care, and she looked after his wants as tenderly as if he were her own child. And like fire fanned by an auspicious wind, like the moon, queen of the stars in the luminous skies, like the morning sun rising over the mountains in the East, Siddhartha grew in strength and stature.

Everyone now delighted in bringing him precious gifts. They gave him toys that would amuse a child of his age: tiny animals, deer and elephants, horses, cows, birds and fish, and little chariots; and they were toys made not of wood or of clay but of gold and of precious stones. And they brought him costly materials and rare gems, pearl necklaces and jeweled bracelets.

One day, while he was playing in a garden not far from the city, Mahaprajapati thought, "It is time I taught him to wear necklaces and bracelets," and she ordered the servants to bring the jewels that had been given to him. She clasped them around his arms and his neck, but it was as if he wore none at all. The gold and the precious stones seemed dull and lifeless, so brilliant was the light he diffused. And the Goddess who lived among the flowers of that garden came to Mahaprajapati and said:

"If the earth were made of gold, a single ray of light emanating from this child, the world's future guide, would be enough to dull its splendor. The light of the stars and the light of the moon, yes, even the light of the sun, are dimmed by his refulgence. And would you have him wear jewels, baubles crudely fashioned by jewelers and goldsmiths? Woman, remove those necklaces, take off those bracelets. They are only fit to be worn by slaves; give them to the slaves. This child will have his thoughts; they are gems of a purer water."

Mahaprajapati gave heed to the words of the Goddess. She unclasped the bracelets and the necklaces, and she never wearied of admiring the prince.

The time came to take Siddhartha to the temple of the Gods. By the king's command, the streets of the city and the public squares were superbly decorated; drums were sounded and bells joyously rung. While Mahaprajapati was dressing him in his richest apparel, the child asked:

"Mother, where are you taking me?"

"To the temple of the Gods, my son," she replied. The child smiled and quietly went with her to meet his father. It was a magnificent sight. In the procession were brahmans from the city, warriors and all the chief merchants. A host of guards followed, and the Sakyas surrounded the chariot that bore the prince and the king. In the streets the air was heavy with incense, flowers were strewn in their path, and the people waved flags and streamers as they passed.

They arrived at the temple. The king took Siddhartha by the hand and led him to the hall where stood the statues of the Gods. As the child stepped across the threshold the statues came to life, and all the Gods, Siva, Skanda, Vishnu, Kuvera, Indra, Brahma, descended from their pedestals and fell at his feet. And they sang:

"Meru, king of the mountains, does not bow before a grain of wheat; the Ocean does not bow before a pool of rainwater; the Sun does not bow before a glowworm; he who will have the true knowledge does not bow before the Gods. Like the grain of wheat, like the pool of rainwater, like the glowworm is the man or the God with stubborn pride; like Meru mountain, like the Ocean, like the Sun is he who will have supreme knowledge. Let the world pay him homage, and the world will be set free!"

6. Siddhartha's First Meditation

THE prince grew older, and the time came for him to study with the teacher who instructed the young Sakyas in the art of writing. This teacher was called Visvamitra.

Siddhartha was entrusted to his care. He was given, to write on, a tablet of gilded sandal-wood, set round with precious stones. When he had it in his hands, he asked:

"Which script, master, would you have me learn?"

And he enumerated the sixty-four varieties of script. Then again he asked:

"Master, which of the sixty-four would you have me learn?"

Visvamitra made no answer: he was struck dumb with astonishment. Finally, he replied:

"I see, my lord, that there is nothing I can teach you. Of the scripts you mentioned, some are known to me only by name, and others are unknown to me even by name. It is I who should sit at your feet and learn. No, my lord, there is nothing I can teach you." He was smiling, and the prince returned his affectionate glance.

Upon leaving Visvamitra, the prince went into the country and started walking toward a village.

On the way, he stopped to watch some peasants working in the fields, then he entered a meadow where stood a clump of trees. They attracted him, for it was noon and very hot. The prince went and sat down in the shade of a tree; there, he began to ponder, and he was soon lost in meditation.

Five itinerant hermits passed near the meadow. They saw the prince meditating, and they wondered:

"Is he a God, he who is seated there, resting? Could he be the God of riches, or the God of love?

Could he be Indra, bearer of thunder, or the shepherd Krishna?"

But they heard a voice saying to them:

"The splendor of the Gods would pale before the splendor of this Sakya who sits under the tree and ponders majestic truths!"

Whereupon they all exclaimed:

"Verily, he who sits and meditates under the tree bears the marks of omnipotence; he will doubtless become the Buddha!"

Then they sang his praises, and the first one said: "To a world consumed by an evil fire, he has come like a lake. His law will refresh the world." The second one said: "To a world darkened by ignorance, he has come like a torch. His law will bring light into the world."

The third one said: "Over the sea of suffering, that sea so difficult to sail, he has come like a ship. His law will bring the world safely into harbor."

The fourth one said: "To those bound in chains of evil, he has come like a redeemer. His law will set the world free."

The fifth one said: "To those tormented by old age and sickness, he has come like a savior. His law will bring deliverance from birth and death."

Three times they bowed, then continued on their way.

In the meanwhile, King Suddhodana wondered what had become of the prince, and he sent many servants out to search for him. One of them found him absorbed in meditation. The servant drew near, then suddenly stopped, overcome with admiration. For the shadows of all the trees had lengthened, except of that tree under which the prince was seated. Its shadow had not moved; it still sheltered him.

The servant ran back to the palace of the king.

"My lord," he cried, "I have seen your son; he is meditating under a tree whose shadow has not moved, whereas the shadows of all the other trees have moved and lengthened." Suddhodana left the palace and followed the servant to where his son was seated. Weeping for joy, he said to himself:

"He is as beautiful as fire on a mountain-top. He dazzles me. He will be the light of the world, and my limbs tremble when I see him thus in meditation."

The king and his servant dared neither move nor speak. But some children passed by, drawing a little chariot after them. They were making a noise. The servant said to them, in a whisper:

"You must not make a noise."

"Why?" asked the children.

"See him who meditates under the tree? That is Prince Siddhartha. The shadow of the tree has not left him. Do not disturb him, children; do you not see that he has the brilliance of the sun?"

But the prince awoke from his meditations. He rose and approaching his father, he said to him:

"We must stop working in the fields, father; we must seek the great truths."

And he returned to Kapilavastu.

7. The Marriage of Siddhartha

SUDDHODANA kept thinking of what Asita had told him. He did not want his family to die out, and he said to himself: "I will arouse in my son a desire for pleasure; then, perhaps, I shall have grandchildren, and they shall prosper."

So he sent for the prince, and he spoke to him in these words:

"My child, you are at an age when it would be well to think of marriage. If there is some maid that pleases you, tell me."

Siddhartha replied:

"Give me seven days to consider, father. In seven days you shall have my answer."

And he mused:

"Endless evil, I know, comes of desire. The trees that grow in the forest of desire have their roots n suffering and strife, and their leaves are poisonous. Desire burns like fire and wounds like a sword. I am not one of those who seek the company of women; it is my lot to live in the silence of the woods. There, through meditation, my mind will find peace, and I shall know happiness. But does not the lotus grow and flourish even amid the tangle of swamp-flowers? Have there not been men with wives and sons who found wisdom? Those who, before me, have sought supreme knowledge spent many years in the company of women. And when the time came to leave them for the delights of meditation, theirs was but a greater joy. I shall follow their example."

He thought of the qualities he would value most highly in a woman. Then, on the seventh day, he returned to his father.

"Father," said he, "she whom I shall marry must be a woman of rare merit. If you find one endowed with the natural gifts I shall enumerate, you may give her to me in marriage."

And he said:

"She whom I shall marry will be in the bloom of youth; she whom I shall marry will have the flower of beauty; yet her youth will not make her vain, nor will her beauty make her proud. She whom I shall marry will have a sister's affection, a mother's tenderness, for all living creatures. She will be sweet and truthful, and she will not know envy. Never, not even in her dreams, will she think of any other man but her husband. She will never use haughty language; her manner will be unassuming; she will be as meek as a slave. She will not covet that which belongs to others; she will make no inconsiderate demands, and she will be satisfied with her lot. She will care nothing for wines, and sweets will not tempt her. She will be insensible to music and perfume; she will be indifferent to plays and festivals. She will be kind to my attendants and to her maidens. She will be the first to awaken and the last to fall asleep. She whom I shall marry will be pure in body, in speech and in thought."

And he added:

"Father, if you know a maid who possesses these qualities, you may give her to me in marriage."

The king summoned the household priest. He enumerated the qualities the prince sought in the woman he would marry, then:

"Go," said he, "go, brahman. Visit all the homes of Kapilavastu; observe the young girls and question them. And if you find one to possess the necessary qualities, bring her to the prince, even though she be of the lowest caste. For it is not rank nor riches my son seeks, but virtue."

The priest scoured the city of Kapilavastu. He entered the houses, he saw the young girls, he cleverly questioned them; but not one could he find worthy of Prince Siddhartha. Finally, he came to the home of Dandapani who was of the Sakya family. Dandapani had a daughter named Gopa. At the very sight of her, the priest's heart rejoiced, for she was beautiful and full of grace. He spoke a few words to her, and he doubted no longer.

The priest returned to King Suddhodana. "My lord," he

exclaimed, "I have found a maid worthy of your son."

"Where did you find her?" asked the king. "She is the daughter of the Sakya, Dandapani," the brahman replied.

Though he had great confidence in his household priest, Suddhodana hesitated to summon Gopa and Dandapani. "Even the wisest men can make mistakes," he thought. "The brahman may be exaggerating her perfections. I must put the daughter of Dandapani to a further test, and my son himself shall judge her."

He had many jewels made out of gold and silver, and by royal command a herald was sent through the streets of Kapilavastu, crying:

"On the seventh day from this day, Prince Siddhartha, son of King Suddhodana, will present gifts to the young girls of the city. So may all the young girls appear at the palace on the seventh day!"

On the day announced, the prince sat on a throne in the great hall of the palace. All the young girls of the city were present, and they filed before him. To each one he presented a jewel, but, as they approached the throne, his striking beauty so intimidated them that they lowered their gaze or turned their heads away. They hardly took the time to receive their presents; some were even in such haste to leave that they merely touched the gift with the tips of their fingers, and it fell to the floor.

Gopa was the last one to appear. She advanced fearlessly, without even blinking her eyes. But the prince had not a single jewel left. Gopa smiled and said to him:

"Prince, in what way have I offended you?"

"You have not offended me," replied Siddhartha.

"Then why do you treat me with disdain?"

"I do not treat you with disdain," he replied. "You are the last one, and I have no jewel to give you."

But suddenly he remembered that on his finger he was wearing a ring of great value. He took it off and handed it to the young girl.

She would not take the ring.

She said, "Prince, must I accept this ring from you?"

"It was mine," replied the prince, "and you must accept it."

"No," said she, "I would not deprive you of your jewels. It is for me, rather, to give you a jewel." And she left.

When the king heard of this incident he was elated.

"Gopa, alone, could face my son," he thought; "she alone is worthy of him. Gopa, who would not accept the ring that you took from your finger, Gopa, O my son, will be your fairest jewel."

And he summoned Gopa's father to the palace.

"Friend," said he, "the time has come for my son Siddhartha to marry. I believe your daughter Gopa has found favor in his eyes. Will you marry her to my son?"

Dandapani did not answer at once. He hesitated, and again the king asked him:

"Will you marry your daughter to my son?" Then Dandapani said:

"My lord, your son has been brought up in luxury; he has never been outside the palace-gates; his physical and intellectual abilities have never been proven. You know that the Sakyas only marry their daughters to men who are skillful and strong, brave and wise. How can I give my daughter to your son who, so far, has shown a taste only for indolence?"

These words disturbed King Suddhodana. He asked to see the prince. Siddhartha came immediately.

"Father," said he, "you look very sad. What has happened?"

The king did not know how to tell him what Dandapani had so bluntly expressed. He remained silent. The prince repeated:

"Father, you look very sad. What has happened?"

"Do not ask me," replied Suddhodana.

"Father, you are sad, what has happened?"

"It is a painful subject; I would rather not speak of it."

"Explain yourself, father. It is always well to be explicit."

The king finally decided to relate the interview he had

had with Dandapani. When he had finished, the prince began to laugh.

"My lord," said he, "you are needlessly disturbed. Do you believe there is anyone in Kapilavastu who is my superior in strength or in intellect? Summon all who are famous for their attainments in any field whatsoever; command them to measure their skill with mine, and I shall show you what I can do."

The king recovered his serenity. He had it proclaimed throughout the city:

"That on the seventh day from this day, Prince Siddhartha will compete with all who excel in any field whatsoever."

On the day designated, all those who claimed to be skillful in the arts or in the sciences appeared at the palate. Dandapani was present, and he promised his daughter to the one, whether of noble or of humble birth, who would be victorious in the contests which were to take place.

First, a young man, who knew the rules of writing, sought to challenge the prince, but the learned Visvamitra stepped before the assembly and said:

"Young man, such a contest would be futile. You are already defeated. The prince was still a child when he was placed in my care; I was to teach him the art of writing. But he already knew sixty-four varieties of script! He knew certain varieties that were unknown to me even by name!"

Visvamitra's testimony was enough to give the prince a victory in the art of writing.

Then they sought to test his knowledge of numbers. It was decided that a certain Sakya named Arjuna, who had time and again solved intricate problems, would act as judge in the contest.

One young man claimed to be an excellent mathematician, and to him Siddhartha addressed a question, but the young man was unable to reply.

"And yet it was an easy question," said the prince. "But here is one that is still easier; who will answer it?"

No one answered this second question.

"It is now your turn to examine me," said the prince.

They asked him questions that were considered difficult, but he gave the answers even before they had finished stating the problem.

"Let Arjuna himself examine the prince!" came the cry from all sides.

Arjuna gave him the most intricate problems, and never once was Siddhartha at a loss for the correct solution.

They all marveled at his knowledge of mathematics and were convinced that his intelligence had probed to the bottom of all the sciences. They then decided to challenge his athletic skill, but at jumping and at running he won with little effort, and at wrestling he had only to lay a finger upon his adversary, and he would fall to the ground.

Then they brought out the bows, and skillful archers placed their arrows in targets that were barely visible. But when it came the prince's turn to shoot, so great was his natural strength that he broke each bow as he drew it. Finally, the king sent guards to fetch a very ancient, very precious bow that was kept in the temple. No one within the memory of man had ever been able to draw or lift it. Siddhartha took the bow in his left hand, and with one finger of his right hand he drew it to him. Then he took as target a tree so distant that he alone could see it. The arrow pierced the tree, and, burying itself in the ground, disappeared. And there, where the arrow had entered the ground, a well formed, which was called the Well of the Arrow.

Everything seemed to be over, and they led toward the victor a huge white elephant on which, in triumph, he was to ride through Kapilavastu. But a young Sakya, Devadatta, who was very proud of his strength, seized the animal by the trunk and, in fun, struck it with his fist. The elephant fell to the ground.

The prince looked reprovingly at the young man and said:

"You have done an evil thing, Devadatta."

He touched the elephant with his foot, and it stood up and paid him homage.

Then they all acclaimed his glory, and the air rang with their cheers. Suddhodana was happy, and Dandapani, weeping with joy, exclaimed:

"Gopa, my daughter Gopa, be proud to be the wife of such a man."

8. Siddhartha Leads a Life of Pleasure

PRINCE Siddhartha lived happily with his wife, the princess. And the king, whose love for his son now verged on adoration, took infinite care to spare him the sight of anything that might distress him. He built three magnificent palaces for him: one for the winter, one for the summer, and the third for the rainy season; and these he was forbidden ever to leave, to wander over the broad face of the earth.

In his palaces, white as autumn clouds and bright as the celestial chariots of the Gods and Goddesses, the prince drained the cup of pleasure. He led a life of voluptuous ease; he spent languid hours listening to music played by the princess and her maidens, and when beautiful, smiling dancers appeared before him and performed to the sound of golden kettle-drums, with delight he watched them as they swayed with a grace and loveliness rare even among the happy Apsarases.

Women cast furtive glances at him: their eyes boldly offered or archly pleaded, and their drooping lashes were a promise of ineffable delight. Their games amused him, their charms held him in thrall, and he was content to remain in these palaces so full of their laughter and song. For he knew nothing of old age and sickness; he knew nothing of death.

Suddhodana rejoiced at the life his son was leading, though his own conduct he judged with the utmost severity. He strove to keep his soul serene and pure; he refrained from doing evil, and he lavished gifts on those who were virtuous. He never yielded to indolence or pleasure; he was never burned by the poison of avarice. As wild horses are made to bear the yoke, even so did he subdue his passions, and in virtue he surpassed his kinsmen and his friends. The knowledge he acquired he placed at the service of his fellow-men, and he only studied those subjects that were useful to all. He not only sought the welfare of his own people but he also wanted the whole world to be happy. He purified his body with the water from the sacred ponds, and he purified his soul with the holy water of virtue. He never uttered a word that was pleasant and yet a lie; the truths he spoke never gave offense or pain. He tried to be just, and it was by honesty, not by force, that he defeated the pride of his enemies. He did not strike, he did not even look with anger upon those who deserved the penalty of death; instead, he gave them useful advice, and then their freedom.

The king was an example to all his subjects, and Kapilavastu was the happiest and most virtuous of kingdoms.

Then beautiful Gopa bore the prince a son, and he was given the name of Rahula. King Suddhodana was happy to see his family prosper, and he was as proud of the birth of his grandson as he had been of the birth of his son.

He continued in the path of virtue, he lived almost like a hermit, and his actions were saintly; yet he kept urging on his beloved son to new pleasures, so great was his fear to see him leave the palace and the city and seek the austere refuge of the holy forests.

9. The Three Encounters

ONE day, some one spoke in the presence of the prince and told how the grass in the woods had become a tender green and the birds in the trees were singing of the spring, and how, in the ponds, the great lotuses were unfolding. Nature had broken the chains that winter had forged, and, around the city, those gardens so dear to young maidens were now gaily carpeted with flowers. Then, like an elephant too long confined in his stable, the prince had an irresistible desire to leave the palace.

The king learned of his son's desire, and he knew no way to oppose it.

"But," he thought, "Siddhartha must see nothing that will trouble the serenity of his soul; he must never suspect the evil there is in the world. I shall order the road cleared of beggars, of those who are sick and infirm and of all who suffer."

The city was decorated with garlands and streamers; a magnificent chariot was prepared, and the cripples, the aged and the beggars were ordered off the streets where the prince would pass. When the time came, the king sent for his son, and there were tears in his eyes as he kissed him on the brow. His gaze lingered over him, then he said to him, "Go!" And with that word he gave him permission to leave the palace, though his heart spoke differently.

The prince's chariot was made of gold. It was drawn by four horses caparisoned in gold, and the charioteer held gold reins in his hands. Only the rich, the young and the beautiful were allowed on the streets he drove through, and they stopped to watch him as he went by. Some praised him for the kindness of his glance; others extolled his dignified bearing; still others exalted the beauty of his features; while many glorified his exuberant strength. And they all bowed before him, like banners dipped before the statue of some God.

The women in the houses heard the cries in the street. They awoke or left their household tasks and ran to the windows or quickly ascended to the terraces. And gazing at him in admiration, they murmured, "Happy the wife of such a man!"

And he, at the sight of the city's splendor, at the sight of the wealth of the men and the beauty of the women, felt a new joy pour into his soul.

But the Gods were jealous of the celestial felicity enjoyed by this city of the earth. They made an old man, and, in order to trouble Siddhartha's mind, they set him down on the road the prince was traveling.

The man was leaning on a staff; he was worn out and decrepit. His veins stood out on his body, his teeth chattered, and his skin was a maze of black wrinkles. A few dirty grey hairs hung from his scalp; his eyelids had no lashes and were red-rimmed; his head and limbs were palsied.

The prince saw this being, so different from the men around him. He gazed at him with sorrowful eyes, and he asked the charioteer:

"What is this man with grey hair and body so bent? He clings to his staff with scrawny hands, his eyes are dull and his limbs falter. Is he a monster? Has nature made him thus, or is it chance?"

The charioteer should not have answered, but the Gods confused his mind, and without understanding his mistake he said:

"That which mars beauty, which ruins vigor, which causes sorrow and kills pleasure, that which weakens the memory and destroys the senses is old age. It has seized this man and broken him. He, too, was once a child, nursing at his mother's breast; he, too, once crawled upon the floor; he grew, he was young, he had strength and beauty; then he reached the twilight of his years, and now you see him, the ruin that is old age."

The prince was deeply moved. He asked: "Will that be my fate, also?"

The charioteer replied:

"My lord, youth will also leave you some day; to you, too, will come troublesome old age. Time saps our strength and steals our beauty."

The prince shuddered like a bull at the sound of thunder. He uttered a deep sigh and shook his head. His eyes wandered from the wretched man to the happy crowds, and he spoke these solemn words:

"So old age destroys memory and beauty and strength in man, and yet the world is not frantic with terror! Turn your horses around, O charioteer; let us return to our homes. How can I delight in gardens and flowers when my eyes can only see old age, when my mind can only think of old age?"

The prince returned to his palace, but nowhere could he find peace. He wandered through the halls, murmuring, "Old age, oh, old age!" and in his heart there was no longer any joy.

He decided, nevertheless, to ride once more through the city.

But the Gods made a man afflicted with a loathsome disease, and they set him down on the road Siddhartha had taken.

Siddhartha saw the sick man; he stared at him, and he asked the charioteer: "What is this man with a swollen paunch? His emaciated arms hang limp, he is deathly pale and pitiful cries escape from his lips. He gasps for breath; see, he staggers and jostles the bystanders; he is falling. . . . Charioteer, charioteer, what is this man?"

The charioteer answered:

"My lord, this man knows the torment of sickness, for he has the king's evil. He is weakness itself; yet he, too, was once healthy and strong!"

The prince looked at the man with pity, and he asked again:

"Is this affliction peculiar to this man, or are all creatures threatened with sickness?"

The charioteer answered:

"We, too, may be visited with a similar affliction, O

prince. Sickness weighs heavily upon the world."

When he heard this painful truth, the prince began to tremble like a moonbeam reflected in the waves of the sea, and he uttered these words of bitterness and pity:

"Men see suffering and sickness, yet they never lose their self-confidence! Oh, how great must be their knowledge! They are constantly threatened with sickness, and they can still laugh and be merry! Turn your horses around, charioteer; our pleasure trip is ended; let us return to the palace. I have learned to fear sickness. My soul shuns pleasure and seems to close up like a flower deprived of light."

Wrapped in his painful thoughts, he returned to the palace.

King Suddhodana noticed his son's sombre mood. He asked why the prince no longer went out driving, and the charioteer told him what had happened. The king grieved; he already saw himself forsaken by the child he adored. He lost his usual composure and flew into a rage at the man whose duty it was to see that the streets were clear; he punished him, but so strong was his habit of being indulgent that the punishment was light. And the man was astonished at being thus upbraided, for he had seen neither the old man nor the sick man.

The king was more anxious now than ever before to keep his son from leaving the palace. He provided him with rare pleasures, but nothing, it seemed, could arouse Siddhartha. And the king thought, "I shall let him go out once more! Perhaps he will recover the joy he has lost."

He gave strict orders to have all cripples and all who were ill or aged driven out of the city. He even changed the prince's charioteer, and he felt certain that this time there would be nothing to trouble Siddhartha's soul.

But the jealous Gods made a corpse. Four men carried it, and others followed behind, weeping. And the corpse, as well as the men who carried it and the men who were weeping, was visible only to the prince and to the charioteer.

And the king's son asked:

"What is he that is being carried by four men, followed by those others, wearing dark clothes and weeping?"

The charioteer should have held his peace, but it was the will of the Gods that he reply:

"My lord, he has neither intelligence nor feeling nor breath; he sleeps, without consciousness, like grass or a piece of wood; pleasure and suffering are meaningless to him now, and friend and enemy alike have deserted him."

The prince was troubled. He said, "Is this a condition peculiar to this man, or does this same end await all creatures?"

And the charioteer answered: "This same end awaits all creatures. Whether of humble or of noble birth, to every being who lives in this world, death comes inevitably."

Then Prince Siddhartha knew what death was.

In spite of his fortitude, he shuddered. He had to lean against the chariot, and his words were full of distress:

"So to this does destiny lead all creatures! And yet, without fear in his heart, man amuses himself in a thousand different ways! Death is about, and he takes to the world's highroads with a song on his lips! Oh, I begin to think that man's soul has become hardened! Turn your horses around, charioteer; this is no time to wander through the flower-gardens. How can a sensible man, a man who knows what death is, seek pleasure in the hour of anguish?"

But the charioteer kept on driving toward the garden where the king had ordered him to take his son. There, at Suddhodana's command, Udayin, who was a son of the household priest and Siddhartha's friend since childhood, had assembled many beautiful maidens, skilled in the art of dancing and of song, and skillful also in the game of love.

10. Gopa's Dream

THE chariot entered the wood. The young trees were in bloom, birds fluttered about joyously as though intoxicated by the light and atmosphere, and on the surface of the pools the lotuses had cupped their petals to drink in the cool air.

Siddhartha went unwillingly, like a young hermit, still new to his vows, who fears temptation and is taken to some celestial palace where lovely Apsarases are wont to dance. Filled with curiosity, the maidens rose and came forward as though to greet a betrothed. Their eyes were bright with admiration, and the hands they extended were like flowers. They all thought, "This is Kama himself come back to earth." But they did not speak nor even smile, so timid were they in his presence.

Udayin called to the boldest and the most beautiful, and he said to them:

"Why do you fail me to-day, you whom I have chosen from among many to captivate the prince, my friend? What makes you behave like shy, silent children? Your charm, your beauty, your boldness would win even a woman's heart, and you tremble before a man! You mortify me. Come, wake up! Use your charms! Make him yield to love!" One of the maidens spoke up:

"He frightens us, O master; his majestic splendor frightens us."

"Great as it is," replied Udayin, "it should not frighten you. For strange is the power of women. Let him remind you of all those who, in the past, have been at the mercy of a tender glance. Once upon a time the great hermit Vyasa, whom even the Gods were afraid to offend, was kicked by a courtesan called the Belle of Benares, and he was not displeased. The monk Manthalagotama, who was famous for his long penances, became an undertaker's assistant, in order to win the favor of the wanton

Jangha, a woman of the very lowest caste. Santa artfully managed to seduce Rishyasringa, a learned man who had never known woman; and that most pious of all men, glorious Visvamitra, one day, in the forest, yielded to the importunities of the Apsaras Ghritaki. And I could name many more who succumbed to women like you, O lovely maidens! Come, do not be afraid of the king's son. Smile at him, and he will fall in love with you."

Udayin's words encouraged the maidens. Smiling, and with exquisite grace, they gradually formed a ring around the prince. They used the most engaging wiles in order to approach Siddhartha, in order to brush past him or hold him and steal a caress. One pretended to stumble and clung to his girdle. Another drew near and mysteriously whispered in his ear, "Deign to hear my secret, O prince." Another feigned intoxication; she slowly unwound the blue veil that bound her breasts, then came and leaned against his shoulder. Another jumped down from the branch of a mango-tree and laughingly tried to stop him as he passed. Still another offered him a lotus-flower. And one sang: "Look, dear love, this tree is covered with blossoms, with blossoms whose perfume cloys the air; in the branches, rare birds trill their happy songs, as though in a golden cage. Listen to the bees, hovering over the flowers; they are roused and consumed by a burning ardor. Look at those creepers, warmly embracing the tree; the breeze ruffles them with a jealous hand. Over there, in that lovely glade, do you see the silver pool asleep? It is smiling, drowsily, like a maiden caressed by a bold moonbeam."

But the prince was not smiling; he was unhappy, for he was thinking on death.

He thought, "They do not know these maidens, that youth is fleeting, and that old age will come and strip them of their beauty! They are blind to the menace that is sickness, though it is already master of the world! They know nothing of death, of imperious death, of death that destroys everything! And that is why they can laugh, that is why they can play!"

Udayin tried to interrupt Siddhartha's thoughts.

He said, "Why are you so discourteous to these maidens?

Perhaps they do not interest you? What matter! Be kind to them, even at the cost of a few lies. Spare them the shame of being spurned. How can your beauty profit you if you are ungracious? You will be like a forest without flowers."

"What good are lies, what good is flattery?" replied the prince. "I would not deceive these women. Old age and death lie in wait for me. Do not try to tempt me, Udayin; do not ask me to join in any vulgar amusement. I have seen old age, I have seen sickness, I am certain of death; nothing now can give me peace of mind. And you would have me yield to love? Of what metal is that man made who knows of death and still seeks love? A cruel, implacable guard stands at his door, and he does not even weep!"

The sun was setting. The maidens had ceased their laughter; the prince had no eyes for their garlands and their jewels. They felt their charms were of no avail, and slowly they took the road back to the city. The prince returned to the palace. King Suddhodana heard from Udayin that his son was shunning all pleasure, and that night he found no sleep.

Gopa was waiting for the prince. He avoided her. It made her anxious, and when she finally fell asleep, she had a dream:

The whole earth shook; the tallest mountains swayed; a savage wind blew, shattering and uprooting the trees. The sun, the moon and the stars had fallen from the sky to the earth. She, Gopa, was stripped of her clothes and of her ornaments; she it had lost her crown; she was naked. Her hair was cut. The bridal bed was broken; the prince's robes and the precious stones with which they were embroidered were scattered about. Meteors sped across the sky over a darkened city, and Meru, king of the mountains, trembled.

Overcome with terror, Gopa awoke. She ran to her husband.

"My lord, my lord," she cried, "what will happen? I have had a terrible dream! My eyes are full of tears, and my heart is full of fear."

"Tell me your dream," the prince replied.

Gopa related all that she had seen in her sleep. The prince

smiled.

"Rejoice, Gopa," said he, "rejoice. You saw the earth shake? Then one day the Gods themselves shall bow before you. You saw the moon and the sun fall from the sky? Then you shall soon defeat evil, and you shall receive infinite praise. You saw the trees uprooted? Then you shall find a way out of the forest of desire. Your hair was cut short? Then you shall free yourself from the net of passions that holds you captive. My robes and my jewels were scattered about? Then I am on the road to deliverance. Meteors were speeding across the sky over a darkened city? Then to the ignorant world, to the world that is blind, I shall bring the light of wisdom, and those who have faith in my words will know joy and felicity. Be happy, O Gopa, drive away your melancholy; you will soon be singularly honored. Sleep, Gopa, sleep; you have dreamed a lovely dream."

11. Siddhartha is Eager to Know the Great Truths

SIDDHARTHA could no longer find peace. He strode through the halls of his palace like a lion stung by some poisoned dart. He was unhappy.

One day, there came to him a great longing for the open fields and the sight of green meadows. He left the palace, and as he strolled aimlessly through the country, he mused:

"It is indeed a pity that man, weak as he really is, and subject to sickness, with old age a certainty and death for a master, should, in his ignorance and pride, contemn the sick, the aged and the dead. If I should look with disgust upon some fellow-being who was sick or old or dead, I would be unjust, I would not be worthy of understanding the supreme law."

And as he pondered the misery of mankind, he lost the vain illusion of strength, of youth and of life. He knew no longer joy or grief, doubt or weariness, desire or love, hatred or scorn.

Suddenly, he saw a man approaching who looked like a beggar and who was visible to him alone. "Tell me, who are you?" the prince asked him.

"Hero," said the monk, "through fear of birth and death, I became an itinerant monk. I seek deliverance. The world is at the mercy of destruction. I think not as other men; I shun pleasures; I know nothing of passion; I look for solitude. Sometimes I live at the foot of a tree; sometimes I live in the lonely mountains or sometimes in the forest. I own nothing; I expect nothing. I wander about, living on charity, and seeking only the highest good."

He spoke. Then he ascended into the sky and disappeared. A God had taken the form of a monk in order to arouse the prince.

Siddhartha was happy. He saw where his duty lay; he

decided to leave the palace and become a monk.

He returned to the city. Near the gates he passed a young woman who bowed and said to him, "She who is your bride must know supreme blessedness, O noble prince." He heard her voice, and his soul was filled with peace: the thought had come to him of supreme blessedness, of beatitude, of nirvana.

He went to the king; he bowed and said to him:

"King, grant the request I have to make. Do not oppose it, for I am determined. I would leave the palace, I would walk in the path of deliverance. We must part, father." The king was deeply moved. With tears in his voice, he said to his son:

"Son, give up this idea. You're still too young to consider a religious calling. Our thoughts in the springtime of life are wayward and changeable. Besides, it is a grave mistake to perform austere practices in our youth. Our senses are eager for new pleasures; our firmest resolutions are forgotten when we learn the cost in effort. The body wanders in the forest of desire, only our thoughts escape. Youth lacks experience. It is for me, rather, to embrace religion. The time has come for me to leave the palace. I abdicate, O my son. Reign in my stead. Be strong and courageous; your family needs you. And first know the joys of youth, then those of later years, before you betake yourself to the woods and become a hermit."

The prince answered:

"Promise me four things, O father, and I shall not leave your house and repair to the woods."

"What are they?" asked the king.

"Promise me that my life will not end in death, that sickness will not impair my health, that age will not follow my youth, that misfortune will not destroy my prosperity."

"You are asking too much," replied the king. "Give up this idea. It is not well to act on a foolish impulse." Solemn as Meru mountain, the prince said to his father:

"If you can not promise me these four things, do not hold me back, O father. When some one is trying to escape from a burning house, we should not hinder him. The day comes, inevitably, when we must leave this world, but what merits is there in a forced separation? A voluntary separation is far better. Death would carry me out of the world before I had reached my goal, before I had satisfied my ardor. The world is a prison: would that I could free those beings who are prisoners of desire! The world is a deep pit wherein wander the ignorant and the blind: would that I could light the lamp of knowledge, would that I could remove the film that hides the light of wisdom! The world has raised the wrong banner, it has raised the banner of pride: would that I could pull it down, would that I could tear to pieces the banner of pride! The world is troubled, the world is in a turmoil, the world is a wheel of fire: would that I could, with the true law, bring peace to all men!"

With tears in his eyes, he returned to the palace. In the great hall Gopa's companions were laughing and singing. He paid no heed to them. Night came on, and they were silent.

They fell asleep. The prince looked at them. Gone was their studied grace, gone the sparkle of their eyes. Their hair was disheveled, their mouths gaped, their breasts were crushed, and their arms and legs were stiffly outstretched or clumsily twisted under them. And the prince cried:

"Dead! They are dead! I am standing in a graveyard!"

And he left, and made his way toward the royal stables.

12. Siddhartha Leaves His Father's Palace

HE called his equerry, fleet Chandaka.

"Bring me my horse Kanthaka, at once," said he. "I would be off, to find eternal beatitude. The deep joy I feel, the indomitable strength that now sustains my will, the assurance that I have a protector even though I am alone, all these things tell me that I am about to attain my goal. The hour has come; I am on the road to deliverance."

Chandaka knew the king's orders, but he felt some superior power urging him to disobey. He went to fetch the horse.

Kanthaka was a magnificent animal; he was strong and supple. Siddhartha stroked him quietly, then said to him in a gentle voice:

"Many times, O noble beast, my father rode you into battle and defeated his powerful enemies. To-day, I go forth to seek supreme beatitude; lend me your help, O Kanthaka! Companions in arms or in pleasure are not hard to find, and we never want for friends when we set out to acquire wealth; but companions and friends desert us when it is the path of holiness we would take. Yet of this am I certain: he who helps another to do good or to do evil shares in that good or in that evil. Know then, O Kanthaka, that it is a virtuous impulse that moves me. Lend me your strength and your speed; the world's salvation and your own is at stake."

The prince had spoken to Kanthaka as he would have to a friend. He now eagerly climbed into the saddle, and he looked like the sun astride an autumn cloud.

The horse was careful to make no noise, for the night was clear. No one in the palace or in Kapilavastu was awakened. Heavy iron bars protected the gates of the city, an elephant could have raised them only with great difficulty, but, to allow the prince to pass, the gates opened silently, of their own accord.

Leaving his father, his son and his people, Siddhartha went forth from the city. He felt no regret, and in a steady voice, he cried:

"Until I shall have seen the end of life and of death, I shall not return to the city of Kapila."

13. Siddhartha the Hermit

KANTHAKA bravely carried him a great distance. When the sun finally peered between the eyelids of night, the most noble of men saw that he was near a wood where dwelt many pious hermits. Deer were asleep under the trees, and birds fluttered about fearlessly. Siddhartha felt rested, and he thought he need go no further. He dismounted and gently stroked his horse. There was happiness in his glance and in his voice as he said to Chandaka:

"Truly, a horse has the strength and swiftness of a God. And you, dear friend, by bearing me company, have proved to me how great is your affection and your courage. It was a noble deed and pleases me. Those who, like yourself, can combine energy and devotion are indeed rare. You have shown that you are my friend, and you expect no reward from me! Yet it is usually a selfish interest that brings men together. I assure you, you have made me very happy. Take the horse now and return to the city. I have found the forest I was seeking." The hero took off his jewels and handed them to Chandaka.

"Take this necklace," said he, "and go to my father. Tell him to believe in me and not give way to his grief. If I enter a hermitage, it is not because I am wanting in affection for my friends or because my enemies provoke my anger; nor is it because I seek a place among the Gods. Mine is a worthier reason: I will destroy old age and death. Therefore, do not grieve, Chanda, and do not let my father be unhappy. I left my home to be rid of unhappiness. Unhappiness is born of desire; that man is to be pitied who is a slave to his passions. When a man dies, there are always heirs to his fortune, but heirs to his virtues are rarely found, are never found. If my father says to you, 'He left for the forest before the appointed time,' you will answer that life is so uncertain that the practice of virtue is never untimely. Say this to the king, O my friend, and do your best to make him forget me. Tell him that I possess neither virtue nor merit; for a man without virtue is never loved, and he who is never loved is never mourned."

With tears in his eyes, Chandaka replied:

"Oh, how they will weep, those who love you! You are young, you are beautiful, the palace of the Gods should be your home; yet you would live in the woods and sleep on the coarse grass? I knew of your cruel resolve; I should not have gone to fetch Kanthaka; but a supernatural power urged me, deceived me, and I brought him to you. How could I have done such a thing of my own will? Sorrow will now find its way into Kapilavastu. O prince, your father loves you dearly, do not forsake him! And Mahaprajapati? What has she not done for you! She is your foster-mother; do not be ungrateful! And is there not still another woman who loves you? Do not abandon faithful Gopa! Raise your son with her help, and one day he will bring you glory!"

He wept bitterly. The hero was silent. Chanda continued:

"You are going to leave your family for ever! Oh, if you must cause them grief, spare me, at least, the anguish of imparting the sad news! What would the king say to me if he saw me return without you? What would your mother say to me? What would Gopa say? And when I appear before your father, you ask me to deny your merit and your virtue! How can I do that, my lord? I can not lie. And even if I should decide to lie, who would believe me? Who can be made to believe that the moon has fiery beams?"

He seized the hero's hand.

"Do not forsake us! Come back, oh, come back!" Siddhartha still remained silent. Finally, he said in a solemn voice:

"We must part, Chanda. There comes a time when people who are bound by the closest ties must go their own ways. If, out of love for my family, I were not to leave, death would still separate us, in spite of everything. What am I now to my mother? What is she to me? Birds that sleep in the same tree at night scatter to the four winds at the first flush of dawn; clouds that some puff of wind has brought together by another puff of wind are again dispersed. I can no longer live in a world that is but a dream. We must part, my friend. Tell the people of Kapilavastu that I have done nothing worthy of blame, tell them to forget their affection for me; and tell them also that they will see me again, soon, the conqueror of old age and death, unless I should fail miserably and die."

Kanthaka was licking his feet. The hero gently stroked his horse and spoke to him as though to a friend:

"Do not weep. You have shown that you are a noble animal. Be patient. The time is near when your toil will be rewarded."

Then he took a sword that Chandaka was holding. The hilt was of gold and was studded with jewels; the blade was sharp. With one blow he cut off his hair, then tossed the sword into the air where it glistened like a new star. The Gods caught it and held it in great reverence.

But the hero was still wearing his gorgeous robe. He wanted a plain one, one suitable to a hermit. Whereupon a hunter appeared, wearing a coarse garment made of a reddish material. Siddhartha said to him:

"Your peaceful robe is like those worn by hermits; it offers a strange contrast to your savage bow. Give me your clothes and take mine in exchange. They will suit you better."

"Thanks to these clothes," said the hunter, "I can deceive the beasts in the forests. They do not fear me, and I can kill them at close range. But if you have need of them, my lord, I shall willingly give them to you and take yours in exchange.

Siddhartha joyfully donned the coarse, reddish-colored clothes belonging to the hunter, and the hunter reverently accepted the hero's robe, then he disappeared into the sky. Siddhartha realized that the Gods themselves had wished to present him with his hermit's robe, and he rejoiced. Chandaka was filled with wonder.

Arrayed in his reddish-colored robes, the saintly hero set out on the path to the hermitage. He was like the king of the

mountains wrapped in clouds at dusk.
    And Chandaka, with a heavy heart, took the road back to Kapilavastu.

4. Gopa and Suddhodana Grieve

GOPA had awakened in the deep of night. A strange uneasiness possessed her. She called to her beloved, Prince Siddhartha, but there was no answer. She rose. She ran through the halls of the palace; he was nowhere to be found. She became frightened. Her maidens were asleep. A cry escaped her lips:

"Oh, wicked, wicked! You have betrayed me! You have allowed my beloved to escape!"

The maidens awoke. They searched every room. There was no longer any doubt: the prince had left the palace. Gopa rolled on the ground; she tore her hair, and her face bore the marks of her deep despair.

"He once told me that he would go away, far away, he, the king of men! But I never thought the cruel parting would come so soon. Oh, where are you, my well-beloved? Where are you? I can not forget you, I, who am forlorn, so forlorn! Where are you? Where are you? You are so beautiful! Your beauty is unrivalled among men. Your eyes sparkle. You are good, and you are beloved, my well-beloved! Were you not happy? Oh, my dear, my beloved, where have you gone?" Her companions tried in vain to console her.

"Hereafter, I will drink only to quench my thirst, I will eat only to still my hunger. I will sleep on the bare ground, for crown I will wear a hermit's braid, no more sweet-scented baths will I take, I will mortify my flesh. The gardens are bare of flowers and of fruit; the faded garlands are heavy with dust. The palace is deserted. No longer will it ring with the happy songs of yesterday."

Mahaprajapati learned from one of her maidens of Siddhartha's flight. She went to Gopa. The two women wept in each other's arms.

King Suddhodana heard the lamentation. He asked the reason. A servant went to inquire and returned with this answer:

"My lord, the prince can not be found anywhere in the palace."

"Close the gates of the city," cried the king, "and search for my son in the streets, in the gardens, in the houses."

He was obeyed, but the prince was nowhere to be found. The king broke down.

"My son, my only child!" he sobbed, and fell into a swoon. He was soon brought to, and he ordered:

"That horsemen be dispatched in all directions, and that they bring me back my son!" In the meanwhile, Chandaka and the horse Kanthaka were slowly returning from the hermitage. As they approached the city, they both hung their heads in dejection. Some horsemen espied them.

"It is Chandaka! It is Kanthaka!" they cried, and they galloped their horses. They saw that Chandaka was carrying the prince's jewels. They asked, anxiously:

"Was the prince murdered?"

"No, no," Chandaka quickly replied. "He entrusted me with his jewels that I might return them to his family. He has donned a hermit's robe, and he has entered a forest where dwell some holy men."

"Do you think," said the horsemen, "that if we went to him, we could persuade him to return with us?"

"Your words would be futile. He is obdurate. He said, 'I shall not return to Kapilavastu until I have conquered old age and death.' And what he has said, he will do."

Chandaka followed the horsemen to the palace. The king summoned him at once.

"My son! My son! Where has he gone, Chandaka?"

The equerry told him what the prince had done. The king grieved, yet he could not help admiring his son's greatness. Gopa and Mahaprajapati entered; they had heard of Chandaka's return. They questioned him, and they learned of Siddhartha's high resolve.

"O you who were my joy," said Gopa through her tears, "you whose voice was so sweet, you who had such strength and such grace, such knowledge and such virtue! When you spoke to me, I thought I was listening to some lovely song, and when I leaned over you, I inhaled the perfume of all the flowers. Now I am far away from you, and I weep. What shall become of me, now, for he is gone, he who was my guide? I shall know poverty, for I have lost my treasure. He was my eyes; I can no longer see the light; I am blind. Oh, when will he return, he who was my joy?"

Mahaprajapati saw the jewels Chandaka had brought back with him. She stood looking at them a great while. She was weeping. Then, taking the jewels, she left the palace.

Still weeping, she walked through the garden until she came to a pool. Once again, she looked at the jewels, then threw them into the water.

Kanthaka had returned to the stables. The other horses were happy at his return and neighed in a friendly manner. But he did not hear them; he did not see them. He was very sad. He whinnied pitifully once or twice, and, suddenly, fell dead.

15. The Doctrine of Arata Kalama

SIDDHARTHA had entered the hermitage where holy Arata Kalama taught the doctrine of renunciation to a great number of disciples. Whenever he appeared, they all admired him; wherever he went, there shone a marvelous light. The monks listened with joy when he spoke, for his voice was sweet and powerful, and he was persuasive. One day, Arata Kalama said to him:

"You understand the law as well as I understand it; all that I know, you know. Hereafter, if you wish, we will share the work; we will both teach the disciples."

The hero asked himself: "Is the law that Arata teaches the true law? Does it lead to deliverance?"

He thought: "Arata and his disciples lead lives of great austerity. They refuse food prepared by man; they will eat only fruit, leaves and roots; they will drink only water. They are more abstemious than the birds that peck at minute seeds, than the deer that nibble at the grass, than the serpents that inhale the breeze. When they sleep, it is under a canopy of branches; the heat of the sun scorches them; they expose their bodies to the bitter winds; they bruise their feet and their knees on the stones of the highway. To them, virtue comes only with suffering. And they think they are happy, for they believe that by practicing perfect austerity, they will earn the right to ascend to the sky! Yes, they will ascend to the sky! But the human race will continue to suffer old age and death! To lead a life of austerity and be indifferent to the constant evil of birth and death is simply to add suffering to suffering. Men tremble in the presence of death, yet they do their utmost to be reborn; they keep plunging deeper and deeper into the very pit they fear. If it is an act of piety to mortify the flesh, then it must be impious to indulge in sensuality, but mortifications in this world are followed by gratifications in the next, and thus the reward of piety is impiety. If, to be sanctified, it is enough simply to be abstemious, then the deer would be saints, and those men also would be saints who have lost caste, for to them an evil fate has made pleasure unattainable. But, it will be said, it is the intention to suffer that develops religious virtue. The intention! We can intend to gratify our senses as well as we can intend to suffer, and if the intention to gratify our senses is worth nothing, why should the intention to suffer be of any value?" Thus did he ponder in the hermitage of Arata Kalama. He saw the vanity of the doctrine that the master was teaching, and he said to him:

"I will not teach your doctrine, Arata. Who knows it will not find deliverance. I shall leave your hermitage, and I shall seek the rule to which we must submit before we can have done with suffering."

And the hero set out for the country of Magadha, and there, alone and absorbed in meditation, he dwelt on the slope of a mountain, near the city of Rajagriha.

16. Siddhartha and King Vimbasara

ONE morning, the hero took his alms-bowl and entered the city of Rajagriha. The people who passed him on the road admired his beauty and his noble bearing. "What is this man?" they wondered. "He is like a God, like Sakra or Brahma himself." Presently, it was noised abroad that a marvelous being was wandering through the city, begging. Every one wanted to see the hero; they followed him about, and women rushed to the windows as he passed by. But he gravely pursued his way, while over the city a strange light appeared.

A man ran to inform the king that a God, no less, was begging in the streets of the city. King Vimbasara went out on the terrace of the palace; he saw the hero. His splendor dazzled him. He sent him alms, and he gave orders to have him followed, in order to discover his retreat. Thus did the king learn that the magnificent beggar lived on the slope of the mountain, near the city.

The following day, Vimbasara drove out of the city and came to the mountain. He left his chariot, and, quite alone, walked toward a tree in whose shade the hero was seated. The king paused near the tree, and, speechless with wonder, reverently gazed at the beggar.

Then, bowing humbly, he said:

"I have seen you and great is my joy! Do not remain here on the lonely mountain-side; sleep no longer on the hard ground. You are beautiful, you are resplendent with youth; come to the city. I will give you a palace, and all your desires shall be gratified."

"My lord," replied the hero, in a gentle voice, "my lord, may you live many years! Desires mean nothing to me. I lead the life of a hermit; I know peace."

"You are young," said the king, "you are beautiful, you are ardent; be rich. You shall have the loveliest maidens in my kingdom to serve you. Do not go away; stay and be my companion."

"I have given up great riches," said the hero.

"I will give you half my kingdom."

"I have given up the most beautiful of kingdoms."

"Here you may gratify all your desires."

"I know the vanity of all desire. Desires are like poison; wise men despise them. I have thrown them away as one would throw away a wisp of dry straw. Desires are as perishable as the fruit on a tree, they are as wayward as the clouds in the sky, they are as treacherous as the rain, they are as changeable as the wind! Suffering is born of desire, for no man has ever gratified all his desires. But they that seek wisdom, they that ponder the true faith, they are the ones that find peace. Who drinks salt water increases his thirst; who flees from desire finds his thirst appeased. I no longer know desire. I seek the true law."

The king said:

"Great is your wisdom, O beggar! Which is your country? Where is your father? Where is your mother? Which is your caste? Speak."

"Perhaps you have heard of the city of Kapilavastu, O king? A prosperous city it is. The king, Suddhodana, is my father. I left him in order to wander and beg."

The king replied:

"Good fortune attend you! I am happy now that I have seen you. Between your family and mine there is a friendship of long standing. Be gracious to me, and when you have gained enlightenment, deign to teach me, O master."

He bowed three times, then returned to Rajagriha.

The hero heard that there lived near Rajagriha a famous hermit named Rudraka, son of Rama. This hermit had many disciples whom he instructed in the law. The hero went to listen to his teachings, but like Arata Kalama, Rudraka knew nothing of the true law, and the hero did not tarry.

Presently he came to the banks of the Nairanjana. Five of Rudraka's disciples: Kaundinya, Asvajit, Vashpa, Mahanaman and Bhadrika, had joined him.

17. Siddhartha Deserted by His First Disciples

THE clear waters of the Nairanjana flowed through a rich and fertile land. Little villages drowsed in the shade of magnificent trees, and great meadows stretched away into the distance. The hero thought, "How pleasant it is here; what an inviting spot in which to meditate! Perhaps, here, I shall find the path to wisdom. Here I shall dwell."

He became deeply absorbed in contemplation. He was so engrossed with his thoughts that he stopped breathing, and, one day, he fell into a swoon. The Gods, who were watching him from the sky, thought he was dead, and they cried:

"Is he dead, this child of the Sakyas? Has he died and left the world to its suffering?"

Maya, the hero's mother, lived among the Gods. She heard their cries and plaints, and she feared for the life of her son. Attended by a host of Apsarases, she descended to the banks of the Nairanjana, and when she saw Siddhartha, so stiff, so inert, she wept.

She said: "When you were born in the garden, I was assured, O my son, that you would behold the truth. And later, Asita predicted that you would set the world free. But they were all lies, these predictions. You did not win fame by any royal conquest, you did not attain supreme knowledge! You died, pitifully and alone. Who will help you, O my son? Who will bring you back to life? For ten moons I carried you in my womb, O my jewel, and now I can only grieve."

She scattered flowers over the body of her son, whereupon he stirred and spoke to her in a gentle voice:

"Have no fear, mother; your labor was not in vain; Asita told you no lie. Even if the earth crumble into dust, even if Meru sink below the waters, even if the stars fall like rain upon the earth, I shall not die. I, alone, of all men, will survive the world's ruin! Do not weep, mother! The time is approaching when I shall attain supreme knowledge."

Maya smiled at her son's words; three times she bowed, then ascended to the sky, to the music of celestial lutes.

For six years, the hero remained on the banks of the river and meditated. He never sought shelter from the wind, from the sun or from the rain; he allowed the gadflies, the mosquitoes and the serpents to sting him. He was oblivious to the boys and girls, the shepherds and woodcutters, who jeered at him as they passed by and who sometimes threw dust or mud at him. He hardly ate: a fruit and a few grains of rice or of sesame composed his fare. He became very thin; his bones showed prominently. But under his gaunt forehead, his dilated eyes shone like stars.

And yet true knowledge did not come to him. He felt he was becoming very weak, and he realized that if he wasted away, he would never reach the goal he had set for himself. So he decided to take more nourishment.

There was a village called Uruvilva near the spot where Siddhartha spent long hours in meditation. The head man of this village had ten daughters. They revered the hero, and they brought him grain and fruit by way of alms. He rarely touched these gifts, but, one day, the girls noticed that he had eaten all they had offered him. The next day, they came with a large dish full of boiled rice, and he emptied that. The following day, each one brought a different delicacy, and the hero ate them all. He began to gain flesh, and, presently, he started going to the village to beg his food. The inhabitants vied with one another in giving him alms, and, before long, he had regained his strength and his beauty. But the five disciples who had joined him said to each other:

"His austerities did not lead him into the path of true knowledge, and now he has ceased to practice them. He takes abundant nourishment; he seeks comfort. He no longer thinks of doing holy deeds. How can he, now, attain true knowledge? We considered him a wise man, but we were mistaken: he is a madman and a fool."

And they left him and went to Benares.

18. Siddhartha Under the Tree of Knowledge

THE hero's clothes had become threadbare in the six years he had been wearing them, and he thought: "It would be well if I had some new clothes; otherwise I shall have to go naked, and that would be immodest."

Now, Sujata, the most devout of the ten young girls who had been bringing him food, had a slave who had just died. She had wrapped the body in a shroud made of a reddish material and had had it carried to the cemetery. The dead slave was lying in the dust. The hero saw the body as he passed; he went over to it and removed the shroud.

It was very dusty, and the hero had no water in which to wash it. Sakra, from the sky, saw his perplexity. Coming down to earth he struck the ground, and a pool appeared before the eyes of the Saint.

"Good," said he, "here is water, but I still need a washstone."

Sakra made a stone and set it down on the edge of the pool.

"Man of virtue," said the God, "give me the shroud; I shall wash it for you." "No, no," replied the Saint. "I know the duties of a monk; I myself shall wash the shroud."

When it was clean, he bathed. Now, Mara, the Evil One, had been watching for him for some time. He suddenly raised the banks of the pool, making them very steep. The Saint was unable to climb out of the water. Fortunately, there was a tall tree growing near the pool, and the Saint addressed a prayer to the Goddess who lived in it.

"O Goddess, may a branch of this tree bend over me!"

A branch immediately bent over the pool. The Saint caught hold of it and pulled himself out of the water. Then he went and sat down under the tree, and he began to sew on the shroud and make a new garment for himself.

Night came on. He fell asleep, and he had five dreams.

First, he saw himself lying in a large bed that was the whole earth; under his head, there was a cushion which was the Himalaya; his right hand rested on the western sea, his left hand on the eastern sea, and his feet touched the southern sea.

Then he saw a reed coming out of his navel, and the reed grew so fast that it soon reached the sky.

Then he saw worms crawling up his legs and completely covering them.

Then he saw birds flying toward him from all points of the horizon, and when the birds were near his head, they seemed to be of gold.

Finally, he saw himself at the foot of a mountain of filth and excrement; he climbed the mountain; he reached the summit; he descended, and neither the filth nor the excrement had defiled him.

He awoke, and from these dreams he knew that the day had come when, having attained supreme knowledge, he would become a Buddha.

He rose and set out for the village of Uruvilva, to beg.

Sujata had just finished milking eight wonderful cows that she owned. The milk they gave was rich, oily and of a delicate savor. She added honey and rice flour to it, then set the mixture to boil in a new pot, on a new stove. Huge bubbles began to form and kept floating off to the right, without the liquid rising or spilling a single drop. The stove did not even smoke. Sujata was astonished, and she said to Purna, her servant:

"Puma, the Gods are favoring us to-day. Go and see if the holy man is approaching the house."

Purna, from the doorstep, saw the hero walking toward Sujata's house. He was diffusing a brilliant light, a golden light. Puma was dazzled. She ran back to her mistress.

"Mistress, he is coming! He is coming! And your eyes will be blinded by his splendor!" "Let him come! Oh, let him come!" cried Sujata. "It is for him that I have prepared this wonderful milk."

She poured the milk mixed with honey and flour into a golden bowl, and she awaited the hero.

He entered. The house was lighted up by his presence. Sujata, to do him honor, bowed seven times. He sat down. Sujata kneeled and bathed his feet in sweet-scented water; then she offered him the golden bowl full of milk mixed with rice flour and honey. He thought:

"The Buddhas of old, it is said, had their last meal served to them in a golden bowl, before attaining supreme knowledge. Since Sujata offers me this milk and honey in a golden bowl, the time has come for me to be a Buddha."

Then he asked the young girl:

"Sister, what must I do with this golden bowl?"

"It belongs to you," she replied.

"I have no use for such a bowl," said he.

"Then do as you please with it," said Sujata. "It would be contemptible of me to offer the food and not offer the bowl."

He left, carrying the bowl in his hands, and he walked to the banks of the river. He bathed; he ate. When the bowl was empty, he threw it into the water, and he said:

"If I am to become Buddha this very day, may the bowl go upstream; if not, may it go with the current."

The bowl floated out to the middle of the river, then rapidly started upstream. It disappeared in a whirlpool, and the hero heard the muffled ring as it landed, in the subterranean world, among those other bowls the former Buddhas had emptied and thrown away.

The hero sauntered along the banks of the river. Night slowly descended. The flowers wearily closed their petals; a sweet fragrance rose from the fields and gardens; the birds timidly rehearsed their evensongs.

It was then the hero walked toward the tree of knowledge.

The road was sprinkled with gold-dust; rare palms,

covered with precious stones, lined the way. He skirted the edge of a pool whose blessed waters exhaled an intoxicating perfume. White, yellow, blue and red lotuses spread their massive petals over the surface, and the air rang with the clear songs of the swans. Near the pool, under the palms, Apsarases were dancing, while in the sky the Gods were admiring the hero.

He approached the tree. On the side of the road, he saw Svastika, the reaper.

"They are tender, these grasses you are mowing, Svastika. Give me some grass; I want to cover the seat I shall occupy when I attain supreme knowledge. They are green, these grasses you are mowing, Svastika. Give me some grass, and you will know the law some day, for I shall teach it to you, and you may teach it to others."

The reaper gave the Saint eight handfuls of grass.

There stood the tree of knowledge. The hero went to the east of it and bowed seven times. He threw the handfuls of grass on the ground, and, suddenly, a great seat appeared. The soft grass covered it like a carpet.

The hero sat down, his head and shoulders erect, his face turned to the east. Then he said in a solemn voice:

"Even if my skin should parch, even if my hand should wither, even if my bones should crumble into dust, until I have attained supreme knowledge I shall not move from this seat."

And he crossed his legs.

19. Mara's Defeat

THE light emanating from the hero's body reached even to those realms where Mara, the Evil One, reigned supreme. It dazzled Mara, and he seemed to hear a voice saying:

"The hero who has renounced royalty, the son of Suddhodana, is now seated under the tree of knowledge. He is concentrating his mind, he is making the supreme effort, and soon he will bring to all creatures the help which they need. The road he will have taken, others will take. Once set free, he will set others free. Once he has found peace, he will bring peace to others. He will enter nirvana, and he will cause others to enter. He will find wisdom and happiness, and he will give them to others. Because of him, the city of the Gods will be crowded; because of him, the city of the Evil One will be deserted. And you, Mara, a commander without an army, a king without subjects, will not know where to take refuge."

Mara was filled with apprehension. He tried to sleep, but his slumber was disturbed by terrible dreams. He awoke and summoned his servants and his soldiers. When they saw him, they became alarmed, and Sarthavaha, one of his sons, said to him:

"Father, you look pale and unhappy; your heart beats fast and your limbs tremble. What have you heard? What have you seen? Speak."

"Son," replied Mara, "the days of my pride are over. I heard a voice crying in the light, and it told me that the son of the Sakyas was seated under the tree of knowledge. And I had horrible dreams. A black cloud of dust settled over my palace. My gardens were bare of leaves, of flowers and of fruit. My ponds had dried up, and my swans and peacocks had their wings clipped. And I felt alone, amid this desolation. You had all deserted me. My queen was beating her breast and tearing her hair, as though haunted by remorse. My daughters were crying out in their anguish, and you, my son, were bowing before this man who meditated under the tree of knowledge! I wanted to fight my enemy, but I could not draw my sword from the scabbard. All my subjects fled in horror. Impenetrable darkness closed in upon me, and I heard my palace crashing to the ground."

Sarthavaha said:

"Father, it is disheartening to lose a battle. If you have seen these omens, bide your time, and do not run the chance of being ingloriously defeated."

But Mara, at the sight of the legions that surrounded him, felt his courage return. He said to his son:

"To the man of energy, a battle can end only in victory. We are brave; we will surely win. What strength can this man have? He is alone. I shall advance against him with a vast army, and I shall strike him down at the foot of the tree."

"Mere numbers do not make the strength of an army," said Sarthavaha, "The sun can outshine a myriad of glowworms. If wisdom is the source of his power, a single hero can defeat countless soldiers."

But Mara paid no heed. He ordered the army to advance at once, and Sarthavaha thought:

"He who is insane with pride will never recover."

Mara's army was a fearful sight. It bristled with pikes, with arrows and with swords; many carried enormous battle-axes and heavy clubs. The soldiers were black, blue, yellow, red, and their faces were terrifying. Their eyes were cruel flames; their mouths spewed blood. Some had the ears of a goat, others the ears of a pig or of an elephant. Many had bodies shaped like a jug. One had the paws of a tiger, the hump of a camel and the head of a donkey; another had a lion's mane, a rhinoceros' horn and a monkey's tail. There were many with two, four and five heads, and others with ten, twelve and twenty arms. In place of ornaments, they wore jawbones, skulls and withered human fingers. And shaking their hairy heads, they advanced with hideous laughter and savage cries:

"I can shoot a hundred arrows at one time; I shall seize the body of the monk." "My hand can crumple up the sun, the moon and the stars; how easy it will be to crush this man and his tree." "My eyes are full of poison: they would dry up the sea; I shall look at him, and he will burn to a cinder."

Sarthavaha kept to himself. A few friends had gathered around him, and they were saying:

"Fools! You think he is mad because he meditates; you think he is craven because he is calm. It is you who are madmen, it is you who are cowards. You do not know his power; because of his great wisdom he will defeat you all. Were your numbers as infinite as the grains of sand on the banks of the Ganges, you would not disturb a single hair of his head. And you believe you can kill him! Oh, turn back! Do not try to harm him; bow before him in reverence. His reign has come. The jackals howl in the forests when the lion is away, but when the lion roars, the jackals scamper off in terror. Fools, fools! You shout with pride while the master is silent, but when the lion speaks you will take to your heels," The army listened with contempt to these words of wisdom spoken by Sarthavaha and his friends. It kept advancing.

Before attacking the hero, Mara sought to frighten him. He roused against him the fury of the winds. Fierce gales rushed toward him from the horizon, uprooting trees, devastating villages, shaking mountains, but the hero never moved; not a single fold of his robe was disturbed.

The Evil One summoned the rains. They fell with great violence, submerging cities and scarring the surface of the earth, but the hero never moved; not a single thread of his robe was wet.

The Evil One made blazing rocks and hurled them at the hero. They sped through the air but changed when they came near the tree, and fell, not as rocks, but flowers.

Mara then commanded his army to loose their arrows at his enemy, but the arrows, also, turned into flowers. The army rushed at the hero, but the light he diffused acted as a shield to protect him; swords were shivered, battle-axes were dented by it, and whenever a weapon fell to the ground, it, too, at once changed into a flower.

And, suddenly, filled with terror at the sight of these prodigies, the soldiers of the Evil One fled.

And Mara wrung his hands in anguish, and he cried: "What have I done that this man should defeat me? For they are not a few, those whose desires I have granted! I have often been kind and generous! Those cowards who are fleeing could bear witness to that."

The troops that were still within hearing answered:

"Yes, you have been kind and generous. We will bear witness to that."

"And he, what proof has he given of his generosity?" continued Mara. "What sacrifices has he made? Who will bear witness to his kindness?"

Whereupon a voice came out of the earth, and it said:

"I will bear witness to his generosity."

Mara was struck dumb with astonishment. The voice continued:

"Yes, I, the Earth, I, the mother of all beings, will bear witness to his generosity. A hundred times, a thousand times, in the course of his previous existences, his hands, his eyes, his head, his whole body have been at the service of others. And in the course of this existence, which will be the last, he will destroy old age, sickness and death. As he excels you in strength, Mara, even so does he surpass you in generosity."

And the Evil One saw a woman of great beauty emerge from the earth, up to her waist. She bowed before the hero, and clasping her hands, she said: "O most holy of men, I bear witness to your generosity."

Then she disappeared.

And Mara, the Evil One, wept because he had been defeated.

20. Siddhartha Becomes the Buddha

BY sunset the army of the Evil One had fled. Nothing had disturbed the hero's meditation, and, in the first watch of the night, he arrived at the knowledge of all that had transpired in previous existences. In the second watch, he learned the present state of all beings. In the third, he understood the chain of causes and effects.

He now clearly saw all creatures being continually reborn, and, whether of high or of low caste, in the path of virtue or of evil, he saw them going through the round of existences, at the mercy of their actions. And the hero thought:

"How miserable is this world that is born, grows old and dies, then is reborn only to grow old and die again! And man knows no way out!"

And in profound meditation, he said to himself:

"What is the cause of old age and death? There is old age and death because there is birth. Old age and death are due to birth. What is the cause of birth? There is birth because there is existence. Birth is due to existence. What is the cause of existence? There is existence because there are ties. Existence is due to ties. What is the cause of ties? There are ties because there is desire. Ties are due to desire. What is the cause of desire? There is desire because there is sensation. Desire is due to sensation. What is the cause of sensation? There is sensation because there is contact. Sensation is due to contact. What is the cause of contact? There is contact because there are six senses. Contact is due to the six senses. What is the cause of the six senses? There are six senses because there is name and form. The six senses are due to name and form. What is the cause of name and form? There is name and form because there is perception. Name and form are due to perception. What is the cause of perception? There is perception because there is impression. Perception is due to impression. What is the cause of impression? There is impression because there is ignorance. Impression is due to ignorance."

And he thought:

"Thus does ignorance lie at the root of death, of old age, of suffering, of despair. To suppress ignorance is to suppress impression. To suppress impression is to suppress perception. To suppress perception is to suppress name and form. To suppress name and form is to suppress the six senses. To suppress the six senses is to suppress contact. To suppress contact is to suppress sensation. To suppress sensation is to suppress desire. To suppress desire is to suppress ties. To suppress ties is to suppress existence. To suppress existence is to suppress birth. To suppress birth is to suppress old age and death. To exist is to suffer. Desire leads from birth to rebirth, from suffering to further suffering. By stifling desire, we prevent birth, we prevent suffering. By leading a life of holiness, desire is stifled, and we cease to endure birth and suffering."

When dawn appeared, this most noble of men was a Buddha. He exclaimed:

"I have had numerous births. In vain have I sought the builder of the house. Oh, the torment of perpetual rebirth! But I have seen you at last, O builder of the house. You no longer build the house. The rafters are broken; the old walls are down. The ancient mountain crumbles; the mind attains to nirvana; birth is no more for desire is no more."

Twelve times the earth shook; the world was like a great flower. The Gods sang:

"He has come, he who brings light into the world; he has come, he who protects the world! Long blinded, the eye of the world has opened, and the eye of the world is dazzled by the light. O conqueror, you will give all beings that which they hunger after. Guided by the sublime light of the law, all creatures will reach the shores of deliverance. You hold the lamp; go now and dispel the darkness!"

PART TWO
I. Trapusha and Bhallika

THE Buddha never moved. He remained under the tree, his legs crossed. He was filled with bliss at having attained perfect knowledge. He thought, "I have found deliverance." One whole week he remained under the tree of knowledge, without moving.

The second week he went on a long journey; he traveled through all the worlds.

The third week he again remained under the tree of knowledge, and he never once blinked his eyes.

The fourth week he went on a short journey, from the eastern sea to the western sea.

It was then that Mara, whom defeat had left inconsolable, went to the Buddha and spoke these evil words:

"Blessed One, why do you tarry, you who know the path to deliverance? Blow out the lamp, quench the flame; enter nirvana, O Blessed One; the hour has come."

But the Blessed One answered:

"No, Mara, I shall not quench the flame, I shall not enter nirvana. I must first gain many disciples, and they, in turn, must win others over to my law. By word and by deed I must silence my adversaries. No, Mara, I shall not enter nirvana until the Buddha is glorified throughout the world, until his beneficent law is recognized."

Mara left him. He was crestfallen, and he seemed to hear divine voices mocking him.

"You have been defeated, Mara," they were saying, "and you stand wrapped in thought, like an old heron. You are powerless, Mara, like an aged elephant stuck fast in a swamp. You thought you were a hero, and you are weaker than a sick man abandoned in a forest. Of what avail were your insolent words?

They were as futile as the chattering of crows."

He picked up a piece of dead wood, and began drawing figures in the sand. His three daughters, Rati, Arati and Trishna, saw him. They were taken aback at the sight of his grief.

"Father, why are you so melancholy?" asked Rati.

"I have been defeated by a saintly man," replied Mara. "He is proof against my strength and my cunning."

"Father," said Trishna, "we are beautiful; we have seductive ways."

"We shall go to this man," continued Arati; "we shall bind him with the chains of love, and we shall bring him to you, humbled and craven."

They went to the Buddha, and they sang:

"Spring is here, friend, the loveliest of the seasons. The trees are in blossom; we must be merry. Your eyes are beautiful, they shine with a lovely light, and you bear the marks of omnipotence. Look at us: we were made to give pleasure and happiness to both men and Gods. Rise and join us, friend; make the most of your shining youth; dismiss all solemn thoughts from your mind. Look at our hair, see how soft it is; flowers lend their fragrance to its silkiness. See our eyes wherein slumbers the sweetness of love. See our warm lips, like fruit ripened in the sun. See our firm, rounded breasts. We glide with the stately grace of swans; we know songs that charm and please, and when we dance, hearts beat faster and pulses throb. Come, friend, do not spurn us; he is foolish, indeed, who would throw away a treasure. Look at us, dear Lord; we are your slaves."

But the Blessed One was unmoved by the song. He frowned at the young girls, and they turned into hags.

In despair they returned to their father. "Father," cried Rati, "see what he has done to our youth and our beauty."

"Love will never hurt him," said Trishna, "for he was able to resist our charms." "Oh," sighed Arati, "how cruelly he has punished us."

"Father," implored Trishna, "cure us of this hideous old age."

"Give us back our youth," cried Rati.

"Give us back our beauty," cried Arati.

"My poor daughters," replied Mara, "I grieve for you. Yes, he has defeated love; he is beyond my power, and I am sad. You plead with me to give you back your youth and your beauty, but how can I? The Buddha alone can undo what the Buddha has done. Return to him; admit that you were blameworthy; tell him that you are repentant, and perhaps he will give you back your charms."

They implored the Buddha.

"Blessed One," said they, "forgive us our offense. Our eyes were blind to the light, and we were foolish. Forgive us!"

"Yes, you were foolish," replied the Blessed One; "you were trying to destroy a mountain with your finger-nails, you were trying to bite through iron with your teeth. But you acknowledge your offense; that already is a sign of wisdom. O maidens, I forgive you."

And the three daughters of the Evil One left his presence, more beautiful than ever before.

The fifth week the Blessed One remained under the tree. But, suddenly, there blew a bitter wind, and a cold rain fell. Then Mucilinda, the serpent-king, said to himself: "The Blessed One must not suffer from the rain or from the cold." He left his home. Seven times he coiled himself around the Buddha, and he spread his hood above the Buddha's head to shelter him. And thus the Buddha suffered not at all during this period of bad weather.

The sixth week he went to a fig-tree where goatherds often forgathered. There, some Gods awaited him, and they humbly bowed as he approached. He said.

"Meekness is sweet to him who knows the law; kindness is sweet to him who can see; meekness is sweet to all creatures; kindness is sweet to all creatures. Blessed is he who has not a desire in the world; blessed is he who has conquered sin; blessed is he who has escaped the torture of the senses; blessed is he who no longer thirsts for existence!"

The seventh week he remained under the tree of

knowledge.

Two brothers, Trapusha and Bhallika, were returning to the northern countries. They were merchants and had five hundred chariots in their train. As they came near the tree, the chariots stopped. In vain did the drivers try to encourage or goad the beasts that drew them; they could not advance a step. The wheels kept sinking in the mud up to the hubs. Trapusha and Bhallika became alarmed, but a God appeared who reassured them and said:

"Walk a little way, O merchants, and you will find one to whom you should do homage."

Trapusha and Bhallika saw the Blessed One. His face was radiant.

"Is it the God of some river or the God of the mountain?" they wondered. "Could it be Brahma himself?"

But upon looking at his garments, they thought:

"It must be some monk. Perhaps he would like something to eat."

Trapusha and Bhallika went to the chariot that carried the provisions. They found flour and honey cakes, and they brought them to the Buddha.

"Take them, saintly man," they said, offering him the cakes, "take them and be gracious to us."

The Blessed One had no bowl in which to receive alms. He did not know what to do. The Gods, who were watching at the four quarters of the earth, saw his perplexity, and they quickly brought him bowls made of gold. But the Blessed One said to himself:

"Truly, it would be unseemly for a monk to receive alms in a golden bowl."

And he refused the golden bowls. The Gods then brought him silver bowls, which he also refused. He likewise refused emerald bowls, and he would only accept bowls made of stone.

He then received the cakes the merchants offered him. When he had finished eating, he said:

"The blessing of the Gods be with you, merchants! Prosper and be happy!"

Trapusha and Bhallika bowed, and they heard a God say to them:

"He who is before you has arrived at supreme knowledge. This was his first meal since he found the path to deliverance, and to you fell the signal honor of offering it to him. He will now go through the world and teach the true law."

Trapusha and Bhallika rejoiced, and they were the first to profess their faith in the Buddha and in the law.

2. The Buddha is Prepared to Preach the Doctrine

THE Buddha began to wonder how he would propagate the knowledge. He said to himself:

"I have discovered a profound truth. It was difficult to perceive; it will be difficult to understand; only the wise will grasp it. In a world full of confusion, men lead restless lives, yet men enjoy living in a world full of confusion. How then can they understand the chain of causes and effects? How can they understand the law? They will never be able to stifle their desires; they will never break away from earthly pleasures; they will never enter nirvana. If I preach the doctrine, I shall not be understood. Perhaps no one will even listen to me. What is the use of revealing to mankind the truth I had to fight to win? Truth stays hidden from those controlled by desire and hatred. Truth is hard to find; it remains ever a mystery. The vulgar mind will never grasp it. He will never know truth whose mind is lost in darkness, who is a prey to earthly desires."

And the Blessed One was not inclined to preach the doctrine. Then Brahma, by virtue of his supreme intelligence, knew of the doubts that beset the Blessed One. He became frightened. "The world is lost," he said to himself, "the world is undone, if the Perfect One, the Holy One, the Buddha, now stands aloof, if he does not go among men to preach the doctrine and propagate the knowledge."

And he left the sky. It took him less time to reach the earth than it takes a strong man to bend or stretch his arm, and he appeared before the Blessed One. To show his deep reverence, he uncovered one shoulder, then kneeling, he raised his folded hands to the Blessed One and said:

"Deign to teach the knowledge, O Master, deign to teach the knowledge, O Blessed One. There are men of great purity in the world, men whom no filth has ever defiled, but, if they are not instructed in the knowledge, how will they find salvation? They must be saved, these men; oh, save them! They will listen to you; they will be your disciples."

Thus spoke Brahma. The Blessed One remained silent. Brahma continued:

"Till now an evil law has prevailed in the world. It has led men into sin. It behooves you to destroy it. O Man of Wisdom, open for us the gates of eternity; tell us what you have found, O Savior! You are he who has climbed the mountain, you stand on the rocky summit, and you survey mankind from afar. Have pity, O Savior; think of the unhappy peoples who suffer the anguish of birth and of old age. Go, conquering hero, go! Travel through the world, be the light and the guide. Speak, teach; there will be many to understand your word."

And the Blessed One answered:

"Profound is the law that I have established; it is subtle and hard to understand; it lies beyond ordinary reasoning. The world will scoff at it; only a few wise men perhaps will grasp the meaning and decide to accept it. If I set out, if I speak and am not understood, I risk an ignominious defeat. I shall stay here, Brahma; men are the sport of ignorance."

But Brahma spoke again:

"You have attained sublime wisdom; the rays of your light reach even into space, yet you are indifferent, O Sun! No, such conduct is unworthy of you; your silence is reprehensible; you must speak. Rise up! Beat the drums, sound the gong! Let the law blaze like a burning torch, or like refreshing rain, let it fall upon the parched earth. Deliver those who are tormented by evil; bring peace to those consumed by a vicious fire! You, who are like a star among men, you alone can destroy birth and death. See, I fall at your feet and implore you, in the name of all the Gods!"

Then the Blessed One thought:

"Among the blue and white lotuses that flower in a pool, there are some that stay under water, others that rise to the surface, and still others that grow so tall that their petals are not even wet. And in the world I see good men and evil men; some have sharp minds and others are dull; some are noble, others ignoble; some will understand me, others will not; but I shall take pity on them all. I shall consider the lotus that opens under water as well as the lotus that flaunts its great beauty."

And he said to Brahma:

"May the gates of eternity be open to all! May all who have ears hear the word and believe! I was thinking of the weariness in store for me and fearing the effort would come to nothing, but my pity outweighs these considerations. I rise, O Brahma, and I shall preach the law to all creatures."

3. The Buddha Leaves for Benares

THE Blessed One wondered who was worthy of being the first to hear the word of salvation. "Where is there a man of virtue, intelligence and energy, to whom I can teach the law?" he asked himself. "His heart must be innocent of hatred, his mind must be tranquil, and he must not keep the knowledge to himself as if it were some dark secret."

He thought of Rudraka, son of Rama. He remembered that he had been free from hatred and had tried to lead a life of virtue, and that he was not the sort of man who would make a secret of the knowledge. He decided to teach him the law, and this question arose in his mind: "Where is Rudraka, now?" Then he learned that Rudraka, son of Rama, had been dead seven days, and he said:

"It is a great pity that Rudraka, son of Rama, should have died without hearing the law. He would have understood it, and he, in turn, could have taught it."

He thought of Arata Kalama. He remembered his clear intellect and his virtuous life, and he decided that Arata Kalama would be glad to propagate the knowledge. And this question arose in his mind: "Where is Arata Kalama now?" Then he learned that Arata Kalama had been dead three days, and he said:

"Arata Kalama died without hearing the law; great is Arata Kalama's loss."

He thought again, and he remembered Rudraka's five disciples who had once joined him. They were virtuous; they were energetic; they would certainly understand the law. The Blessed One knew, by virtue of his intelligence, that Rudraka's five disciples were living in the Deer Park at Benares. So he set out for Benares.

At Mount Gaya he met a monk named Upaka. At the

sight of the Blessed One, Upaka uttered a cry of admiration.

"How beautiful you are!" he exclaimed. "Your face is radiant. Fruit that has ripened in the sun has less bloom. Yours is the beauty of a clear autumn. My Lord, may I ask who your master was?"

"I had no master," answered the Blessed One. "There is no one like me. I alone am wise, calm, incorruptible."

"What a great master you must be!" said Upaka. "Yes, I am the only master in this world; my equal can not be found on earth or in the sky." "Where are you going?" asked Upaka. "I am going to Benares," said the Blessed One, "and there I shall light the lamp that will bring light into the world, a light that will dazzle even the eyes of the blind. I am going to Benares, and there I shall beat the drums that will awaken mankind, the drums that will sound even in the ears of the deaf. I am going to Benares, and there I shall teach the law."

He continued on his way, and he came to the banks of the Ganges. The river was high, and the Blessed One looked for a boatman to take him across. He found one and said to him:

"Friend, will you take me across the river?"

"Certainly," replied the boatman, "but first pay me for the trip."

"I have no money," said the Blessed One.

And he flew through the air to the opposite bank.

The boatman was heart-broken. He cried, "I did not take him across the river, he who was such a saintly man! Oh, woe is me!" And he rolled on the ground in his great distress.

4. The Buddha Finds His Former Disciples

THE Blessed One entered the great city of Benares. He wandered through the streets, asking for alms; he ate the food that was given him, then he went to the Deer Park where he knew he would find Rudraka's former disciples.

The five disciples saw him in the distance. They thought they recognized him, and they said to each other:

"Do we not know this man, walking toward us? Is he not the one whose austerities, formerly, used to astonish us, and who, one day, revolted against the severe self-discipline he had been observing? If his mortifications did not show him the way to supreme knowledge then, how can his thoughts profit us to-day when he is swayed by greed and cowardice? Let us not go and meet him, or rise when he approaches; let us not relieve him of his cloak or of his alms-bowl; let us not even offer him a seat. We will say to him, 'All the seats here are taken.' And we will give him nothing to eat or drink."

Thus did they decide. But the Blessed One kept drawing nearer, and the closer he came the more uncomfortable they felt. They were seized with a great desire to rise from their seats. They were like birds frantically trying to escape from a cage under which a fire has been kindled. They were restless; they seemed to be ill. Finally, they broke their resolution. They rose as one man; they ran to the Blessed One, and they greeted him. One took his alms-bowl, another his cloak; a third offered him a seat. They brought him water to bathe his feet, and with one voice they cried:

"Welcome, friend, welcome. Take a seat in our midst."

The Blessed One sat down and bathed his feet. Then he said to the five hermits:

"Do not address me as friend, O monks. I am the Saint,

the Perfect One, the supreme Buddha. Open your ears, O monks; the path is discovered that leads to deliverance. I will show you the path; I will teach you the law. Listen well, and you will learn the sacred truth."

But they answered:

"Formerly, in spite of your austere practices, you did not arrive at perfect knowledge, so how could you have attained it, now that you lead a life of self-indulgence?"

"O monks," replied the Blessed One, "I do not lead a life of self-indulgence; I have renounced none of the blessings to which I aspired. I am the Saint, the Perfect One, the supreme Buddha. Open your ears, O monks; the path is discovered that leads to deliverance. I will show you the path; I will teach you the law. Listen well, and you will learn the sacred truth."

He added, "O monks, will you admit that I have never before addressed you in this manner?" "We admit it, Master."

"I say unto you: I am the Saint, the Perfect One, the supreme Buddha. Open your ears, O monks; the path is discovered that leads to deliverance. Listen well."

And the five monks listened as he spoke.

"There are two extremes that he must avoid who would lead a life governed by his intelligence. Some devote themselves to pleasure; their lives are a constant round of dissipations; they seek only to gratify their senses. Such beings are contemptible; their conduct is ignoble and futile; it is unworthy of him who would acquire intelligence. Others devote themselves to self-mortification; they deprive themselves of everything; their conduct is gloomy and futile; it is unworthy of him who would acquire intelligence. From these two extremes, O monks, the Perfect One stands aloof. He has discovered the middle path, the path that opens the eyes and opens the mind, the path that leads to rest, to knowledge, to nirvana. This sacred path, O monks, has eight branches: right faith, right resolve, right speech, right action, right living, right effort, right thought, right meditation. This, O monks, is the middle path, the path that I, the Perfect One, discovered, the path that leads to rest, to knowledge, to nirvana."

All five held their breath, the better to hear him. He paused a moment, then continued:

"O monks, I will tell you the truth about suffering. Suffering is birth, suffering is old age, suffering is sickness, suffering is death. You are bound to that which you hate: suffering; you are separated from that which you love: suffering; you do not obtain that which you desire: suffering. To cling to bodies, to sensations, to forms, to impressions, to perceptions: suffering, suffering, suffering. O monks, I will tell you the truth about the origin of suffering. The thirst for existence leads from rebirth to rebirth; lust and pleasure follow. Power alone can satisfy lust. The thirst for power, the thirst for pleasure, the thirst for existence; there, O monks, is the origin of suffering. O monks, I will tell you the truth about the suppression of suffering. Quench your thirst by annihilating desire. Drive away desire. Forgo desire. Free yourselves of desire. Be ignorant of desire. O monks, I will tell you the truth about the path that leads to the extinction of suffering. It is the sacred path, the noble eight-fold path: right faith, right resolve, right speech, right action, right living, right effort, right thought, right meditation. O monks, you know the sacred truth about suffering; no one before me had discovered it; my eyes opened, and suffering was revealed to me. I understood the truth about suffering; you, O monks, must now understand it. O monks, you know the sacred truth about the origin of suffering; no one before me had discovered it; my eyes opened, and the origin of suffering was revealed to me. I understood the truth about the origin of suffering; you, O monks, must now understand it. O monks, you know the sacred truth about the suppression of suffering; no one before me had discovered it; my eyes opened, and the suppression of suffering was revealed to me. I understood the truth about the suppression of suffering; you, O monks, must now understand it. O monks, you know the sacred truth about the path that leads to the extinction of suffering; no one before me had discovered it; my eyes opened, and the path that leads to the extinction of suffering was revealed to me. I understood the truth about the path that leads to the extinction of suffering; you must now understand it, O monks."

The five disciples listened with rapture to the words of the Blessed One. He spoke again: "O monks, as long as I did not have a complete understanding of these four truths, I knew that neither in this world nor in the world of the Gods, in Mara's world nor in Brahma's world I knew that among all beings, men, Gods, hermits or brahmans, I had not attained the supreme rank of Buddha. But, O monks, now that I have a complete understanding of these four truths, I know that in this world as in the world of the Gods, in Mara's world and in Brahma's world, I know that among all beings, men, Gods, hermits or brahmans, I have attained the supreme rank of Buddha. I am for ever set free: for me there will be no new birth."

Thus spoke the Blessed One, and the five monks joyfully acclaimed him and glorified him.

5. The Story of the Hermit and the Hare

KAUNDINYA was the first of the five monks to approach the Blessed One. Fie said: "I have listened, O Master, and if you consider me worthy, I will be your disciple."

"Did you understand me, Kaundinya?" the Blessed One asked.

"I have faith in the Buddha and the Buddha. I would follow," said Kaundinya. "I would follow him who has the knowledge, who knows the worlds, who is a Saint; I would follow him who tames all beings as one tames wild bulls, whose words are heeded by both Gods and men; I would follow him who is the supreme Buddha. I have faith in the law and the law I would follow. The Blessed One has expounded it; it has been clearly set forth; it leads to salvation, and the wise must acknowledge its beneficent power. According to your precepts would I live, according to your saintly precepts, to your precepts that the wise shall praise."

"You have understood, Kaundinya," said the Blessed One. "Come nearer. Well preached is the law. Lead a saintly life, and have done with suffering." Then Vashpa came to the Buddha to profess his faith, and he was followed by Bhadrika, Mahanaman and Asvajit. And presently there were six saints in the world.

The Blessed One was still in the Deer Park when a young man named Yasas arrived. Yasas was the son of a wealthy merchant of Benares. He had been leading a worldly existence, but he had learned the vanity of such things, and he was now seeking the sacred peace of the woods. The Blessed One saw Yasas; he spoke to him, and Yasas announced that he was ready to walk in the path of holiness.

The father of Yasas came to the Deer Park to look for

his son. He wanted to discourage him, to make him turn aside from the path of holiness. But he heard the Buddha speak; his words impressed him, and he believed in him. The mother and the wife of Yasas also professed their belief in the truth of the law, but while Yasas joined the monks, his father, his mother and his wife returned to their home in Benares.

Four friends of Yasas, Vimala, Subahu, Purnajit and Gavampati, were amused at the step he had taken. They said:

"Let us go to the Deer Park and look for Yasas. We shall convince him of his mistake, and he will return with us." Upon entering the wood, they found the Buddha instructing his disciples. He was saying:

"There was once a hermit who dwelt in a ravine far up in the mountains. He lived miserably and alone. His clothes were made out of bark; he drank only water, and he ate nothing but roots and wild fruit. His sole companion was a hare. This hare could speak like a human being, and he liked to talk to the hermit. He derived great benefit from his teachings, and he strove earnestly to attain wisdom. Now, one year, there was a terrible drought: the mountain springs dried up, and the trees failed to flower or bear fruit. The hermit could no longer find food or water; he became weary of his mountain retreat, and, one day, he cast aside his hermit's robe. The hare saw him and said, 'Friend, what are you doing?' 'You can see for yourself,' replied the hermit. 'I have no further use for this robe.' 'What!' exclaimed the hare, 'are you going to leave the ravine?' 'Yes, I shall go among people. I shall receive alms, and they will give me food, not just roots and fruit.' At these words the hare became frightened; he was like a child abandoned by its father, and he cried, 'Do not go, friend! Do not leave me alone! Besides, many are ruined who go to live in cities! The solitary life of the forest is alone praiseworthy.' But the hermit was determined: he had decided to go, he would go. Then the hare said to him: 'You would leave the mountains? Then leave! But grant me this favor: wait a day longer, just one day. Stay here to-day, to-morrow you may do as you please.' The hermit thought, 'Hares are good foragers; they often have a store of provisions hidden away. To-morrow this one may bring me something to eat.' So he promised not to leave until the following day, and the hare scampered off joyously. The hermit was one of those who held Agni in great reverence, and he was careful always to keep a fire burning in the ravine. 'I have no food,' he said to himself, 'but at least I can keep warm until the hare returns.' At dawn the following day, the hare reappeared, empty-handed. The hermit's face betrayed his disappointment. The hare bowed to him and said, 'We animals have neither sense nor judgment; forgive me, worthy hermit, if I have done wrong.' And he suddenly leaped into the flames. 'What are you doing?' cried the hermit. He sprang to the fire and rescued the hare. Then the hare said to him, 'I would not have you fail in your duty; I would not have you leave this retreat. There is no longer any food to be had. I have given my body to the flames; take it, friend; feed upon my flesh. and stay in the ravine.' The hermit was deeply moved. He replied, 'I shall not take the road to the city; I shall remain here, even if I must die of starvation.' The hare was happy; he looked up at the sky and murmured this prayer: 'Indra, I have always loved the life of solitude. Deign to hear me, and cause the rain to fall.' Indra heard the prayer. The rail fell in torrents, and presently the hermit and his friend found all the food they wanted in the ravine."

After a moment of silence, the Blessed One added:

"At that time, O monks, the hare was I. As for the hermit, he was one of the evil-minded young men who have just entered the Deer Park. Yes, you were he, Vimala!"

He rose from his seat.

"Just as I kept you from following the evil path when I was a hare living in the ravine, Vimala, so shall I show you the way to holiness, now that I have become the supreme Buddha, and your eyes will see, your ears will hear. Why, you are already blushing with shame at having tried to prevent your best friend from finding salvation!"

Vimala fell at the feet of the Blessed One. He professed his faith in him, and he was received among the disciples. Then

Subahu, Purnajit and Gavampati also decided to accept the sacred word.

Each day the number of disciples increased, and soon the master had sixty monks ready to propagate the knowledge. He said to them: "O disciples, I am free of all bonds, human and divine. And you, too, are now free. So start on your way, O disciples, go, out of pity for the world, for the world's happiness, go. It is to you that Gods and men will owe their welfare and their joy. Set out on the road, singly and alone. And teach, O disciples, teach the glorious law, the law glorious in the beginning, glorious in the middle, glorious in the end; teach the spirit of the law; teach the letter of the law; to all who hear, proclaim the perfect, the pure, the saintly life. There 'are some who are not blinded by the dust of the earth, but they will not find salvation if they do not hear the law proclaimed. So go, O disciples, go and teach them the law."

The disciples scattered, and the Blessed One took the road to Uruvilva.

6. The Story of Padmaka

THE Blessed One had been walking a long while. He was weary. Coming to a small wood, he entered and sat down at the foot of a tree. He was about to fall asleep when a band of thirty young men entered the wood. He watched them.

From their words and behavior, it was evident that they were looking for some one. They finally addressed the Buddha.

"Did you see a woman pass by?" they asked. "No. Who are you?"

"We are musicians. We wander from city to city. We have often played before kings, for our skill is greatly admired. We brought a young girl along with us to-day, for our pleasure, but while we were sleeping, over there; by the side of the road, she stole all that she could take with her and fled. It is she we are seeking."

"Which is better," the Buddha asked: "that you go in search of this woman, or that you go in search of yourselves?"

The musicians laughed at the Master. "Play your lute," he then said to the one who was laughing the loudest.

The musician played. He was skillful; it was easy to believe that kings delighted in his playing. When he had finished the Master said:

"Give me your lute."

And he played. The musicians listened with amazement. They never knew such sweet notes could be plucked from a lute. Even the wind was silent, and the Goddesses of the wood left their verdant retreats, the better to hear him.

The Blessed One stopped playing.

"Master," said the musicians, "we thought we were skilled in our art, and we are ignorant of its first principles. Deign to teach us all you know."

The Blessed One replied, "You suspect, now, that your knowledge of music is superficial, yet you once thought you had mastered the art. And so you think you know yourselves, but your knowledge is only superficial. You earnestly ask me to teach you all I know about music, yet you laugh when I tell you to go in search of yourselves!"

The musicians were no longer laughing.

"We understand you, Master," they cried, "we understand you! We shall go in search of ourselves."

"It is well," said the Buddha. "You will learn the law from me. Then, like King Padmaka, who sacrificed his body to save his people, you will give your intelligence to save mankind."

And the musicians listened with rapt attention while he told the story of King Padmaka.

"There once reigned in Benares a just and powerful king named Padmaka. Now, a strange epidemic suddenly swept through the city. Those who were stricken turned completely yellow, and, even in the sunshine, they shivered with cold. The king took pity on his subjects, and he tried to find some way to cure them. He consulted the most famous physicians; he distributed medicines, and he himself helped to nurse the sick. But it was hopeless; the epidemic continued to rage. Padmaka grieved. One day, an old physician came to him and said, 'My lord, I know a remedy that will cure the inhabitants of Benares.' 'What is it?' asked the king. 'It is a large fish named Rohita. Have him caught, and give a piece, no matter how small, to all who are sick, and the epidemic will disappear.' The king thanked the old physician; he ordered the fish Rohita to be sought in the seas and in the rivers, but nowhere could it be found. The king was in despair. Sometimes in the morning or in the evening, he would hear plaintive voices crying outside the palace walls, 'We are suffering, O king; save us!' And he would weep bitterly. Finally, he thought: 'What good is wealth or royalty, what good is life, if I can not succor those who are racked with pain?' He summoned his eldest son, and he said to him, 'My son, I leave you my fortune and my kingdom.' Then he ascended to the terrace of the palace; he offered perfume and flowers to the Gods, and he cried, 'Gladly do I sacrifice a life that I consider useless. May the sacrifice benefit those who are afflicted! May I become the fish Rohita and be found in the river that flows through the city!' He threw himself from the terrace and immediately reappeared in the river as the fish Rohita. He was caught; he was still alive when they cut him into pieces to distribute among the sick, but he never felt the knives, and he quivered with love for all creatures. The epidemic soon disappeared, and over the city of Benares, a celestial choir sang: 'It was Padmaka, the holy king, who saved you! Rejoice!' And they all did honor to Padmaka's memory."

The musicians listened to the Master, and they promised to follow him, to receive the knowledge.

In Uruvilva, the Blessed One found the three Kasyapa brothers. These virtuous brahmans had a thousand disciples. For some time they had been bothered by a dangerous serpent that kept disturbing their sacrifices, and they brought their troubles to the Buddha. The Buddha smiled; he watched for the serpent and ordered it, in the future, to leave them in peace. The serpent obeyed, and the sacrifices were no longer interrupted.

The Kasyapas asked the Buddha to stay with them a few days. He consented. He astounded his hosts by performing innumerable prodigies, and presently they all decided to accept the law. The eldest of the Kasyapas alone refused to follow the Buddha. He thought:

"True, this monk is very powerful; he performs great prodigies, but he is not my equal in holiness."

The Blessed One read Kasyapa's thoughts. He said to him:

"You think you are a very holy man, Kasyapa, and you are not even in the path that leads to holiness."

Kasyapa was astonished that the Buddha should have guessed his secret thoughts. The Blessed One added:

"You do not even know how to find the path that leads to holiness. Hearken to my words, Kasyapa, if you would dispel the darkness in which you live."

Kasyapa thought for a moment; then he fell at the feet of the Blessed One, and he said:

"Instruct me, O Master! Let me walk no longer in the night!"

Then the Blessed One ascended a mountain, and he addressed the Kasyapa brothers and their disciples.

"O monks," said he, "everything in the world is aflame. The eye is aflame; all that it sees is aflame; all that we behold in the world is aflame. Why? Because the fire of love and of hatred is not extinguished. You are blinded by the flames of this fire, and you suffer the torment of birth and of old age, of death and of misery. O monks, everything in the world is aflame! Understand me, and for you the fire will be extinguished; your eyes will no longer be blinded by the flames, and you will no longer enjoy the blazing spectacle in which you delight to-day. Understand me, and you will know that there is an end to birth, you will know that to this earth we need never return."

7. The Buddha at the Bamboo Grove

THE Blessed One remembered that King Vimbasara had once expressed a desire to know the law, and he resolved to go to Rajagriha. He set out with the eldest Kasyapa and a few of his new disciples, and he went to live in a wood, near the city.

Vimbasara soon learned of the arrival of the monks. He decided to pay them a visit. Accompanied by a host of retainers, he went to the wood. He recognized the Master, and he exclaimed:

"You did not forget my wish, O Blessed One; great is my gratitude and my reverence."

He prostrated himself, and when the Master bade him rise, he stood at a distance, to show his respect.

But in the crowd there were some who knew Kasyapa, and who considered him a very saintly man. They had never seen the Buddha before, and they were astonished that the king should do him such honor.

He has surely made a mistake," said one brahman; "he should have prostrated himself before Kasyapa."

"Yes," said another, "Kasyapa is a great master." "The king has made a strange blunder," a third added; "he has mistaken the pupil for the master."

They were speaking in whispers, yet the Blessed One heard them, for what could escape his notice? He said to Kasyapa:

"Who persuaded you to leave your hermitage, O man of Uruvilva? Who made you admit your weakness? Answer, Kasyapa; how did you come to leave your familiar retreat?"

Kasyapa understood what the Master had in mind. He replied:

"I know now where my former austerities were tending; I know the vanity of all that I once taught. My discourse was evil, and I began to hate the life I was leading."

As he said these words, he fell at the Master's feet, and he added:

"I am your devoted pupil. Let me lay my head upon your feet! You are the Master; it is you who command. I am your pupil, your servant. You will I heed and you will I obey."

Seven times he prostrated himself, and the crowd exclaimed in admiration:

"Mighty is he who has convinced Kasyapa of his ignorance! Kasyapa thought he was the greatest of teachers, and now see him bow before another! Oh, mighty is he who is Kasyapa's master!" Then the Blessed One spoke to them of the four great truths. When he had finished, King Vimbasara approached him, and, in front of them all, boldly uttered these words:

"I believe in the Buddha, I believe in the law, I believe in the community of the saints."

The Blessed One gave the king leave to sit beside him, and the king spoke again:

"In my lifetime I have had five great hopes: I hoped that some day I would be king; I hoped that some day the Buddha would come into my kingdom; I hoped that some day my gaze would rest upon his countenance; I hoped that some day he would teach me the law; I hoped that some day I would profess my faith in him. To-day, all these hopes are realized. I believe in you, my Lord, I believe in the law, I believe in the community of the saints."

He rose.

"O Master, deign to take your meal at my palace, to-morrow."

The Master consented. The king left; he knew great happiness.

Many of those who had accompanied the king now followed his example, and professed their faith in the Buddha, in the law and in the community of the saints.

The next day, the inhabitants of Rajagriha left their

homes and went to the wood; they were eager to see the Blessed One; They all admired him, and they praised his power and his glory.

The time came for him to go to the king's palace, but the road was so crowded with spectators that it was impossible to advance a step. Suddenly, a young brahman appeared before the Master. No one knew whence he came. He said:

"The gentle Master is among gentle folk; he brings deliverance. He who shines like gold has come to Rajagriha."

He had a pleasant voice. He beckoned to the crowd to make way, and they obeyed without a thought of resisting. And he sang:

"The Master has dispelled the darkness; night will never be reborn; he who knows the supreme law has come to Rajagriha."

"Where does he come from, this young brahman with the clear, sweet voice?" the people wondered.

He continued to sing:

"He is here, he who is omniscient, the gentle Master, the sublime Buddha. He is supreme in the world; I am happy to serve him. Not to serve the ignorant, but humbly to serve the wise and to venerate those who are noble: is there in the world a holier joy? To live in a land of peace, to do many good works, to seek the triumph of righteousness: is there in the world a holier joy? To have skill and knowledge, to love acts of generosity, to walk in the path of justice: is there in the world a holier joy?"

The young brahman managed to make a way through the crowd, and he led the Master to the palace of King Vimbasara. Then, his work done, he rose from the earth, and upon attaining the highest reaches of the sky, vanished into the light. And the people of Rajagriha knew that a God had deemed it an honor to serve the Buddha and exalt his grandeur.

Vimbasara received the Blessed One with great reverence. At the end of the meal, he said to him:

"I rejoice at your presence, my Lord. I must see you often, and often hear the sacred word from your lips. You must now accept a gift from me. Nearer the city than that forest where you dwell, there is a pleasant wood, known as the Bamboo Grove. It is vast; you and your disciples can live there in comfort. I give you the Bamboo Grove, my Lord, and if you will accept it, I shall feel that you have done me a great service."

The Buddha smiled with pleasure. A golden basin was brought, filled with sweet-scented water. The king took the basin and poured the water over the Master's hands. And he said:

"As this water pours from my hands into your hands, my Lord, so may the Bamboo Grove pass from my hands into your hands, my Lord."

The earth trembled: the law now had soil in which to take root. And that same day, the Master and his disciples went to live in the Bamboo Grove.

8. Sariputra and Maudgalyayana

TWO young brahmans, Sariputra and Maudgalyayana, were living at that time in the city of Rajagriha. They were intimate friends and were both pupils of the hermit Sanjaya. To each other they had made this promise: "Whichever one of us first obtains deliverance from death will immediately tell the other."

One day, Sariputra saw Asvajit collecting alms in the streets of Rajagriha. He was struck by his pleasant countenance, his noble and modest demeanor, his quiet and dignified bearing. He said to himself:

"Verily, there is a monk who, already in this world, has found the sure path to saintliness. I must go up to hip; I must ask him who his master is and what law he obeys."

But then he thought:

"This is not the proper time to question him. He is collecting alms; I must not disturb him. I shall follow him, and when he is satisfied with the offerings he has received, I shall approach and speak to him." The venerable Asvajit presently stopped asking for alms. Then Sariputra went up to him and greeted him in a friendly manner. Asvajit returned Sariputra's greeting.

"Friend," said Sariputra, "serene is your countenance, clear and radiant your glance. Who persuaded you to renounce the world? Who is your master? What law do you obey?"

"Friend," replied Asvajit, "that great monk, the son of the Sakyas, is my master."

"What does your master say, friend; what does he teach?"

"Friend, I left the world but recently; I have known the law only a short time; I can not expound it at great length, but I can give you briefly the spirit of it."

"Do, friend," cried Sariputra. "Say little or say much, as you please; but give me the spirit of the law. To me the spirit only matters."

The venerable Asvajit spoke this one sentence:

"The Perfect One teaches the cause, the Perfect One teaches the ends."

Sariputra rejoiced at these words. It was as if the truth had been revealed to him. "All that is born has an end," he thought. He thanked Asvajit, and, filled with hope, he went to find Maudgalyayana.

"Friend," said Maudgalyayana when he saw Sariputra, "friend, how serene is your countenance! How clear and radiant your glance! Have you obtained deliverance from death?"

"Yes, friend. Near Rajagriha, there is a master who teaches deliverance from death."

Sariputra told of his encounter, and the two friends decided to go to the Blessed One. Their master, Sanjaya, tried to dissuade them.

"Stay with me," said he; "I will give you a position of eminence among my disciples. You will become masters and be my equals."

"Why should we want to be your equals? Why should we disseminate ignorance? We know now what your teaching is worth. It would make us masters of ignorance."

Sanjaya continued to urge them; suddenly, warm blood gushed from his mouth. The two friends drew back in horror.

They left and went to the Buddha.

"Here," said the Master as he saw them approach, "here are the two men who will be the foremost among my disciples."

And he joyfully welcomed them to the community.

9. The Buddha Pacifies the Malcontents of Rajagriha

THE number of believers was constantly increasing, and King Vimbasara gave repeated evidence to the Master of his faith and friendship. He often invited him to the palace and offered him a seat at his table, and at such times he would order the city to have a festive appearance. The streets were carpeted with flowers, and the houses decorated with banners. The sweetest perfumes filled the air, and the inhabitants dressed in their brightest clothes. The king himself would come forward to greet the Blessed One and would shade him from the sun with his golden parasol.

Many young nobles put all their faith in the law taught by the Blessed One. They wanted to become saints; they abandoned family and fortune, and the Bamboo Grove was soon filled with devout disciples.

But there were many in Rajagriha who were disturbed to see the great number of converts the Buddha was making, and they went about the city, voicing their anger. "Why has he settled in our midst, this son of the Sakyas?" they would ask. "Were there not enough monks already, preaching to us about virtue? And they did not lure our young men away like this master. Why, even our children are leaving us. Because of this son of the Sakyas, how many women are widows! Because of this son of the Sakyas, how many families are childless! Evil will befall the kingdom, now that this monk has settled in our midst!"

The Master soon had a great many enemies among the inhabitants of the city. Whenever they met his disciples, they would taunt them or make sarcastic remarks.

"The great monk came to the city of Rajagriha and conquered the Bamboo Grove; will he now conquer the entire kingdom of Magadha?" said one as he went by.

"The great monk came to the city of Rajagriha and took Sanjaya's disciples away from him; who will he lure away to-day?" said another.

"A plague would be less harmful than this great monk," said a third; "it would kill fewer children."

"And it would leave fewer widows," a woman sighed.

The disciples made no reply. But they felt the anger of the populace growing, and they told the Master of the evil words they had heard.

"Do not let it disturb you, O disciples," replied the Buddha. "They will soon stop. To those who follow you with jeers and insults, speak quiet, gentle words. Say to them, 'It is because they know the truth, the real truth, that the heroes convince, that the perfect ones convert. Who dares offend the Buddha, the Saint who converts by the power of truth?' Then they will be silent, and in a few days, when you wander through the city, you will meet only with respect and praise."

It happened as the Buddha had said. The evil voices were silenced, and every one in Rajagriha did honor to the Master's disciples.

10. Suddhodana Sends Messengers to His Son

KING Suddhodana heard that his son had attained supreme knowledge and that he was living at Rajagriha, in the Bamboo Grove. He had a great desire to see him again, and he sent a messenger to him, with these words: "Your father, King Suddhodana, longs to see you, O Master."

When the messenger arrived at the Bamboo Grove, he found the Master addressing his disciples.

"There is a forest clinging to the slope of a mountain, and at the foot of the mountain, a wide, deep pool. Wild beasts live on the banks of this pool. A man appears who would harm these beasts, who would make them suffer, who would let them die. He closes up the good path that leads away from the pool, the path that is safe to travel, and he opens up a treacherous path that ends in a dreadful swamp. The beasts are now in danger; one by one, they will perish. But let a man appear who, on the contrary, seeks the welfare of these wild beasts, who seeks their comfort, their prosperity. He will destroy the treacherous path that ends in a swamp, and he will open up a safe path that leads to the peaceful mountain top. Then the beasts will no longer be in danger; they will thrive and multiply. Now understand what I have told you, O disciples. Like these beasts on the banks of the wide, deep pool, man lives near the pleasures of the world. He who would do him harm, who would make him suffer, who would let him die, is Mara, the Evil One. The swamp wherein all beings perish is pleasure, desire, ignorance. He who seeks the welfare, the comfort, the prosperity of all is the Perfect One, the Saint, the blessed Buddha. It was I, O disciples, who opened up the safe path; it was I who destroyed the treacherous path. You will not go to the swamp; you will climb the mountain and reach the bright summit. All that a master can do who pities his disciples and who seeks their welfare, I have done for you, O my disciples."

The messenger listened in a transport of delight. Then he fell at the Master's feet and said:

"Receive me among your disciples, O Blessed One."

The Master extended his hands and said: "Come, O monk."

The messenger stood up, and, suddenly, his clothes, of their own accord, took the shape and color of a monk's robe. He forgot everything, and the message that Suddhodana had entrusted to him was never delivered.

The king became weary of waiting for his return. Each day, the desire to see his son became more intense, and he sent another messenger to the Bamboo Grove. But for this man's return he also waited in vain. Nine times he sent messengers to the Blessed One, and nine times the messengers, upon hearing the sacred word, decided to remain and become monks.

Suddhodana finally summoned Udayin.

"Udayin," said he, "as you know, of the nine messengers who set out for the Bamboo Grove, not one has returned, not one has sent me word how my message was received. I do not know if they spoke to my son, if they even saw him. It grieves °me, Udayin. I am an old man. Death lies in wait for me. I may live till to-morrow, but it would be rash to count on the days that follow after. And before I die, Udayin, I want to see my son. You were once his best friend; go to him now. I can think of no one who would be more welcome. Tell him of my grief; tell him of my wish, and may he not be indifferent!"

"I shall go, my lord," replied Udayin.

He went. Long before he arrived at the Bamboo Grove, he had made up his mind to become a monk, but King Suddhodana's words had affected him deeply, and he thought, "I shall tell the Master of his father's grief. He will be moved to pity and will go to him."

The Master was happy to see Udayin become one of his disciples.

Winter was almost over. It was a favorable time to travel, and Udayin said to the Buddha, one day:

"The trees are budding; they will soon be in leaf. See the bright rays of the sun shining through the branches. Master, this is a good time to travel. It is no longer cold, nor it is yet too warm; and the earth wears a lovely mantle of green. We shall have no trouble finding food on the way. Master, this is a good time to travel."

The Master smiled at Udayin and asked:
"Why do you urge me to travel, Udayin?"
"Your father, King Suddhodana, would be happy to see you, Master."

The Buddha considered a moment, then he said: "I shall go to Kapilavastu; I shall go and see my father."

11. The Story of the Crane and the Fish

WHEN Vimbasara heard that the Master was leaving the Bamboo Grove, to be gone for some time, he went to see him with his son, Prince Ajatasatru.

The Master looked at the young prince; then turning to the king, he said:

"May Ajatasatru be worthy of your love, O king."

Again he looked at the prince, and he said to him:

"Now listen well, Ajatasatru, and ponder my words. Cunning does not always succeed; wickedness does not always prevail. A story will prove this, the story of something that happened long ago, something I saw with my own eyes. I was then living in a forest; I was a tree-God. This tree grew between two pools, one small and unattractive, the other wide and beautiful. The little pool was full of fish; in the larger one, lotuses grew in great profusion. During a certain summer of oppressive heat, the little pool almost completely dried up; while the large pool, sheltered from the sun as it was by the lotuses, always had plenty of water and remained pleasantly cool. A crane, passing between these two pools, saw the fish and stopped. Standing on one leg, he began to think: 'These fish would be a lawful prize. But they are quick; they are likely to escape if I attack them too hastily. I must use cunning Poor fish! They are so uncomfortable in this dried-up pool! And over there is that other pool, full of deep, cool water, where they could swim about to their heart's content!' A fish saw the crane deep in thought and looking as solemn as a hermit, and he asked, 'What are you doing there, venerable bird? You seem immersed in thought.' 'I am meditating, O fish,' said the crane, 'yes, indeed, I am meditating. I am wondering how you and your friends can escape your sad fate.' 'Our sad fate! What do you mean?' 'You suffer in that shallow water, O unhappy fish! And each day, as the heat becomes more intense, the water will fall still further, and then what will become of you? For presently the pool will be completely dry, and you will all perish! Poor, poor fish! I weep for you.' All the fish had heard what the crane said. They were filled with dismay. 'What will become of us,' they cried, 'when the heat will have dried up the pool?' They turned to the crane. 'Bird, O venerable bird, can you not save us?' The crane again pretended to be lost in thought; finally, he replied, 'I believe I see a way out of your misery.' The fish listened eagerly. The crane said, 'There is a marvelous pool quite near here. It is considerably larger than the one in which you live, and the lotuses that cover the surface have protected the water from the summer's thirst. Take my word for it, go live in that pool. I can pick you up in my bill, one at a time, and carry you there. In that way, you will all be saved.' The fish were happy. They were about to accept the crane's suggestion when a crayfish spoke up. 'I have never heard anything quite so strange,' he exclaimed. The fish asked him, 'What is there to astonish you about that?' 'Never,' said the crayfish, 'never, since the beginning of the world, did I know a crane to take an interest in fish, unless it was perhaps to eat them.' The crane assumed an offended air and said, 'What, you wicked crayfish, you suspect me of trying to deceive these poor fish who are in imminent danger of death! O fish, I only want to save you; it is your welfare I seek. Put my good faith to a test if you wish. Choose one of your number, and I shall carry him in my bill to the lotus pool. He will see it; he can even swim around a few times; then I shall pick him up and bring him back here. He will tell you what to think of me.' 'That seems quite fair,' said the fish. To make this trip to the pool, they chose one of the older fish who, although half blind, was considered quite a sage. The crane carried him to the pool, dropped him in, and let him swim about as much as he pleased. The old fish was delighted, and when he returned to his friends, he had only words of praise for the crane. The fish were now convinced that they would owe their lives to him. 'Take us,' they cried, 'take us and carry us to the lotus pool.' 'Just as you wish,' said the crane, and with his bill he again picked up the old, half-blind fish. But this time he did not carry him to the pool. Instead, he dropped him on the ground and stabbed him with his bill; then he ate him and left the bones at the foot of a tree, the tree of which I was the God. This done, the crane returned to the small pool and said, 'Who will come with me now?' The fish were eager to see their new home, and the crane had only to make a choice that would satisfy his appetite. Presently, he had eaten them all, one after another. Only the crayfish remained. The crayfish had already shown that he distrusted the bird, and he was now saying to himself, 'I doubt very much that the fish are in the lotus pool. I am afraid the crane has taken advantage of their faith in him. Still, it would be well for me to leave this miserable pool and go to the other one which is so much larger and more comfortable. The crane must carry me, but I must run no risk. And if he has deceived the others, I must avenge them.' The bird approached the crayfish. 'It is your turn, now,' said the crane. 'How will you carry me?' asked the crayfish. 'In my bill, like the others,' replied the crane. 'No, no,' said the crayfish; 'my shell is slippery; I might fall out of your bill. Rather, let me hold on to your neck with my claws; I shall be careful not to hurt you.' The crane agreed. He stopped at the foot of the tree. 'What are you doing?' asked the crayfish. 'We are only half-way. Are you tired? Yet the distance is not great between the two pools!' The crane was at a loss for an answer. Besides, the crayfish was beginning to tighten the hold on his neck. 'And what have we here!' exclaimed the crayfish. 'This pile of fish-bones at the foot of the tree is evidence of your treachery. But you will not deceive me as you deceived the others. I shall kill you, if I must die in the attempt.' The crayfish tightened his claws. The crane was in great pain; with tears in his eyes, he cried, 'Dear crayfish, do not hurt me. I shall not eat you. I shall carry you to the pool.' 'Then go,' said the crayfish. The crane walked to the edge of the pool and extended his neck over the water. The crayfish had only to drop into the pool. Instead, he tightened his grip, and so powerful were his claws that the crane's neck was severed. And the tree-God could not help exclaiming, 'Well done, crayfish!' " The Master added: "Cunning does not always succeed. Wickedness does not always prevail. Sooner or later the treacherous crane meets a crayfish. Always remember that, Prince Ajatasatru!"

Vimbasara thanked the Master for the valuable lesson he had taught his son. Then he said:

"Blessed One, I have a request to make."

"Speak," said the Buddha.

"When you are gone, O Blessed One, I shall be unable to do you honor, I shall be unable to make you the customary offerings, and it will grieve me. Give me a lock of your hair, give me the parings of your finger-nails; I shall place them in a temple in the midst of my palace. Thus, I shall retain something that is a part of you, and, each day, I shall decorate the temple with fresh garlands, and I shall burn rare incense."

The Blessed One gave the king these things for which he had asked, and he said:

"Take my hair and take these parings; keep them in a temple, but, in your mind, keep what I have taught you."

And as Vimbasara joyfully returned to his palace, the Master left for Kapilavastu.

12. The Story of Visvantara

IT was a great distance from Rajagriha to Kapilavastu, and the Master was walking slowly. Udayin decided to go ahead and inform Suddhodana that his son was on his way to see him, for the king would then be patient and would cease to grieve.

Udayin flew through the air, and, in a trice, had arrived at Suddhodana's palace. He found the king in deep despair.

"My lord," said he, "dry your tears. Your son will be in Kapilavastu before long."

"Oh, it is you, Udayin!" exclaimed the king. "I thought that you, too, had forgotten to deliver my message, and I had given up hope of ever seeing my beloved son. But you have come at last, and joyful is the news you bring. I shall weep no more; I shall now patiently await the blessed moment when these eyes shall look again upon my son."

He ordered that Udayin be served a splendid repast.

"I will not eat here, my lord," said Udayin. "Before I touch any food, I must know if my master has been properly served. I shall return to him the way I came."

The king protested.

"It is my wish, Udayin, that you receive your food from me, each day; and it is also my wish that my son receive his food from me, each day of this journey which he has undertaken to please me. Eat, and I shall then give you food to take to the Blessed One."

When Udayin had eaten, he was given a bowl of delicious food to take to the king's son. He tossed the bowl into the air; then he rose from the ground and flew away. The bowl fell at the Buddha's feet, and the Buddha thanked his friend. Each day thereafter, Udayin flew to the palace of King Suddhodana to fetch the Master's food, and the Master was pleased with the zeal his disciple showed in serving him.

He finally arrived at Kapilavastu. To receive him, the Sakyas had assembled in a park bright with flowers. Many of those present were extremely proud, and they thought, "There are some here who are older than Siddhartha! Why should they pay him homage? Let the children, let the young men and young maidens, bow before him; his elders will hold their heads high!"

The Blessed One entered the park. All eyes were dazzled by the brilliant light he diffused. King Suddhodana was deeply moved; he made a few steps in his direction. "My son . . ." he cried. His voice faltered; tears of joy coursed down his cheeks, and he slowly bowed his head.

And when the Sakyas saw the father paying homage to the son, they all humbly prostrated themselves.

A magnificent seat had been prepared for the Master. He sat down. Then the sky opened, and a shower of roses descended on the park. Earth and atmosphere were impregnated with the perfume. The king and all the Sakyas gazed in wonderment. And the Master spoke.

"I have already, in some former existence, seen my family grouped around me and heard them sing my praises as with one voice. At that time King Sanjaya was reigning in the city of Jayatura. His wife's name was Phusati, and they had a son, Visvantara. When he came of age, Visvantara married Madri, a princess of rare beauty. She bore him two children: a son, Jalin, and a daughter, Krishnajina. Visvantara owned a white elephant that had the marvelous power to make the rain fall at will. Now, the distant kingdom of Kalinga was visited by a terrible drought. The grass withered; the trees bore no fruit; men and beasts died of hunger and of thirst. The king of Kalinga heard of Visvantara's elephant and of the strange power it possessed. He sent eight brahmans to Jayatura to get it and return with it to their unfortunate country. The brahmans arrived during a festival. Riding on the elephant, the prince was on his way to the temple, to distribute alms. He saw these envoys of the foreign king. 'What brings you here?' he asked them. 'My lord,' replied the brahmans, 'our kingdom, the kingdom of Kalinga, has been visited by drought and famine. Your elephant can save us, by bringing us the rain; will you part with him?' 'It is little you ask,' said Visvantara. 'You could have asked me for my eyes or my flesh! Yes, take the elephant, and may a refreshing rain fall upon your fields and upon your gardens!' He gave the elephant to the brahmans, and they joyfully returned to Kalinga. But the inhabitants of Jayatura were greatly distressed; they feared a drought in their own country. They complained to King Sanjaya. 'My lord,' said they, 'your son's action was reprehensible. His elephant protected us from famine. What will become of us now, if the sky withholds its rain? Show him no mercy, O king; let Visvantara pay for this folly with his life.' The king wept. He tried to put them off with promises, and at first they would not listen, but they finally relented and asked that the prince be exiled to some remote and rocky desert. The king was obliged to give his consent. 'When my son hears of his exile,' thought Sanjaya, 'he will take it to heart.' But this was not the case. Visvantara simply said, 'I shall leave tomorrow, father, and I shall take none of my treasures with me.' Then he went to look for Madri, his princess. 'Madri,' said he, 'I must leave the city; my father has exiled me to a cruel desert, where it will be hard to find a livelihood. Do not come with me, O beloved; too great are the hardships you will have to endure. You will have to leave the children behind, and they will die of loneliness. Stay here with them; remain on your golden throne; it was I my father exiled, not you.' 'My lord,' replied the princess, 'if you leave me behind I shall kill myself, and the crime will lie at your door.' Visvantara was silent. He gazed at Madri; he embraced her. 'Come,' said he. Madri thanked him, and she added, 'I shall take the children with me; I can not leave them here, to die of loneliness.' The following day, Visvantara had his chariot made ready; he got in with Madri, Jalin and Krishnajina, and as they drove out of the city, King Sanjaya and Queen Phusati wept and sobbed pitifully. The prince, his wife and the children were already far from the city when they saw a brahman approaching. 'Traveler,' said the brahman, 'is this the road to Jayatura?' 'Yes,' replied Visvantara, 'but why are you going to Jayatura?' 'I come from a distant country,' said the brahman. 'I heard that there lived in Jayatura a generous prince named Visvantara. He once owned a marvelous elephant that he gave to the king of Kalinga. He is very charitable, they say. I want to see this kindly man; I want to ask him for a donation. I know that no one has ever appealed to him in vain.' Visvantara said to the brahman, 'I am the man you seek; I am Visvantara, son of King Sanjaya. Because I gave my elephant to the king of Kalinga, my father sent me into exile. What can I give you, O brahman?' When he heard these words, the brahman complained bitterly. He said in a pitiful voice: 'So they deceived me! I left my home, full of hope, and, disappointed, I must now return!' Visvantara interrupted him. 'Console yourself, brahman. Not in vain have you appealed to Prince Visvantara.' He unharnessed the horses and gave them to him. The brahman thanked his benefactor and left. Visvantara then continued on his way. He was now drawing the chariot himself. Presently, he saw another brahman approaching. He was a little, frail old man, with white hair and yellow teeth. 'Traveler,' he said to the prince, 'is this the road to Jayatura?' 'Yes,' replied the prince, 'but why are you going to Jayatura?' 'The king of that city has a son, Prince Visvantara,' said the brahman. 'Visvantara, according to the stories I have heard, is extremely charitable; he saved the kingdom of Kalinga from famine, and whatever is asked of him is never refused. I shall go to Visvantara, and I know he will not deny my request.' 'If you go to Jayatura,' said the prince, 'you will not see Visvantara; his father has exiled him to the desert.' 'Woe is me!' cried the brahman. 'Who now will help me in my feeble old age? All hope has fled, and I shall return to my home as poor as when I left!' He wept. 'Do not weep,' said Visvantara; 'I am the man you seek. You have not met me in vain. Madri, Jalin, Krishnajina, get down from the chariot! It is no longer mine: I have given it to this old man.' The brahman was overjoyed. The four exiles continued on their way. They were now on foot, and when the children were tired, Visvantara would carry Jalin, and Madri

Krishnajina. A few days later, they saw a third brahman approaching. He was going to Jayatura to see Prince Visvantara and ask him for alms. The prince stripped himself of his clothes, in order that the brahman should not leave him empty-handed. Then he walked on. And a fourth brahman approached. His skin was dark, his glance fierce and imperious. 'Tell me,' he said in a harsh voice, 'is this the road to Jayatura?' 'Yes,' replied the prince, 'and what takes you to Jayatura?' The brahman wanted to see Visvantara, who was sure to give him a magnificent present. When he learned that he was in the presence of the unhappy, exiled prince, he did not weep; in an angry voice, he said, it was a hard road I traveled, and it must not have been in vain. You have undoubtedly brought along some valuable jewelry which you can give me.' Madri was wearing a necklace of gold. Visvantara asked her for it; she smiled and handed it to him, and the brahman took the necklace and went away. Visvantara, Madri, Jalin and Krishnajina kept on walking. They crossed raging torrents; they ascended ravines covered with underbrush; they traveled over rocky plains seared by a merciless sun. Madri's feet were cut by the stones; Visvantara's heels were worn to the bone, and wherever they passed, they left a trail of blood. One day, Visvantara, who was walking ahead, heard some one sobbing. He turned around and saw Madri sitting on the ground, lamenting her fate. He was seized with anguish, and he said, 'I begged and pleaded with you, my beloved, not to follow me into exile, but you would not listen. Come, stand up; however great our weariness, the children must not suffer for it; we must not mind our wounds.' Madri saw that his feet were bleeding, and she cried, 'Oh, how much greater is your suffering than mine! I shall control my grief.' She tried to stand up, but her limbs gave way, and once again she burst into tears. 'All my strength has left me,' she sobbed; 'even the love I bear my husband and my children is not enough to sustain my courage. I shall die of hunger and of thirst in this dreadful land; my children will die, and perhaps my well-beloved.' From the sky, Indra had been watching Visvantara and his family. He was touched by Madri's grief, and he decided to come down to earth. He assumed the form of a pleasant old man, and, astride a swift horse, he advanced to meet the prince. He accosted Visvantara and addressed him in an engaging manner. 'From your appearance it is evident, my lord, that you have suffered great hardship. There is a city not far from here. I shall show you the way. You and your family must come to my home and stay as long as you please.' The old man was smiling. He urged the four exiles to get on his horse, and as Visvantara seemed to hesitate, he said, 'The horse is powerful, and you are not heavy. As for me, I shall walk; it will not tire me, for we have not far to go.' Visvantara was astonished to learn that a city had been built in this cruel desert; besides, he had never heard of the city. But the old man's voice was so pleasant that he decided to follow him, and Madri was so weary that he accepted the invitation to ride with her and the children. They had gone about three hundred paces when a magnificent city appeared before them. It was immense. A wide river flowed through it, and there were many beautiful gardens and orchards full of ripe fruit. The old man led his guests to the gates of a shining palace. 'Here is my home,' said he; 'here, if you wish, you may dwell the rest of your days. Please enter.' In the great hall, Visvantara and Madri sat on thrones of gold; at their feet, the children played on heavy rugs, and the old man presented them with many beautiful robes. Exquisite food was then served to them, and they appeased their hunger. But Visvantara was lost in thought. Suddenly, he rose from his seat, and he said to the old man, 'My lord, I am disobeying my father's commands. He banished me from Jayatura, where he is king, and he ordered me to spend the rest of my life in the desert. I must not enjoy these comforts, for they were forbidden. My lord, permit me to leave your house.' The old man tried to dissuade him, but it was futile; and followed by Madri and the children, Visvantara left the city. Outside the gates, he turned around to take a last look, but the city had disappeared; where it had once stood, there was now only burning sand. And Visvantara was happy that he had not remained longer. He finally came to a mountain, overrun by an immense forest, and there he found a hut that a hermit had once occupied. Out of leaves, he made a couch for himself and his family, and there, at last, undisturbed by remorse, he found rest and peace. Every day, Madri went into the forest to gather wild fruit; it was the only food they had, and they drank the water of a clear, bubbling spring they had discovered near the hut. For seven months they saw no one; then, one day, a brahman passed by. Madri was away, gathering fruit, and Visvantara was watching the children while they played in front of the hut. The brahman stopped and observed them carefully. 'Friend,' he said to the father, 'will you give me your children?' Visvantara was so taken aback that he was unable to reply. He glanced anxiously at the brahman and finally questioned him. 'Yes, will you give me your children? I have a wife, much younger than myself. She is rather a haughty woman. She is tired of doing household work, and she asked me to find two children who could be her slaves. Why not give me yours? You seem to be very poor; it must be hard for you to feed them. In my home they will have plenty to eat, and I shall try to have my wife treat them as kindly as possible.' Visvantara thought, 'What a painful sacrifice I am being asked to make. What shall I do? In spite of what the brahman says, my children will be very unhappy in his home; his wife is cruel, she will beat them and will give them only scraps of food. But since he has asked me for them, have I the right to refuse?' He thought a while longer, then he finally said, 'Take the children with you, brahman; let them be your wife's slaves.' And Jalin and Krishnajina, their faces wet with tears, went away with the brahman. Madri, in the meanwhile, had been gathering pomegranates, but each time she picked one off the tree, it slipped out of her hand. This frightened her, and she hurried back to the hut. She missed the children, and turning to her husband she asked, 'Where are the children?' Visvantara was sobbing. 'Where are the children?' Still no reply. She repeated the question a third time. 'Where are the children?' And she added, 'Answer, answer quickly. Your silence is killing me.' Visvantara spoke; in a pitiful voice, he said, 'A brahman came; he wanted the children for slaves!' 'And you gave them to him!' cried Madri.

'Could I refuse?' Madri swooned; she was unconscious a long time. When she recovered, her lamentations were pitiful. She cried, 'Oh, my children, you who would rouse me from my slumber at night; you who would be given the choicest fruit I had gathered, a wicked man has taken you away! I can see him forcing you to run, you who have just learned to walk. In his home, you will go hungry; you will be brutally beaten. You will be working in the house of a stranger. You will furtively watch the roads, but neither father nor mother will you ever see again. And your lips will be parched; your feet will be hurt by the sharp stones; the sun will burn your cheeks. Oh, my children, we were always able to spare you the hardships we had to endure. We carried you across the fearful desert; you did not suffer then, but now, what will you suffer?' She was still weeping when another brahman came through the forest. He was an old man and walked with great difficulty. He stared at the princess with watery eyes, then he addressed Prince Visvantara. 'My lord, as you see, I am old and feeble. I have no one at home to help me when I get up in the morning or when I go to bed at night; I have neither son nor daughter to look after me. Now, this woman is young; she seems quite strong. Let me take her for a servant. She will help me to get up; she will put me to bed; she will watch over me while I sleep. Give me this woman, my lord; you will be doing a good deed, a saintly deed, that will be praised throughout the world.' Visvantara had listened attentively; he was pensive. He looked at Madri. 'Beloved, you heard what the brahman said; what would you answer?' She replied, 'Since you have given away our children: Jalin, the best-beloved, and darling Krishnajina, you can give me to this brahman; I shall not complain.' Visvantara took Madri's hand and placed it in the brahman's hand. He felt no remorse; he was not even weeping. The brahman received the woman; he thanked the prince and said, 'May you know great glory, Visvantara; may you become the Buddha some day!' He started away, but turned, suddenly, and came back to the hut. And he said, 'I shall look for a servant in some other land; I shall leave this woman here, to remain with the Gods of the mountain, and the Goddesses of the forest and of the spring; and, hereafter, you must give her to no one.' While the old brahman was speaking, his appearance gradually changed; he became very beautiful; his face was gloriously radiant. Visvantara and Madri recognized Indra. They fell at his feet and worshipped him; and the God said to them, 'Each one of you may ask one favor of me, and it shall be granted.' Visvantara said, 'Oh, that I might become the Buddha some day and bring deliverance to those who are born and who die in the mountains!' Indra replied, 'Glory be to you who, one day, shall be the Buddha!' Madri spoke next. 'My lord, grant me this favor: may the brahman, to whom my children were given, decide to sell them instead of keeping them in his home, may he find a buyer only in Jayatura, and may that buyer be Sanjaya himself.' Indra replied, 'So be it!' As he ascended to the sky, Madri murmured, 'Oh, that King Sanjaya might forgive his son!' And she heard the God say, 'So be it!' In the meantime, Jalin and Krishnajina had arrived at their new home. The brahman's wife was very pleased with these two young slaves, and she lost no time putting them to work. She delighted in giving orders, and the children had to obey her slightest whim. At first, they did their best to carry out her wishes, but she was such an exacting mistress that they soon lost all desire to please, and many were the reprimands and the blows they received. The more harshly, they were treated, the more discouraged they became, and the woman finally said to the brahman, 'I can do nothing with these children. Sell them and bring me other slaves, slaves who know how to work and obey.' The brahman took the children and went from city to city, trying to sell them, but no one would buy: the price was too high. He finally arrived in Jayatura. One of the king's counselors passed them in the street; he stared at the children, at their emaciated bodies and sun-burned faces, and, suddenly, he recognized them by their eyes. He stopped the brahman and asked, 'Where did you get these children?' 'I got them in a mountain forest, my lord,' replied the brahman. 'They were given to me for slaves; they were unruly, and I am now trying to sell them.' The king's counselor became anxious; turning to the children, he asked, 'Does this servitude mean that your father is dead?' 'No,' replied Jalin, 'both our parents are alive, but father gave us to this brahman.' The counselor ran to the palace of the king. 'My lord,' he cried, 'Visvantara has given your grandchildren, Jalin and Krishnajina, to a brahman. They are his slaves. He is dissatisfied with their service, and is taking them from city to city, in order to sell them!' King Sanjaya ordered the brahman and the children brought before him at once. They were soon found, and when the king saw the misery that had come to these children of his race, he wept bitter tears. Jalin addressed him in a pleading voice. 'Buy us, my lord, for We are unhappy in the Brahman's home, and we want to live with you, who love us. But do not take us by force; our father gave us to the brahman, and from this sacrifice he expects to receive great blessings, for himself and for all creatures.' 'What price do you want for these children?' the king asked the brahman. 'You may have them for a thousand head of cattle,' replied the brahman. 'Very well.' The king turned to his counselor and said, 'You who will now rank next to me in my kingdom, give this brahman a thousand head of cattle, and pay him also a thousand measures of gold.' Then the king, accompanied by Jalin and Krishnajina, went to Queen Phusati. At the sight of her grandchildren, she laughed and wept for joy; she dressed them in costly clothes, and she gave them rings and necklaces to wear. Then she asked them about their father and mother. 'They live in a rude hut, in a forest, on the slope of a mountain,' said Jalin. 'They have given away all their possessions. They live on fruit and water, and their only companions are the wild beasts of the forest.' 'Oh, my lord' cried Phusati, 'will you not recall your son from exile?' King Sanjaya sent a messenger to Prince Visvantara; he pardoned him, and ordered him to return to Jayatura. When the prince drew near the city, he saw his father, his mother and his children advancing to greet him. They were accompanied by a great crowd of people who had heard of Visvantara's sufferings and of his virtue, and who now forgave him and admired him. And the king said to the prince, 'Dear son, I have done you a grave injustice; know my remorse. Be kind to me: forget my blunder; and be kind to the inhabitants of the city: forget that they ever wronged you. Never again will your acts of charity give us offense.' Visvantara smiled and embraced his father, while Madri fondled Jalin and Krishnajina, and Phusati wept for joy. And when the prince passed through the gates of the city, he was acclaimed as with one voice. Now, Visvantara was I, O Sakyas! You acclaimed me as they once acclaimed him. Walk in the path that leads to deliverance."

The Blessed One was silent. The Sakyas had listened attentively; they now bowed before him and withdrew. However, not one of them had thought of offering him his meal on the morrow.

13. The Story of Dharmapala

THE following day, the Master went through the city, begging his food from house to house. He was soon recognized, and the people of Kapilavastu exclaimed:

"What a strange sight! Prince Siddhartha, who once drove through these streets, dressed in magnificent robes, now wanders from door to door, begging his food, in the humble garb of a monk."

And they rushed to the windows; they ascended to the terraces, and great was their admiration for the beggar.

One of Gopa's maidens heard the excitement as she was leaving the palace. She asked the reason and was told. She immediately ran back to her mistress.

"Your husband, Prince Siddhartha," said she, "is wandering through the city, like a mendicant monk!"

Gopa gave a start. She thought, "He who once, for all his gorgeous jewels, was radiant with light, now wears coarse clothes, now has for sole adornment the divine brilliance of his person." And she murmured, "How beautiful he must be!" She ascended to the terrace of the palace. Surrounded by a crowd of people, the Master was approaching. A majestic splendor emanated from his person. Gopa trembled with joy, and in a voice full of fervor she sang:

"Soft and shining is his hair, brilliant as the sun his forehead, radiant and smiling his sweeping glance! He stalks like a lion through the golden light!"

She went to the king.

"My lord," said she, "your son is begging in the streets of Kapilavastu. An admiring throng follows him about, for he is more beautiful than ever before."

Suddhodana was greatly disturbed. He left the palace,

and approaching his son, he said to him:

"What are you doing? Why do you beg your food? Surely you must know that I expect you at the palace, you and your disciples."

"I must beg," replied the Blessed One; "I must obey the law."

"We are a race of warriors," said the king; "no Sakya was ever a beggar."

"You belong to the Sakya race; I, in the course of my previous existences, have sought supreme knowledge; I have learned the beauty of charity; I have known the joy of self-sacrifice. When I was the child Dharmapala, the queen, my mother, was playing with me one day, and she forgot to greet my father, King Brahmadatta, as he passed by. In order to punish her, he ordered one of the guards to cut off my hands, for he thought it would hurt her more to see me suffer than to suffer herself. My mother pleaded with him and offered her hands instead, but he was inexorable, and he was obeyed. I was smiling, and to see me smile, soon brought a smile to my mother's face. My father then ordered the guard to cut off my feet. This was done, and still I kept smiling. In a violent rage, he cried, 'Cut off his head!' My mother became terrified; she cowered before him. 'Cut off my head,' she begged, 'but spare your son, O king!' The king was about to yield when I spoke up in a childish voice. 'Mother, it is for your salvation that I give my head. When I am dead, let my body be placed on a pike and exposed to view; let it be food for the birds of the air.' And, as the executioner seized me by the hair, I added, 'Oh, that I might become the Buddha and set free all who are born and who die in the worlds!' And now, King Suddhodana, now at last I have attained wisdom; I am the Buddha; I know the path that leads to deliverance. Do not disturb me at my task. Be wide awake; be quick of apprehension; follow the sacred path of virtue. He sleeps in peace who leads a life of holiness, he sleeps on earth and in the other worlds." King Suddhodana wept with admiration. The Buddha continued:

"Learn to distinguish true virtue from false virtue; learn

to know the true path from the false path. He sleeps in peace who lead a life of holiness, he sleeps on earth and in the other worlds!"

The king fell at his feet; he believed in him, completely. The Blessed One smiled, then entered the palace and sat down at his father's table.

4. Gopa's Great Virtue

PRESENTLY the women of the palace came to pay homage to the Master. Gopa, alone, was missing. The king evinced his surprise.

"I asked her to come with us," said Mahaprajapati. "'I shall not go with you,' she answered. 'I may be wanting in virtue; I may not deserve to see my husband. If I have done nothing wrong, he will come to me of his own accord, and I shall then show him the respect that is his due.'"

The Master left his seat and went to Gopa's apartments. She had discarded her costly raiment and her soft veils; she had flung aside her bracelets and her necklaces; she was wearing a reddish-colored robe, made of some coarse material. At the sight of her thus attired, he smiled with happiness. She fell at his feet and worshipped him.

"You see," said she, "I wanted to dress as you are dressed; I wanted to know about your life in order to live as you live. You eat but once a day, and I eat but once a day. You gave up sleeping in a bed; look around: no bed will you see, for here is the bench on which I sleep. And from now on I shall have done with sweet perfumes, and no longer shall I put flowers in my hair."

"I was aware of your great virtue, Gopa," replied the Master. "It has not failed you, and I praise you for it. How many women are there in this world who would have had the courage to do as you did?"

And seating himself, he spoke these words:

"Women are not to be trusted. For one who is wise and good, more than a thousand can be found who are foolish and wicked. Woman is more mysterious than the path of a fish through the water; she is as fierce as a robber, and like the robber, she is deceitful; she will rarely tell the truth, for to her a lie is like the truth and the truth like a lie. Often have I told my disciples to avoid women. It displeases me even to have them speak to them. Yet you, Gopa, are not false; I believe in your virtue. Virtue is a flower not easily found; a woman must have clear eyes in order to see it; she must have pure hands in order to gather it Mara hides his pointed arrows under flowers oh, how many women love treacherous flower, flowers that inflict wounds which never heal! Unhappy women! The body is but foam and they know it not. They cling to this world, then the day comes when King Death claims them for his own. The body is less substantial than a mirage: who knows that will break Mara's flowered arrows, who knows that will never meet King Death. Death carries away the woman who heedlessly gathers flowers, even as the torrent, swollen by the storm, carries away the drowsy village. Gather flowers, O woman, take joy in their colors, drink in their perfume; Death lies in wait for you, and before you are satisfied, you will be his. Consider the bee: it goes from flower to flower, and, harming no one, simply takes the nectar from which honey is made."

5. Nanda Renounces Royalty

WHEN Siddhartha had retired from the world, King Suddhodana had chosen Nanda, another one of his sons, to succeed him to the throne. Nanda was happy to think that one day he would be king, and he was also happy at the thought of his coming marriage to Princess Sundarika, to beautiful Sundarika whom he loved dearly.

The Master feared for his brother; he was afraid he would stray into the path of evil. One day, he went to him and said:

"I have come to you, Nanda, because I know you are very happy, and I want to hear from your own lips the reason for this happiness. So speak, Nanda; bare your heart to me."

"Brother," replied Nanda, "I doubt if you would understand, for you once spurned sovereign power I and you deserted loving Gopa!"

"You expect to be king some day, and that is why you are happy, Nanda!"

"Yes. And I am also happy because I love Sundarika, and because Sundarika will soon be my bride."

"Poor man!" cried the Master. "How can you be happy, you who live in darkness? Would you see the light? Then first rid yourself of happiness: fear is born of happiness, fear and suffering. He neither fears nor suffers who no longer knows happiness. Rid yourself of love: fear is born of love, fear and suffering. He neither fears nor suffers who no longer knows love. If you seek happiness in the world, your efforts will come to nothing, your pleasure will turn to pain; death is always present, ready to swoop down on the unfortunate and still their laughter and their song. The world is but flame and smoke, and everything in the world suffers from birth, from old age and from death. Since you first began pitifully to wander from existence to existence, you have shed more tears than there is water in the rivers or in the seas. You have grieved and you have wept at being thwarted in your desires, and you have wept and you have grieved when that happened which you dreaded. A mother's death, a father's death, a brother's death, a sister's death, the death of a son, the death of a daughter, oh, how many times, down through the ages, have these not caused you heartache? And how many times have you not lost your fortune? And each time you had cause for grief, you wept and you wept and you wept, and you have shed more tears than there is water in the rivers or in the seas!" Nanda, at first, paid little heed to what the Buddha was saying, but as he began to listen the words moved him deeply. The Master continued:

"Look upon the world as a bubble of foam; let it be but a dream, and sovereign death will pass you by."

He was silent.

"Master, Master," cried Nanda, "I will be your disciple! Take me with you."

The Master took Nanda by the hand and left the palace. But Nanda was pensive; he was afraid he had been hasty. Perhaps he would bitterly regret what he had done. For whatever might be said of it, it was pleasant and noble to exercise sovereign power. And Sundarika? "How beautiful she is," he thought; "shall I ever see her again?" And he uttered a deep sigh.

But he still followed the Master. He was afraid, to speak to him. He feared his rebuke as he feared his scorn.

Suddenly, as they turned the corner of a street, he saw a young girl approaching. She was smiling. He recognized Sundarika, and he lowered his eyes.

"Where are you going?" she asked him.

He did not answer. She turned to the Master. "Are you taking him with you?"

"Yes," replied the Master. "But he will come back soon?"

Nanda wanted to cry, "Yes, I shall come back soon, Sundarika!" But he was afraid, and without a word, his eyes still downcast, he went off with the Master.

Then Sundarika knew that Nanda was lost to her, and she wept.

16. The Buddha Leaves Kapilavastu

ONE day, gentle Gopa stood looking at her son Rahula.

"How beautiful you are, my child!" she exclaimed. "How your eyes sparkle! Your father owes you a pious heritage; you must go and claim it.

Mother and child ascended to the terrace of the palace. The Blessed One was passing in the street below. Gopa said to Rahula:

"Rahula, do you see that monk?"

"Yes, mother," replied the child. "His body is covered with gold."

"He is as beautiful as the Gods of the sky! It is the light of holiness that makes his skin shine like gold. Love him, my son, love him dearly, for he is your father. He once possessed great treasures; he had gold and silver and glittering jewels; now, he goes from house to house, begging his food. But he has acquired a marvelous treasure: he has attained supreme knowledge. Go to him, my son; tell him who You are, and demand your heritage."

Rahula obeyed his mother. He was presently standing before the Buddha. He felt strangely happy.

"Monk," said he, "it is nice to stand here, in your shadow."

The Master looked at him. It was a kindly glance, and Rahula, taking heart, began walking beside him. Remembering his mother's words, he said:

"I am your son, my Lord. I know that you possess the greatest of treasures. Father, give me my heritage."

The Master smiled. He made no reply. He continued to beg. But Rahula remained at his side; he followed him about and kept repeating:

"Father, give me my heritage."

At last the Master spoke:

"Child, you know nothing about this treasure that you have heard men praise. When you claim your heritage, you think you are claiming material things of a perishable nature. The only treasures known to you are those dear to human vanity, treasures that greedy death wrests from the false rich. But why should you be kept in ignorance? You are right to claim your heritage, Rahula. You shall have your share of the jewels that are mine. You shall see the seven jewels; you shall know the seven virtues, and you shall learn the true value of faith and purity, modesty and reserve, obedience, abnegation and wisdom. Come, I shall give you in charge of holy Sariputra; he will teach you."

Rahula went with his father, and Gopa rejoiced. King Suddhodana, alone, was sad: his family was deserting him! He could not help speaking his mind to the Master.

"Do not grieve," replied the Master, "for great is the treasure they will share who hearken to my words and follow me! Bear your grief in silence; be like the elephant wounded in battle by the arrows of the enemy: no one hears him complain. Kings ride into battle on elephants that are under perfect control; in the world, the great man is the man who has learned to control himself, the man who bears his grief in silence. He who is truly humble, he who curbs his passions as one curbs wild horses, is envied by the Gods. He does no evil. Neither in the mountain-caves nor in the caverns of the sea can you escape the consequences of an evil deed; they follow you about; they sear you; they drive you mad, for they give you no peace! But if you do good, when you leave the earth your good deeds greet you, like friends upon your return from a voyage. We live in perfect happiness, we who are without hatred in a world full of hatred. We live in perfect happiness, we who are without sickness in a world full of sickness. We live in perfect happiness, we who are without weariness in a world full of weariness. We live in perfect happiness, we who possess nothing. Joy is our food, and we are like radiant Gods. The monk who lives in solitude preserves a soul that is full of peace; he contemplates the truth with a clear, steady gaze, and enjoys a felicity unknown to ordinary mortals."

  Having consoled King Suddhodana with these words, the Blessed One left Kapilavastu and returned to Rajagriha.

17. Anathapindika's Offering

THE Master was in Rajagriha when a rich merchant named Anathapindika arrived from Cravasti. Anathapindika was a religious man, and when he heard that a Buddha was living in the Bamboo Grove, he was eager to see him.

He set out one morning, and as he entered the Grove, a divine voice led him to where the Master was seated. He was greeted with words of kindness; he presented the community with a magnificent gift, and the Master promised to visit him in Cravasti.

When he returned home, Anathapindika began to wonder where he could receive the Blessed One. His gardens did not seem worthy of such a guest. The most beautiful park in the city belonged to Prince Jeta, and Anathapindika decided to buy it.

"I will sell the park," Jeta said to him, "if you cover the ground with gold coins."

Anathapindika accepted the terms. He had chariot-loads of gold coins carried to the park, and presently only a small strip of ground remained uncovered. Then Jeta joyfully exclaimed:

"The park is yours, merchant; I will gladly give you the strip that is still uncovered."

Anathapindika had the park made ready for the Master; then he sent his most faithful servant to the Bamboo Grove, to inform him that he was now prepared to receive him in Cravasti.

"O Venerable One," said the messenger, "my master falls at your feet. He hopes you have been spared anxiety and sickness, and that you are not loath to keep the promise you made to him. You are awaited in Cravasti, O Venerable One."

The Blessed One had not forgotten the promise he had made to the merchant Anathapindika; he wished to abide by it, and he said to the messenger, "I will go."

He allowed a few days to pass; then he took his cloak and his alms-bowl, and followed by a great number of disciples, he set out for Cravasti. The messenger went ahead, to tell the merchant he was coming.

Anathapindika decided to go and meet the Master. His wife, his son and his daughter accompanied him, and they were attended by the wealthiest inhabitants of the city. And when they saw the Buddha, they were dazzled by his splendor; he seemed to be walking on a path of molten gold. They escorted him to Jeta's park, and Anathapindika said to him:

"My Lord, what shall I do with this park?" "Give it to the community, now and for all time," replied the Master.

Anathapindika ordered a servant to bring him a golden bowl full of water. He poured the water over the Master's hands, and he said:

"I give this park to the community, ruled by the Buddha, now and for all time."

"Good!" said the Master. "I accept the gift. This park will be a happy refuge; here we shall live in peace, and find shelter from the heat and from the cold. No vicious animals enter here: not even the humming of a mosquito disturbs the silence; and here there is protection from the rain, the biting wind and the ardent sun. And this park will inspire dreams, for here we shall meditate hour after hour. It is only right that such gifts be made to the community. The intelligent man, the man who does not neglect his own interests, should give the monks a proper home; he should give them food and drink; he should give them clothes. The monks, in return, will teach him the law, and he who knows the law is delivered from evil and attains nirvana."

The Buddha and his disciples established themselves in Jeta's park, Anathapindika was happy; but, one day, a solemn thought occurred to him.

"I am being loudly praised," he said to himself, "and yet what is so admirable about my actions? I present gifts to the Buddha and to the monks, and for this I am entitled to a future reward; but my virtue benefits me alone! I must get others to share in the privilege. I shall go through the streets of the city, and from those whom I meet, I shall get donations for the Buddha and for the monks. Many will thus participate in the good I shall be doing."

He went to Prasenajit, king of Cravasti, who was a wise and upright man. He told him what he had decided to do, and the king approved. A herald was sent through the city with this royal proclamation:

"Listen well, inhabitants of Cravasti! Seven days from this day, the merchant Anathapindika, riding an elephant, will go through the streets of the city. He will ask all of you for alms, which he will then offer to the Buddha and to his disciples. Let each one of you give him whatever he can afford."

On the day announced, Anathapindika mounted his finest elephant and rode through the streets, asking every one for donations for the Master and for the community. They crowded around him: this one gave gold, that one silver; one woman took off her necklace, another her bracelet, a third an anklet; and even the humblest gifts were accepted.

Now, there lived in Cravasti a young girl who was extremely poor. It had taken her three months to save enough money to buy a piece of coarse material, out of which she had just made a dress for herself. She saw Anathapindika with a great crowd around him.

"The merchant Anathapindika appears to be begging," she said to a bystander.

"Yes, he is begging," was the reply.

"But he is said to be the richest man in Cravasti. Why should he be begging?"

"Did you not hear the royal proclamation being cried through the streets, seven days ago?"

"No."

"Anathapindika is not collecting alms for himself. He wants every one to participate in the good he is doing, and he is asking for donations for the Buddha and his disciples. All those who give will be entitled to a future reward."

The young girl said to herself, "I have never done anything deserving of praise. It would be wonderful to make an offering to the Buddha. But I am poor. What have I to give?" She walked away, wistfully. She looked at her new dress. "I have only this dress to offer him. But I can not go through the streets naked."

She went home and took off the dress. Then she sat at the window and watched for Anathapindika, and when he passed in front of her house, she threw the dress to him. He took it and showed it to his servants.

"The woman who threw this dress to me," said he, "probably had nothing else to offer. She must be naked, if she had to remain at home and give alms in this strange manner. Go; try to find her and see who she is."

The servants had some difficulty finding the young girl. At last they saw her, and they learned that their master had been correct in his surmise: the dress thrown out of the window was the poor child's entire fortune. Anathapindika was deeply moved; he ordered his servants to bring many costly, beautiful clothes, and he gave them to this pious maiden who had offered him her simple dress.

She died the following day and was reborn a Goddess in Indra's sky. But she never forgot how she had come to deserve such a reward, and, one night, she came down to earth and went to the Buddha, and he instructed her in the holy law.

18. The New Disciples

THE Master remained in Cravasti for some time; then he left, to return to Rajagriha where King Vimbasara awaited him. He had stopped to rest in a village that was about halfway, when he saw seven men approaching. He recognized them. Six were relatives, and they were among the wealthiest and most powerful of the Sakyas. Their names were Anuruddha, Bhadrika, Bhrigu, Kimbala, Devadatta and Ananda. The seventh was a barber named Upali.

Anuruddha, one day had said to himself that it was a disgrace that none of the Sakyas had seen fit to follow the Buddha. He decided to set a good example, and as there was no reason for hiding his intention, he mentioned it first to Bhadrika, who was his best friend. Bhadrika approved of his decision, and after giving it some thought, resolved to do likewise. These two then won over Ananda, Bhrigu, Kimbala and Devadatta, by convincing them that there was no higher calling than that of a monk.

The six princes then set out to join the Buddha. They had hardly left Kapilavastu when Ananda, glancing at Bhadrika, exclaimed:

"How now, Bhadrika! You would lead a life of holiness, and you keep all your jewels?"

Bhadrika blushed; but then he saw that Ananda was also wearing his jewelry, and he laughingly replied:

"Look at yourself, Ananda."

It was now Ananda's turn to blush.

Whereupon they all looked at one another, and they found they were still wearing their jewels. It made them feel ashamed; they lowered their eyes, and were walking along the road in silence when they met the barber Upali.

"Barber," said Ananda, "take my jewels; I give them to you."

"And take mine," said Bhadrika.

The others also handed their jewels to Upali. He was at a loss for an answer. Why should these princes, who had never seen him before, give him such presents? Should he accept them? Should he refuse?

Anuruddha understood the barber's hesitation. He said to him:

"Do not be afraid to accept these jewels. We are on our way to join the great hermit who was born to the Sakyas, we are on our way to join Siddhartha, who has become the Buddha. He will instruct us in the knowledge, and we shall submit to his rule."

"Princes," asked the barber, "are you going to become monks?"

"Yes," they answered.

He then took the jewels and started for the city. But, suddenly, he thought, "I am acting like a fool. Who will ever believe that princes thrust these riches upon me? I shall be taken for a thief, or perhaps for an assassin. The least that can happen to me is that I shall incur the deep displeasure of the Sakyas. I shall not keep the jewels." He hung them on a tree that stood beside the road. And he thought, "Those princes are setting a noble example. They had the courage to leave their palaces; do I, who am nothing, lack the courage to leave my shop? No. I shall follow them. I, too, shall see the Buddha, and may he receive me into the community!"

He followed the princes at a distance. He was shy about joining them. Bhadrika happened to turn around. He saw Upali; he called him.

"Barber, why did you throw away our jewels?" he asked.

"I, too, want to become a monk," replied the barber.

"Then walk with us," said Bhadrika. But Upali still hung back. Anuruddha said to him:

"Walk beside us, barber. Monks make no distinctions, except for age and for virtue. When we stand before the Buddha, you must even be the first to address him, and the first to ask him to receive you into the community. For by yielding to you, the princes will show that they have put aside their Sakya pride."

They continued on their way. Suddenly, a hawk swooped down on Devadatta's head and carried off a diamond he had been wearing in his hair. This exposed his vanity, and it made the princes smile. Devadatta, now, had not a single jewel left, but his companions, in their hearts, still questioned the sincerity of his faith.

19. Nanda's Pride

THE Master was happy to number these relatives among his disciples, and he took them with him to the Bamboo Grove. There, poor Nanda was suffering. He kept thinking of Sundarika; she often appeared to him in his dreams, and he regretted having left her. The Buddha knew of his unhappiness, and he decided to cure him.

One day, he took him by the hand and led him to a tree where a hideous monkey was sitting.

"Look at that monkey," said he, "is she not beautiful?"

"I have rarely seen one as ugly," replied Nanda.

"Really?" said the Master. "And yet she resembles Sundarika, your former betrothed."

"What are you talking about!" exclaimed Nanda. "Do you mean to say that this monkey looks like Sundarika, who is grace, who is beauty itself?"

"In what way is Sundarika different? Are they not both females, do they not both awaken the desire of the male? I believe you would be willing to leave the path of holiness and run to Sundarika's arms, just as somewhere in this wood there is a monkey that can be roused to a frenzy of love by the violent ardor of this female. They will both become old and decrepit, and then you, as well as the monkey, will wonder what could have caused your folly. They will both die, and perhaps you and the monkey will then understand the vanity of passion. Sundarika is no different from this monkey."

But Nanda was not listening. He was sighing. He was dreaming that he saw slender, graceful Sundarika wandering in a garden bright with flowers.

"Take the hem of my cloak!" the Blessed One said, imperiously.

Nanda obeyed. He felt the earth suddenly give way under him, and a fierce wind sweep him to the sky. When he regained his feet, he found himself in a marvelous park. He was walking on a path of gold, and the flowers were living jewels, fashioned out of rubies and fragrant sapphires.

"You are in Indra's sky," said the Blessed One. "Open your sightless eyes."

Nanda saw a house of shining silver surrounded by an emerald field. An Apsaras, far lovelier than Sundarika, was standing at the door. She was smiling. Maddened by desire, Nanda rushed to her, but she stopped him with a sudden gesture. "Be pure on earth," she said to him; "keep your vows, Nanda. After your death, you will be reborn here; then you may come to my arms."

The Apsaras disappeared. Nanda and the Master returned to earth.

Nanda forgot Sundarika. He was haunted by the lovely vision he had seen in the celestial gardens, and, out of love for the Apsaras, he now resolved to lead a pure life.

But the monks still looked at him with disapproval. They would not speak to him; often, when they met him in the Bamboo Grove, they would smile at him scornfully. This made him unhappy. He thought, "They seem to bear me ill will; I wonder why?" One day, he stopped Ananda who was passing, and he asked him:

"Why do the monks avoid me? Why do you not speak to me any more, Ananda? Formerly, in Kapilavastu, we were friends as well as relatives. What have I done to offend you?"

"Poor man!" replied Ananda. "We, who meditate on the saintly truths, have been forbidden by the Master to speak to you, who meditate on the charms of an Apsaras!"

And he left.

Nanda was very disturbed. He ran to the Master; he fell at his feet and wept. The Master said to him: "Your thoughts are evil, Nanda. You are a slave to your feelings. First it was Sundarika, now it is an Apsaras, who turns your head. And you would be reborn! Reborn among the Gods? What folly, what vanity! Strive to attain wisdom, Nanda; give heed to my teachings, and kill your devouring passions."

Nanda pondered the Buddha's words. He became a most obedient disciple, and gradually he purified his mind. Sundarika no longer appeared to him in his dreams, and now, when he thought of the Apsaras, he laughed at having wanted to become a God for her sake. One day, when he saw a hideous monkey watching him from a tree-top, he cried in a triumphant voice:

"Hail, you that Sundarika can not equal in grace; hail, you that are lovelier far than the loveliest Apsaras!"

He took great pride in having conquered his passions. "I am a true saint," he said to himself, "and in virtue I will not yield even to my brother."

He made a robe for himself of the same size as the Master's. Some monks saw him in the distance, and they said:

"Here comes the Master. Let us rise and greet him."

But as Nanda drew near, they saw their mistake. They were embarrassed, and as they sat down again, they said:

"He has not been in the community as long as we have; why should we rise in his presence?"

Nanda had been pleased to see the monks rise at his approach; he was abashed to see them sit down again. But he was afraid to complain; he felt they would blame him. Yet it was no lesson to him; he continued to walk through the Bamboo Grove, wearing a robe that was like the Buddha's. In the distance, he was taken for the Master, and the monks would rise from their seats; but at his approach, they would laugh and sit down again.

Finally, a monk went to the Buddha and told him. He was very displeased. He assembled the monks, and in front of them all, he asked Nanda:

"Nanda, did you really wear a robe of the same size as mine?"

"Yes, Blessed One," replied Nanda; "I wore a robe of the same size as yours."

"What!" said the Master, "a disciple dares to make a robe

for himself of the same size as the Buddha's! What do you mean by such audacity? An action of this kind does not tend to arouse the faith of the unbeliever, nor does it help to strengthen the faith of the believer. You must shorten your robe, Nanda, and, in the future, any monk who makes a robe for himself of the same size as the Buddha's, or larger than the Buddha's, will be committing a grave offense, an offense for which he will be severely punished."

Nanda saw the error of his ways, and he realized that to be a true saint, he would have to conquer his pride.

20. The Death of Suddhodana

NEAR the city of Vaisali, there was an immense wood that had been presented to the Master, and there he was living when the news came to him that his father, King Suddhodana, had fallen sick. The king was an old man; the illness was serious; it was feared that he was dying. The Master decided to visit him, and flying through the air he came to Kapilavastu.

The king lay mournfully on his couch. He was gasping for breath. Death was very near. Yet he smiled when he saw his son. And the Master spoke these words:

"Long is the road you have traveled, O king, and always did you strive to do good. You knew nothing of evil desires; your heart was innocent of hatred, and anger never blinded your mind. Happy is he who is given to doing good! Happy is he who looks into a limpid pool and sees his unsullied countenance, but far happier is he who examines his mind and knows the purity thereof! Your mind is pure, O king, and your death as calm as the close of a lovely day." "Blessed One," said the king, "I understand now the inconstancy of the worlds. I am free of all desire; I am free of the chains of life."

Once again, he paid homage to the Buddha. Then he turned to the servants, assembled in the hall.

"Friends," said he, "I must have wronged you many times, yet never once did you show me that you bore malice. You were kind and good. But before I die, I must have your forgiveness. The wrongs I did you were unintentional; forgive me, Friends."

The servants were weeping. They murmured: "No, you have never wronged us, lord!" Suddhodana continued:

"And you, Mahaprajapati, you who were my pious consort, you whom I see in tears, calm your grief. My death is a happy death. Think of the glory of this child you brought up; gaze at him in all his splendor, and rejoice."

He died. The sun was setting.

The Master said:

"Behold my father's body. He is no longer what he was. No one has ever conquered death. He who is born must die. Show your zeal for good works; walk in the path that leads to wisdom. Make a lamp of wisdom, and darkness will vanish of its own accord. Do not follow evil laws; do not plant poisonous roots; do not add to the evil in the world. Like the charioteer who, having left the highroad for a rough path, weeps at the sight of a broken axle, even so does the fool, who has strayed from the law, weep when he falls into the jaws of death. The wise man is the torch that gives light to the ignorant; he guides mankind, for he has eyes, and the others are sightless."

The body was carried to a great funeral pile. The Master set fire to it, and while his father's body was being consumed by the flames, while the people of Kapilavastu wept and lamented, he repeated these sacred truths:

"Suffering is birth, suffering is old age, suffering is sickness, suffering is death. O thirst to be led from birth to birth! Thirst for power, thirst for pleasure, thirst for being, thirsts that are the source of all suffering! O evil thirsts, the saint knows you not, the saint who extinguishes his desires, the saint who knows the noble eight-fold path."

PART THREE
I. Mahaprajapati is Admitted to the Community

MAHAPRAJAPATI was musing. She knew the vanity of this world. She wanted to flee the palace, to flee Kapilavastu, and lead a life of holiness.

"How happy is the Master! How happy are the disciples!" she thought. "Why can I not do as they do? Why can I not live as they live? But they oppose women. We are not admitted to the community, and I must remain in this mournful city, to me deserted; I must remain in this mournful palace, empty in my sight!"

She grieved. She laid aside her costly robes; she gave her jewels to her handmaidens, and she was humble before all creatures.

One day, she said to herself:

"The Master is kind; he will take pity on me. I shall go to him, and perhaps he will be willing to receive me into the community."

The Master was in a wood, near Kapilavastu. Mahaprajapati went to him, and in a timid voice, she said:

"Master, only you and your disciples can be really happy. Yet I, too, like you and those who accompany you, wish to walk in the path of salvation. May the favor be granted me to enter the community, O Blessed One."

The Master remained silent. She continued:

"How can I be happy in a world I despise? I know its meretricious joys. I long to walk in the path of salvation. May the favor be granted me to enter the community, O Blessed One. And I know many women who are willing to follow me. May the favor be granted us to enter the community, O Blessed One."

The Master still remained silent. She continued:

"My palace is cheerless and dreary. The city is wrapped in darkness. The embroidered veils weigh heavily upon my brow; the diadems, the bracelets and the necklaces hurt me. I must walk in the path of salvation. Many earnest women, many women of great piety, are ready to follow me. May the favor be granted women to enter the community, O Blessed One."

For the third time, the Master remained silent. Mahaprajapati, her eyes full of tears, returned to her gloomy palace.

But she would not accept defeat. She resolved to seek the Master once again and plead with him.

He was then in the great wood, near Vaisali. Mahaprajapati cut off her hair, and putting on a reddish-colored robe made of a coarse material, she set out for Vaisali.

She made the trip on foot; she never once complained of weariness. Covered with dust, she finally arrived at the hall where the Buddha was meditating. But she did not dare to enter; she stood outside the door, with tears in her eyes. Ananda happened to pass by. He saw her and asked:

"O queen, why have you come here, dressed in this manner? Why are you standing before the Master's door?"

"I dare not enter his presence. Three times, already, he has denied my plea, and that which he has thrice refused, I have come to ask him again: that the favor be granted me, that the favor be granted women, to enter the community."

"I shall intercede for you, O queen," said Ananda.

He entered the hall. He saw the Master, and he said to him:.

"Blessed One, Mahaprajapati, our revered queen, is standing before your door. She dares not appear before you; she is afraid you will again turn a deaf ear to her plea. Yet it is not the plea of a foolish woman, Blessed One. Would it mean so much to you to grant it? The queen was a mother to you, once; she was always kind to you; surely she deserves to be heard. Why should you not receive women into the community? There are women of great piety, women with the saintly courage to keep in the path of holiness."

"Ananda," said the Master, "do not ask me to permit women to enter the community."

Ananda left. The queen was waiting for him.

"What did the Master say," she asked, anxiously.

"He denies your plea. But do not lose hope."

The following day, .Ananda again went to the Blessed One.

"Mahaprajapati has not left the wood," said he. "She is thinking of the happy days of her youth. Maya was then alive; Maya, the most beautiful of all women; Maya, to whom a son would be born. Maya's sister was a noble woman: she knew nothing of envy: she loved this child, even before it came into the world. And when it was born, to bring joy to all creatures, Queen Maya died. Mahaprajapati was kind to the motherless boy: he seemed so frail. She protected him from harm; she gave him devoted nurses; she shielded him from the influence of evil servants; she lavished her care and her tenderness upon him. He grew older, and still she would not leave him. She anticipated his least wishes; she worshipped him. And he attained the happiest fortune; he is the giant tree that shelters the wise; and now, when she would seek a humble place in his shadow, she is refused the peace and rest to which she aspires. O Master, be not unjust; receive Mahaprajapati into the community."

The Master pondered; then he gravely spoke these words:

"Listen, Ananda. Go to Mahaprajapati and tell her that I am willing to receive her into the community, but that she must conform to certain very strict rules. These are the observances I shall require of the women in the community: a nun, even if she has been a nun for a hundred years, must rise in the presence of a monk and show him every mark of deep respect, even though he has been a monk for only a day; the nuns must go to the monks for a public confession of their transgressions and for instruction in the sacred word; nuns guilty of a grave offense must submit to a fitting punishment, for fifteen days, in front of the whole community of monks and nuns; before nuns are admitted to the community, their constancy and their virtue must be tried for a period of two years; the nuns will not be allowed to exhort the monks, but the monks will be allowed to exhort the nuns. These are the observances which, in addition to the observances already known to the monks, will be required of all the nuns."

Mahaprajapati joyfully promised to observe these rules. She entered the community, and within a few months, many women had followed her example.

But, one day, the Master said to Ananda:

"If women had not been admitted to the community, Ananda, chastity would have been preserved a long time, and the true faith would have lived, vigorous and serene, for a thousand years.. But now that women are admitted to the community, Ananda, chastity will be in danger, and the true faith, in all its vigor, will live only five hundred years."

2. The Buddha Exposes the Imposters

FROM Vaisali, the Master went to Cravasti, to Jeta's park. One day, King Prasenajit came to see him. "My Lord," said the king, "six hermits have recently arrived in Cravasti. They do not believe in your law. They maintain that your knowledge is not equal to theirs, and they have tried to astonish me by performing numerous prodigies. I believe their statements to be untrue, but it would be well, my Lord, if you were to confound their audacity. The world's salvation depends upon your glory. So appear before these cheats and impostors and silence them."

"King," replied the Buddha, "order a great hall to be built near the city. Have it finished in seven days. I shall proceed there. Arrange to have the evil hermits present, and you will then see who performs the greatest prodigies, they or I."

Prasenajit ordered the hall to be built.

While awaiting the day of the trial, the lying hermits sought to delude the Master's faithful followers, and those who refused to listen to their evil words incurred their bitter enmity. Now, the Master had no truer friend in Cravasti than Prince Kala, a brother of Prasenajit. Kala had shown his utter contempt for the hermits, and they decided to take their revenge.

Kala was a very handsome man. One day, as he was walking through the royal gardens, he met one of Prasenajit's wives, and she playfully threw him a garland of flowers. The hermits heard of the incident, and they told the king that his brother had tried to seduce one of his wives. The king flew into a great rage, and without giving Kala a chance to justify himself, he had his hands and feet cut off.

Poor Kala suffered pitifully. His friends stood around his couch, weeping. One of the evil hermits happened to pass by.

"Come, show your power," they said to him. "You know

that Kala is innocent. Make him well again!"

"He believes in the son of the Sakyas," replied the hermit. "It behooves the Sakyas' son to make him well again."

Then Kala began to sing:

"How can the Master of the worlds fail to see my misery? Let us worship the Lord who no longer knows desire; let us adore the Blessed One who takes pity on all creatures." Ananda suddenly appeared before him.

"Kala," said he, "the Master has taught me the words that will heal your wounds."

He recited a few verses, and the prince immediately recovered the use of his limbs.

"Henceforth," he exclaimed, "I shall serve the Master! However humble the tasks which he may assign to me, I shall perform them with joy, to please him."

And he followed Ananda to Jeta's park. The Master received him graciously and admitted him to the community.

The day arrived on which the Master was to compete with the hermits. Early in the morning, King Prasenajit went to the hall he had had built for this occasion. The six hermits were already there. They exchanged glances and smiled.

"King," said one of them, "we are the first to arrive at the place of meeting."

"Do you suppose the one we are expecting will really come?" said another.

"Hermits," said the king, "do not scoff at him. You know how he sent one of his disciples to cure my brother whom I had unjustly punished. He will come. He may even be here, in our midst, without our knowing it."

As the king finished speaking, a luminous cloud filled the hall. It became lighter and lighter; it melted into the daylight, and the Buddha appeared, arrayed in golden splendor. Behind him stood Ananda and Kala. Ananda held a red flower in his hand, Kala a yellow flower, and never, in all the gardens of Cravasti, had any one seen two such flowers as these.

Prasenajit showed his profound admiration. The evil

hermits ceased their laughter.

The Blessed One spoke:

"The glowworm shines for all to see, as long as the sun stays hidden, but when the blazing star appears, the poor worm quenches his feeble light. The impostors spoke loudly as long as the Buddha was silent, but now that the Buddha speaks, they weep with fear and are silent."

The hermits were alarmed. They saw the king viewing them with a scornful eye, and they hung their heads in shame.

Suddenly, the roof of the hall disappeared, and on the dome of the sky, stretching from the east to the west, the Master traced a course over which he proceeded to travel. At the sight of this prodigy, his most insolent rival fled in terror. The hermit imagined he was being pursued by a howling pack of hounds, and he never stopped running until he came to the edge of a pool. There, he tied a stone to his neck and threw himself into the water. A fisherman found his body the following day. In the meanwhile, the Master had created a being in his own image, and, with him, he was now walking in the celestial path. And his great voice was heard, saying:

"O my disciples, I am about to ascend to the abode of the Gods and the Goddesses. Maya, my mother, has summoned me; I must instruct her in the law. I shall remain with her three months. But, each day, I shall descend to earth, and Sariputra, alone, will know where to find me; he will rule the community according to my instructions. And while I am absent from the sky, I shall leave with my mother, to instruct her, this being whom I have created in mine own image."

3. Suprabha

AT the end of three months, the Master descended to earth and took the road to Cravasti. As he was approaching Jeta's park, he met a young girl. She was the servant of a wealthy inhabitant of the city who happened to be working in the fields that day. She was taking him a bowl of rice for his meal. At the sight of the Buddha, she felt strangely happy.

"It is the Master, the Blessed One," she thought. "My eyes behold him; my hands could almost touch him, he is so near. Oh, what a holy joy it would be to give him alms! But I have nothing of my own."

She sighed. Her glance fell on the bowl of rice.

"This rice . . . My master's meal . . . No master can reduce to slavery one who is already a slave. Mine could strike me, but what of that! He could put me in chains, but I would bear them lightly. I shall give the rice to the Blessed One."

She presented the bowl to the Buddha. He accepted it and continued on his way to Jeta's park. The young girl, her eyes shining with happiness, went to look for her master. "Where is my rice?" he asked, as soon as he saw her.

"I gave it to the Buddha as an alms. Punish me if you will, I shall not weep; I am too happy for what I have done."

He did not punish her. He bowed' his head and said:

"No, I shall not punish you. I am asleep and your eyes are open. Go; you are no longer a slave."

The young girl made a deep obeisance.

"With your permission then," said she, "I shall go to Jeta's park, and I shall ask the Blessed One to instruct me in the law."

"Go," said the man.

She went to Jeta's park; she sat at the Buddha's feet, and

she became one of the most saintly women in the community.

Among those who sought instruction from the Blessed One at the same time as this young slave was Suprabha, the daughter of a prominent citizen of Cravasti. Suprabha was very beautiful. To see her was to fall in love with her, and she was courted by all the distinguished young men of the city. This caused her father no little concern. "To which one shall I give her in marriage?" he would repeatedly ask himself; "those whom I refuse will become my bitter enemies." And for hours at a time, he would remain deep in thought.

One day, Suprabha said to him:

"You seem to be troubled, dear father. What is the reason?"

"Daughter," he replied, "you alone are the cause of my anxiety. There are so many in Cravasti who wish to marry you!"

"You are afraid to make a choice from among my suitors," said Suprabha. "Poor men! If they but knew my thoughts! Do not be anxious, father! Tell them to assemble, and, according to the ancient custom, I shall go among them, and I myself shall choose a husband from their number."

"I shall do as you wish, daughter."

Suprabha's father went to King Prasenajit and received permission to have a herald proclaim throughout the city:

"That seven days from this day, there will be held an assembly of all the young men who wish to marry Suprabha. The young girl herself will select a husband from among their number."

On the seventh day, a host of suitors gathered in the magnificent garden belonging to Suprabha's father. She appeared, riding in a chariot. She was holding a yellow banner on which was painted the picture of the Blessed One. She was singing his praises. They all looked at her in amazement, and they wondered, "What will she say to us?" She finally addressed the young men.

"I can not love any of you," said she, "but do not think that I spurn you. Love is not my aim in life; I want to take refuge with the Buddha. I shall go to the park where he dwells, and he will instruct me in the law."

Mournfully, the young men withdrew, and Suprabha went to Jeta's park. She heard the Blessed One speak; she was admitted to the community, and she became a most devoted nun.

One day, as she was leaving the sacred gardens, she was recognized by one of her former suitors who happened to be passing with several friends.

"We must carry off this woman," said he. "I loved her once; I still love her. She shall be mine."

His friends agreed to help him. Before Suprabha was aware of it, she was surrounded, and they suddenly rushed upon her. But as they were about to seize her, she directed her thought toward the Buddha, and, immediately, she rose in the air. A crowd gathered; Suprabha soared above them for a while, then, flying with the grace and majesty of a swan, she returned to her sacred dwelling.

And their cries followed her:

"O saintly one, you make manifest the power of the faithful; O saint, you render manifest the power of the Buddha. It would be unjust to condemn you to the earthly pleasures of love, O saintly one, O saint."

4. Virupa

KING Prasenajit had a daughter named Virupa. She had reached a marriageable age. Unfortunately, she was extremely ugly; no prince or warrior would have her for a wife, and even the merchants looked at her askance.

But presently a wealthy stranger came to live in Cravasti. His name was Ganga. The king thought, "Ganga has never seen my daughter. Perhaps he will not refuse to marry her." And he summoned him to the palace.

Ganga was highly flattered by Prasenajit's offer. He was of humble birth, and although, as a merchant, he had amassed a great fortune, he had never dreamed of marrying a princess. He therefore accepted the proposal.

"Then come to the palace this very evening," said the king, "and take my daughter home with you."

He obeyed. The night was dark, and the wedding took place without Ganga having seen his betrothed. Then Virupa accompanied her husband to his home. Ganga saw his wife the next day. Her ugliness frightened him. He wanted to turn her out of the house, but he did not dare; he feared the king's vengeance. He kept her at home, but she was virtually a prisoner; she was not allowed to go out, for any reason whatsoever.

She was very unhappy. In vain she gave her husband constant proof of her affection; he only showed his aversion and his contempt for her. He never looked at her. He hardly spoke to her. And Virupa felt lonely and forlorn.

One day, Ganga was invited to a feast given by some of his friends. "Whoever comes without wife," he was warned, "will be fined five hundred pieces of gold."

Ganga decided to attend; it would relieve the monotony of his existence. But he did not want to show Virupa to his friends; he was afraid of being ridiculed. "I shall pay the five hundred pieces of gold," he thought, "and they will not make fun of me."

That day, Virupa was sadder than usual. She knew where her husband had gone, and she wept. She said to herself:

"What good is a life as dreary as mine? I never have any pleasure. My master loathes me. And I can not blame him; I am ugly; every one has told me so. I have brought joy to no one. Oh, I loathe myself. Death would be better than this life I lead; death would be sweet. I shall kill myself."

She took a rope and hung herself.

At that same moment, in Jeta's park, the Master was wondering, "Who is suffering to-day in Cravasti? Whom can I save from misery? To what unfortunate being can I lend a helping hand?"

By his power of divination, he learned of Virupa's distress. He flew to Ganga's house; he entered. Virupa was still alive. The Master loosened the rope she had fastened about her neck. She breathed deeply and looked around. She recognized the Master. She fell at his feet and made him a pious offering. Then he said:

"Look at yourself in a mirror, Virupa."

She obeyed. She uttered a cry of joy and astonishment. She was as beautiful as a daughter of the Gods. Again she wanted to worship the Buddha, but he had disappeared.

In the meanwhile, Ganga had not been spared the banter of his friends.

"Why did you come without your wife?" they asked him. "Are you afraid to let us see her? She must be very beautiful. You jealous husband!"

Ganga was at a loss for an answer. The feast bored him. One of his friends handed him a cup of intoxicating wine.

"Drink, Ganga," said he. "We laugh, and you are almost in tears. Come, laugh with us. Drink; this wine will teach you to laugh."

Ganga took the cup. He drank. He became livelier. He

drank again. Presently, he was drunk. And he kept on drinking until, finally, he fell into a heavy sleep.

"Let us hurry over to his house, while he is asleep," said his friends. "We shall see his wife, and we shall find out why he keeps her out of sight."

They entered Ganga's home. Virupa had the mirror in her hand; she was looking at herself. Her eyes were bright with happiness. All the guests admired her, and they went away, quietly, saying, "We now understand Ganga's jealousy."

Ganga was still sleeping. They awoke him and said:

"Great is your felicity, friend. What did you do that was so pleasing to the Gods, to deserve a wife of such rare beauty?"

"This is too much!" cried Ganga. "What have I ever done to you that you should insult me so cruelly?"

And he abruptly left them. He was raging with anger and mortification. He flung open the door of his house; he strode through the halls, muttering imprecations; but, suddenly, the curses died upon his lips. He turned pale with astonishment. Before him was standing a woman of incomparable beauty. She was smiling. He slowly came to his senses; then he, too, smiled, and he asked:

"O you who appear before me like some radiant Goddess new-risen from her bed of flowers, O well-beloved, who made you so beautiful?"

Virupa told him the story. From that day, she and her husband knew true happiness, and they both sought every opportunity to evince their faith in the Buddha and show him their gratitude.

5. Sinca's Deceit

IN the meanwhile, the evil hermits, whose imposture the Buddha had exposed, were being treated with contempt by the populace, and each day their desire for vengeance grew more intense. They had established themselves near Jeta's park, and night and day they spied upon the Buddha and his disciples. But all in vain; they saw nothing that gave them the slightest excuse for slandering the community.

At last, one of the hermits said to his companions:

"We have long been observing the conduct of these monks. Their virtue can not be denied. Still, we must turn the minds of the people against them, and I think I have found a way. I know a young girl of great charm. Her name is Sinca. She is very clever at practicing deceit. She will not refuse to help us, and soon the glory of this Sakya will vanish."

The hermits sent word to Sinca. She came. "Why did you send for me?" she asked.

"Do you know the monk from Kapilavastu, the one who is worshipped as the Buddha?" "No, but I know of his great fame. I have been told of the many prodigies he has performed."

"This man is our bitterest enemy, Sinca. He treats us shamefully and would destroy our power. Now, you believe in us; come, take our part. She who will have conquered the conqueror may well be proud; she will be famous among women, and the world will ring with her praises."

Sinca was carried away by the hermit's words. She assured him that the Buddha would soon be disgraced and his name hated throughout the earth.

Each day, now, she went to Jeta's park, at a time when those who had been listening to the Master preach were beginning to leave. She was dressed in flaming red, and she carried flowers in her arms. And if, by chance, some one asked her, "Where are you going?" she would reply, "What business is it of yours?" When she came to the park, she waited until she was quite alone; then, instead of entering the Buddha's domain, she set out for the dwelling of the evil hermits. There, she spent the night, but at dawn she returned to the gates of the park, and when she was sure to be seen by the early risers on their way to their devotions, she would leave and return home. And to those who asked, "Where do you come from, so early in the morning?" she would reply, "What business is it of yours?"

At the end of one month, she gave a different answer. In the evening she would say, "I am going to Jeta's park, where the Blessed One is waiting for me," and in the morning, "I have just come from Jeta's park, where I spent the night with the Blessed One." And there were some poor, credulous people who believed her and who suspected the Master of unchastity.

The sixth month, she took a piece of cloth and wrapped it around her body. "She is pregnant," they thought, and the fools maintained that the Master's virtue was only a pretense.

When the ninth month arrived, she tied a wooden ball to the thick girdle about her waist, and when she walked, she assumed a languorous gait. Finally, one night, she entered the hall where the Master was expounding the law. Boldly, she faced him, and her strident voice interrupted his speech.

"Sweet is your voice and honeyed your words as you instruct the people in the law. While I, who am pregnant because of you, I, who am soon to become a mother, have not even a place for my confinement! You would deny me the very oil and butter I need. If it would make you blush, now, to look after me, you could at least entrust me to one of your disciples, or to King Prasenajit, or to the merchant Anathapindika. But no! I am nothing to you any more, and little you care about the child that will be born! You would know all the joys of love, but the responsibilities you would ignore!"

"Is that a lie or are you telling the truth, Sinca?" asked the Master, calmly. "Only you and I know."

"You know very well I am not lying," cried Sinca.

The Master retained his composure. But Indra, who had been watching from the sky, decided it was time to expose Sinca's impudence. He had four Gods take the form of mice. They crawled under her robe and gnawed at the string that was holding the wooden ball. The ball fell to the ground.

"There, your child is born," exclaimed the Master with a laugh.

The disciples turned upon. Sinca in their rage. They reviled her; they spat in her face; they beat her. She fled. She was weeping with pain and shame and anger. Suddenly, red flames sprang up around her and enveloped her in a mantle of fire, and she, who had dared to slander the Buddha, came to a cruel and terrible end.

6. The Buddha Tames a Wild Buffalo

THE Master left Jeta's park. He stopped in the cities and in the villages to preach the law, and full many there were to adopt the true faith.

One day, an old man and his wife invited the Master to take his meal with them.

"My Lord," said the old man, "we have long been eager to hear your word. We are happy, now that we know the sacred truths, and among your friends you will find none more devout than we."

"I am not surprised," replied the Buddha, "for you and I were near relations in our former existences."

"Master," said the woman, "my husband and I have lived together since our early youth; we have now attained a ripe old age. Life has been kind to us. Never has the slightest quarrel come between us. We still love each other as in the days gone by, and the evening of our lives is as sweet as was the dawn. May it be granted us, my Lord, to love each other in our next existence as we have loved one another in this life." "It will be granted," said the Master; "the Gods have protected you!"

He continued on his way. He saw an old woman drawing water from a well by the side of the road. He approached her.

"I am thirsty," said he. "Will you give me a drink?"

The old woman stared at him. She was deeply moved. She began to weep. She wanted to embrace the Master, but she was afraid. The tears coursed down her cheeks.

"Embrace me," said the Master.

The old woman ran to his arms, and she murmured:

"Now I can die happy. I have seen the Blessed One, and it was given me to embrace him."

He went on. He came to a vast forest where a herd of

buffaloes lived with their keepers. One of these buffaloes was a very powerful animal. He had an ugly temper. He barely tolerated the presence of his keepers, and at the approach of a stranger he would become aggressive. When the stranger came near, he would attack him with his horns, and he would often wound him seriously. Sometimes he killed him.

The keepers saw the Blessed One walking along, quietly, and they shouted: "Take care, traveler. Do not come near us. There is a vicious buffalo here."

But he paid no attention to the warning. He made straight for the spot where the buffalo was grazing.

All at once, the buffalo raised his head and sniffed noisily; then, lowering his horns, he rushed at the Master. The keepers trembled. "Our voices were not loud enough," they cried; "he did not hear us." But, suddenly, the animal stopped short; he knelt before the Master and began licking his feet. There was a look of pleading in his eyes.

The Master gently stroked the buffalo. He spoke to him in a quiet voice.

"Say to yourself that all earthly things are transitory, that peace is found only in nirvana. Do not weep. Believe in me, believe in my goodness, in my compassion, and your condition will change. You will not be reborn among the animals, and, in time, you will attain the sky and dwell among the Gods."

From that day, the buffalo was extremely docile. And the keepers, who had expressed their admiration for the Master and who had given him what alms they could afford, were instructed in the law, and they became known for their piety, even among the most pious.

7. Dissension Among the Monks

THE Master arrived at the city of Kausambi, and there, at first, he was very happy. The inhabitants eagerly listened to his words, and many of them became monks. King Udayana was among the believers, and he allowed his son Rashtrapala to enter the community.

Yet it was in Kausambi that the Master met with one of his great sorrows. A monk, one day, was reprimanded for committing some minor offense. He would not own himself in the wrong; so he was punished. He refused to submit to the punishment, and, as he was a pleasant man, of great wit and learning, there were many to take his part. In vain the others besought him to return to the straight path.

"Do not assume that conceited air," they said to him; "do not consider yourself incapable of making mistakes. Heed our wise advice. Address the other monks as they should be addressed who profess a faith that is also yours; they will address you as he should be addressed who professes a faith that is also theirs. The community will grow, the community will flourish, only if the monks will take counsel from one another."

"It is not for you to tell me what is right or wrong," he replied. "Stop reproving me."

"Do not say that. Your words offend against the law. You are defying discipline; you are sowing discord in the community. Come, mend your ways. Live at peace with the community. Avoid these quarrels, and be faithful to the law."

It was useless. They then decided to expel the rebel, but, once again, he refused to obey. He would remain in the community: since he was innocent, there was no need to submit to an unjust punishment.

The Master finally intervened. He tried to pacify the monks; he pleaded with them to forget their grievances and to unite, as before, in the performance of their sacred duties, but no one paid any attention. And, one day, a monk even had the audacity to say to him:

"Keep still, O Master; do not bother us with your speeches. You have arrived at a knowledge of the law; meditate upon it. You will find your meditations quite delightful. As for us, we shall know where to go; our quarrels will not keep us from finding the way. Meditate, and be quiet."

The Master was not angry. He tried to speak, but it was impossible, He saw then that he could never convince the monks of Kausambi; they seemed to be possessed with some sudden folly. The Master decided to forsake them, but first he said to them:

"Happy is he who has a faithful friend; happy is he who has a discerning friend. What obstacles could two wise and virtuous friends not overcome? But he who has no faithful friend resembles a king without a country: he must roam in solitude, like the elephant in the wild forest. Yet it is better to travel alone than in the company of a fool. The wise man should follow a lonely path; he should avoid evil and should preserve his serenity, like the elephant in the wild forest."

He left. No one tried to stop him. He went to a village where he knew he would find his disciple Bhrigu. Bhrigu was overjoyed to see him, and the Master was not a little comforted. Then, Anuruddha, Nanda and Kimbala joined him. They gave him every proof of their respect and friendship, and they lived at peace with one another. And the Master thought, "So there are some, among my disciples, who love me and who do not quarrel."

One day, as he sat down in the shade of a tree and began thinking of the troublous times in Kausambi, a herd of elephants stopped to rest not far from him. The biggest elephant went down to the river and drew water which he brought back to the others. They drank; then, instead of thanking him for doing them this service, they abused him, they beat him with their trunks, and, finally, they drove him away. And the Master saw that his own experience was not unlike that of the elephant: they were both victims of gross ingratitude. The elephant noticed the sadness in his face; he drew near and looked at him tenderly; then left, to go in search of food and drink for him.

The Master finally returned to Cravasti and rested in Jeta's park.

But it still grieved him to think of the cruel monks of Kausambi. One morning, however, he saw them enter the park. They were in great distress: alms had been denied them, for every one was indignant at their treatment of the Master. They had come to beg his forgiveness. The guilty monk confessed himself to have been in the wrong, and his punishment was light. His adversaries, as well as his friends, admitted the error of their ways, and all promised strictly to obey the rules. And the Master was happy: there was no longer any dissension in the community.

8. Kuvalaya the Dancer

ONE day, he returned to the country of Rajagriha.

In a field, not far from the city, he came upon a brahman named Bharadvaja. It was the harvest season, and the brahman and his servants were joyously celebrating. They were laughing and singing as the Master went by. He held out his alms-bowl, and those who recognized him, greeted him and made him many friendly offerings. This displeased Bharadvaja. He went up to the Master, and he said to him in a loud voice:

"Monk, tarry not in our midst; you set an evil example. We work, we that are here, and with watchful eyes, we observe the changes of seasons. When it is time to plow, my servants plow; when it is time to sow, they sow; and I plow and sow with them. Then the day comes when we harvest the fruit of our labor. We provide our own food, and when it is stored away, we have good reason to rest and play. While you, you roam the streets and walk the roads, and the only trouble you design to take is to hold out a bowl to those you meet. It would be better far for you to work; it would be better far to plow and sow."

The Master smiled and answered:

"Friend, like you I plow and sow, and when my work is done, I eat."

"You plow? You sow?" said Bharadvaja. "How can I believe that? Where are your cattle? Where is your grain? Where is your plow?"

The Master said:

"Purity of understanding, that is the glorious seed I sow. Works of holiness are the rain that falls upon the fertile earth where the seed sprouts and ripens. And mine is a mighty plow: it has wisdom for its plowshare, the law for its handles, and an active faith is the powerful bullock yoked to its pole. Desire is uprooted like weeds in the fields I plow, and I gather in the richest of harvests, nirvana."

He continued on his way. But the brahman Bharadvaja followed him; he would now hear the sacred word.

They entered the city. On the public square, a large crowd was watching a troop of dancers. The daughter of the leader was attracting particular attention. Such grace and beauty had seldom been seen, and, whenever she appeared, those who were not master of their passions burned with the desire to possess her. Her name was Kuvalaya.

She had just finished dancing. Ardent eyes were still fastened upon her. She was aware of her power, and full of pride and audacity, she shouted 'to the crowd:

"Admire me, my lords! In all Rajagriha is there one who can surpass Kuvalaya in beauty, are there any who can even equal her?"

"Yes, woman," replied the brahman Bharadvaja. "What is your beauty when compared with the beauty of the Master?"

"I would see this Master whose beauty you praise," said Kuvalaya; "lead me to him."

"Here he is," said the Blessed One.

And he came forward.

The dancer stared at him.

"You are beautiful," she said at last. "I shall dance for you."

Kuvalaya danced. The dance began slowly. She had wrapped all her veils about her, even covering her face, and the beauty once so boldly flaunted was now only a dim promise. She was like the moon, hiding behind soft clouds from the gaze of night. A cloud flew away; a faint ray escaped through the rift. The dance became more rapid; one by one the veils fell away, and the queen of the stars appeared in all her glory. Faster and faster she whirled; suddenly, a blinding light flashed in her eyes, and she stopped. She was naked. The crowd gasped and surged forward.

"Unhappy woman!" said the Buddha.

He looked at her intently. Whereupon Kuvalaya's cheeks became sunken, her forehead wrinkled and her eyes grew dull. Only a few ugly teeth were left in her mouth; only a few thin strands of grey hair still hung from her head, and she was stooped as with age. The Blessed One had punished her as he had once punished Mara's daughters when they had tried to tempt him; he had changed the beautiful dancer into a shriveled old woman.

She sighed:

"Master, I know the great wrong I have done. An ephemeral beauty had made me vain. You taught me a bitter lesson, but I feel that some day I shall be happy to have received it. Let me learn the sacred truths; then may I be released for ever from this body that, even when it was the delight of men, was nothing but a loathsome corpse."

The Master granted Kuvalaya's request, and she became one of the most devout of the Buddha's faithful followers.

9. The God Alavaka Defeated by the Buddha

IN the city of Atavi there ruled a king who was very fond of hunting. One day, he saw an enormous deer and started in pursuit. The deer was fleet of foot, and in the heat of the chase, the king lost sight of the other hunters. Finally, the prey escaped, and weary and discouraged, the king sat down under a tree. He fell asleep.

It happened that a wicked God named Alavaka lived in the tree. He liked to feed on human flesh, and he killed and devoured all who came near him. He saw the king; he rejoiced, and the poor hunter was about to be dealt a severe blow when a noise fortunately awoke him. He realized that his life was threatened; he made an attempt to rise, but the God took him by the throat and held him down. Then the king tried to plead with him.

"Spare me, my lord!" said he. "By your terrifying appearance, I know you to be one of the Gods that eat human flesh. Oh, deign to be kind to me. You will have no cause to regret your mercy. I shall reward you with magnificent gifts."

"What care I for gifts!" replied Alavaka. "It is your flesh I want; it will appease my hunger."

"My lord," replied the king, "if you let me return to Atavi, I shall send you a man every day to satisfy your hunger."

"When you get back to your home, you will forget this promise."

"No," said the king, "I never forget a promise. Besides, if I should once fail to make this daily offering, you have only to come to my palace and tell me of your grievance, and, immediately, without resisting, I shall follow you, and you may devour me."

The God allowed himself to be persuaded, and the king

returned to the city of Atavi. But he kept thinking of his cruel promise; there was no way he could evade it, and henceforth he would have to be a hard and ruthless master.

He sent for his minister and told him what had happened. The minister considered for a moment, then said to the king:

"My lord, in the prison of Atavi there are criminals who have been condemned to death. We can send them to the God. When he sees that you are keeping faith with him, perhaps he will relieve you of your promise."

The king approved of the suggestion. Guards were sent to the prison, and to those whose days were numbered they said: "Not far from the city there is a tree inhabited by a God who is very fond of rice. Whoever leaves a plate of rice for him at the foot of the tree will be granted a full pardon."

Whereupon, each day, one of these men, carrying a plate of rice, joyously set out for the tree, never to return.

Presently, there were no men condemned to death left in prison. The minister ordered the judges to be extremely severe and to acquit no one accused of murder except on irrefutable proof of his innocence, but it was in vain; some new way had to be found for appeasing the hunger of the God. Then they began to sacrifice the thieves.

In spite of all their efforts to apprehend the guilty, the prison was again empty, and the king and his minister were compelled to look for victims among the worthy inhabitants of the city. Old people were carried off and forcibly led to the tree, and if the guards were not fleet-footed, the God would sometimes devour them and the victims as well.

A vague uneasiness possessed the city of Atavi. The old people were seen to disappear; no one knew what became of them. And, each day, the king's remorse grew more poignant. But he lacked the courage to sacrifice his life to the welfare of his people. He thought: "Will no one come to my assistance? There lives in Cravasti, and sometimes in Rajagriha, I have been told, a man of great power, a Buddha, whose prodigies are loudly praised. They say he is fond of traveling. Why, then, does he not come into my kingdom?"

By his power of divination, the Buddha knew of the king's desire. He flew through the air and came to Alavaka's tree. There, he sat down.

The God saw him. He started walking toward him, but, suddenly, he became powerless. His knees trembled. Fury seized him.

"Who are you?" he asked, fiercely.

"A being far more powerful than yourself," replied the Buddha.

Alavaka was in a terrible rage. He would have liked to torture this man who was sitting on the ground in front of him, this man whom he could not reach; he would have liked to torture him to death. The Buddha never lost his composure.

Alavaka finally managed to control himself. He thought that cunning would perhaps succeed where strength had failed, and in a pleasant voice he said:

"I see you are a wise man, my Lord; it is always a pleasure for me to interrogate men of wisdom. I ask them four questions. If they can answer, they are free to go wherever they please; if they can not answer, they remain my prisoners, and I devour them when I feel so disposed."

"Ask me the four questions," said the Buddha.

"I must warn you," said Alavaka, "that no one has ever answered them. You will find scattered around the bones of those I interrogated in the past."

"Ask me the four questions," repeated the Buddha.

"Well then," said Alavaka, "how can man avoid the river of passions? How can he cross the sea of existences and find safe harbor? How can he escape the tempests of evil? How can he be left untouched by the storm of desires?"

In a quiet voice, the Buddha replied:

"Man avoids the river of passions if he believes in the Buddha, in the law and in the community; he crosses the sea of existences and finds safe harbor if he understands works of holiness; he will escape the tempests of evil if he performs works of holiness; he will be left untouched by the storm of desires if he knows the sacred path that leads to deliverance."

When Alavaka heard the Master's answers, he fell at his feet and worshipped him, and he promised to change his savage ways. Then, together, they went to Atavi, to the palace of the king.

"King," said the God, "I release you from your pledge." The king was happier than he had ever been before. When he knew who had saved him, he cried:

"I believe in you, my Lord, who have saved me and saved my people; I believe in you, and I shall dedicate my life to proclaiming your glory, the glory of the law and the glory of the community."

10. Devadatta Expelled from the Community

THE monk Devadatta was possessed of an arrogant nature. He was impatient of any restraint. He aspired to supplant the Buddha, but the monks, he knew, would not join him in an open revolt. For that he needed the support of some king or prince.

"King Vimbasara is an old man," he said to himself, one day; "Prince Ajatasatru, who is young and brave, is eager to succeed him to the throne. I could advise the prince to his advantage, and, in return, he could help me to become the head of the community."

He went to see Ajatasatru. He addressed him in flattering terms; he praised his strength, his courage, his beauty.

"Oh, if you were king," said he, "what glory would come to Rajagriha! You would conquer the neighboring states; all the sovereigns of the world would pay you homage: you would be the omnipotent master, and you would be worshipped like a God."

With such words as these, Devadatta won Ajatasatru's confidence. He received many precious gifts, and he became still more arrogant.

Maudgalyayana noticed Devadatta's frequent visits to the prince. He decided to warn the Blessed One.

"My Lord," he began, "Devadatta is very friendly with Prince Ajatasatru."

The Blessed One interrupted him.

"Let Devadatta do as he pleases; we shall soon know the truth. I am aware that Ajatasatru pays him homage; it does not advance him a single step in the path of virtue. Let Devadatta glory in his arrogance! It will be his ruin. As the banana-tree and the bamboo-tree bear fruit only to die, so will the honors Devadatta is receiving simply hasten his downfall."

Devadatta soon reached the height of vanity. He could not abide the Buddha's grandeur, and, one day, he made bold to say to him:

"Master, you are now well along in years; it is a great hardship for you to rule the monks; you should retire. Meditate in peace upon the sublime law you have discovered, and the community let me take charge of."

The Master smiled quizzically.

"Be not concerned about me, Devadatta; you are too kind. I shall know when it is time to retire. For the present, I shall stay in charge of the community. Besides, when the time does come, I shall not give it even to Sariputra or Maudgalyayana, those two great minds that are like blazing torches, and you want it, Devadatta, you who have such a mediocre intelligence, you who shed even less light than a night-lamp!"

Devadatta bowed respectfully before the Master, but he could not hide the fire of anger in his eyes.

The Master then sent for learned Sariputra.

"Sariputra," said he, "go through the city of Rajagriha and cry in a loud voice: 'Beware of Devadatta! He has strayed from the path of righteousness. The Buddha is not responsible for his words or for his actions; the law no longer inspires him, the community no longer interests him. Henceforth, Devadatta speaks only for himself.'"

It grieved Sariputra to have such a painful mission to perform; however, he understood the Master's reasons, and he went through the city crying Devadatta's shame. The inhabitants stopped to listen, and some thought, "The monks envy Devadatta his friendship for Prince Ajatasatru." But the others said, "Devadatta must have committed a serious offense, for the Blessed One thus publicly to denounce him."

11. Ajatasatru's Treachery

DEVADATTA was musing: "Siddhartha thought to humiliate me by making light of my intelligence. I shall show him he is mistaken. My glory will overshadow his: the night-lamp will become the sun. But King Vimbasara is his faithful friend; he protects him. As long as the king is living, I can do nothing. Prince Ajatasatru, on the other hand, honors me and holds me in high esteem; he reposes implicit confidence in me. If he were to reign, I would get everything I desire."

He went to Ajatasatru's palace.

"Oh, prince," said he, "we are living in an unfortunate age! They that are best fitted to govern are likely to die without ever having reigned. Human life is so brief a thing! Your father's longevity causes me no little concern for you."

He kept on talking, and he was presently giving the prince most evil advice. The prince was weak; he listened. Before long, he had decided to kill his father."

Night and day, now, Ajatasatru wandered through the palace, watching for an opportunity to slip into his father's apartments and make away with him. But he could not escape the vigilance of the guards. His restlessness puzzled them, and they said to King Vimbasara:

"O king, your son Ajatasatru has been behaving strangely of late. Could he be planning an evil deed?"

"Be silent," replied the king. "My son is a man of noble character. It would not occur to him to do anything base."

"You ought to send for him, O king, and question him."

"Be silent, guards. Do not accuse my son lightly."

The guards continued to keep a close watch, and at the end of a few days, they again spoke to the king. To convince them that they were mistaken, the king summoned Ajatasatru.

The prince appeared before his father. He was trembling.

"My lord," said he, "why did you send for me?"

"Son," said Vimbasara, "my guards say that you have been behaving strangely of late. They tell me you wander through the palace, acting mysteriously, and that you shun the gaze of those you meet. Son, are they not lying?"

"They are not lying, father," said Ajatasatru Remorse suddenly overwhelmed him. He fell at the king's feet, and out of the depths of his shame, he cried:

"Father, I wanted to kill you."

Vimbasara shuddered. In a voice full of anguish, he asked:

"Why did you want to kill me?"

"In order to reign."

"Then reign," cried the king. "Royalty is not worth a son's enmity."

Ajatasatru was proclaimed king the next day.

The first thing he did was to have great honors paid to his father. But Devadatta still feared the old king's authority; he decided to use his influence against him.

"As long as your father is allowed his freedom," he said to Ajatasatru, "you are in danger of losing your power. He still retains many followers; you must take measures to intimidate them."

Devadatta again was able to impose his will on Ajatasatru, and poor Vimbasara was thrown into prison. Ajatasatru presently decided to starve him to death, and he allowed no one to take him any food.

But Queen Vaidehi was sometimes permitted to visit Vimbasara in his prison, and she would take rice to him which he ate ravenously. Ajatasatru, however, soon put a stop to this; he ordered the guards to search her each time she went to see the prisoner. She then tried to hide the food in her hair, and when this, too, was discovered, she had to use great ingenuity to save the king from dying of hunger. But she was repeatedly found out, and Ajatasatru, finally, denied her access to the prison.

In the meanwhile, he was persecuting the Buddha's faithful followers. They were forbidden to look after the temple where Vimbasara, formerly, had placed a lock of the Master's hair and the parings of his finger-nails. No longer were flowers or perfume left there as pious offerings, and the temple was not even cleaned or swept.

In Ajatasatru's palace there dwelt a woman named Srimati. She was very devout. It grieved her to be unable to perform works of holiness, and she wondered how, in these sad times, she could prove to the Master that she had kept her faith. Passing in front of the temple, she complained bitterly to see it so deserted, and when she noticed how unclean it was, she wept.

"The Master shall know that there is still one woman in this house who would honor him," thought Srimati, and at the risk of her life, she swept out the temple and decorated it with a bright garland.

Ajatasatru saw the garland. He was greatly incensed and wanted to know who had dared to disobey him. Srimati did not try to hide; of her own accord, she appeared before the king.

"Why did you defy my orders?" asked Ajatasatru.

"If I defied your orders," she replied, "I respected those of your father, King Vimbasara."

Ajatasatru did not wait to hear further. Pale with fury, he rushed at Srimati and stabbed her with his dagger. She fell, mortally wounded; but her eyes were shining with joy, and in a happy voice, she sang:

"My eyes have seen the protector of the worlds; my eyes have seen the light of the worlds, and for him, in the night, I have lighted the lamps. For him who dissipates the darkness, I have dissipated the darkness. His brilliance is greater than the brilliance of the sun; his rays are purer than the rays of the sun, and my rapt gaze is dazzled by the splendor. For him who dissipates the darkness, I have dissipated the darkness."

And, dead, she seemed to glow with the light of sanctity.

12. The Death of Devadatta

DEVADATTA was eager to succeed the Buddha as head of the community. One day, he said to King Ajatasatru: "My lord, the Buddha holds you in contempt. He hates you. You must put him to death, for your glory is at stake. Send some men to the Bamboo Grove with orders to kill him; I shall lead the way."

Ajatasatru was easily persuaded. The assassins came to the Bamboo Grove, but when they saw the Master, they fell at his feet and worshipped him. This added fuel to Devadatta's rage. He went to the royal stables where a savage elephant was kept, and he bribed the guards to release him when the Master passed by, so that the animal could gore him with his tusks or trample him underfoot. But at the sight of the Master, the elephant became quite gentle, and going up to him, with his trunk he brushed the dust from the sacred robes. And the Master smiled and said:

"This is the second time, thanks to Devadatta, that an elephant has paid homage to me."

Then Devadatta himself tried to do harm to the Master. He saw him meditating in the shade of a tree; and he had the audacity to throw a sharp stone at him. It struck him in the foot; the wound began to bleed. The Master said:

"You have committed a serious offense, Devadatta; the punishment will be terrible. Vain are your criminal attempts upon the life of the Blessed One; he will not meet with an untimely death. The Blessed One will pass away of his own accord, and at the hour he chooses."

Devadatta fled. He decided he would no longer obey the rules of the community, and, wherever he could, he would seek followers of his own.

In the meanwhile, Vimbasara was starving. But he did not die. A mysterious force sustained him. His son finally decided to have him put to death, and he gave orders to burn the soles of his feet, to slash his limbs and to pour boiling oil and salt on the open wounds. The executioner obeyed, and even he wept to see an old man tortured.

A son was born to Ajatasatru on the day he issued the order for his father's death. When he saw the child, a great joy came to him; he relented, and he hurriedly sent guards to the prison to stop the execution. But they arrived too late; King Vimbasara had died amid frightful suffering.

Then Ajatasatru began to repent. One day, he heard Queen Vaidehi saying to the infant prince, as she carried him in her arms: "May your father be as kind to you as his father was to him. Once, when he was a child, he had a sore on his finger; it hurt him, and he cried; no ointment would heal it; so Vimbasara put the finger to his lips and drew out the pus, and Ajatasatru was able to laugh again and play. Oh, love your father, little child; do not punish him with your cruelty for having been cruel to Vimbasara."

Ajatasatru shed bitter tears. He was overwhelmed with remorse. At night, in his dreams, he saw his father, bleeding from his wounds, and he heard him moan. He was seized with a burning fever, and the physician Jivaka was summoned to attend him.

"I can do nothing for you," said Jivaka. "Your body is not sick. Go to the Perfect Master, the Blessed One, the Buddha; he alone knows the words of consolation that will restore you to health."

Ajatasatru took Jivaka's advice. He went to the Blessed One; he confessed his misdeeds and his crimes, and he found peace.

"Your father," the Buddha said to him, "has been reborn among the most powerful Gods; he knows of your repentance, and he forgives you. Heed me, King Ajatasatru; know the law, and cease to suffer."

Ajatasatru issued a proclamation, banishing Devadatta from the kingdom, and ordering the inhabitants to close their doors to him if he were to seek refuge in their homes.

Devadatta was then near Cravasti where he hoped to be received by King Prasenajit, but he was scornfully denied an audience and was told to leave the kingdom. Thwarted in his attempts to enlist followers, he finally set out for Kapilavastu.

He entered the city as night was falling. The streets were dark, almost deserted; no one recognized him as he passed, for how could this lean, wretched monk, slinking in the shadow of the walls, be identified with the proud Devadatta? He went straight to the palace where princess Gopa dwelt in solitude.

He was admitted to her presence.

"Monk," said Gopa, "why do you wish to see me? Do you bring me a message of happiness? Do you come with orders from a husband I deeply reverence?"

"Your husband! Little he cares about you! Think of the time he wickedly deserted you!"

"He deserted me for the world's salvation." "Do you still love him?"

"My love would defile the purity of his life."

"Then hate him with all your heart."

"With all my heart I respect him."

"Woman, he spurned you; take your revenge." "Be quiet, monk. Your words are evil."

"Do you not recognize me? I am Devadatta, who loves you."

"Devadatta, Devadatta, I knew you were false and evil; I knew you would be a faithless monk, but I never suspected the depths of your villainy."

"Gopa, Gopa, I love you! Your husband scorned you, he was cruel. Take your revenge. Love me!"

Gopa blushed. From her gentle eyes fell tears of shame.

"It is you who scorn me! Your love would be an insult if it were sincere, but you lie when you say you love me. You seldom noticed me in the days when I was young, in the days when I was beautiful! And now that you see me, an old woman, worn out by my austere duties, you tell me of your love, of your guilty love! You are the most contemptible of men, Devadatta! Go away! Go away!"

In his rage he sprang at her. She put out her hand to protect herself, and he fell to the ground. As he rolled over, blood gushed from his mouth.

He fled. The Sakyas heard that he was in Kapilavastu; they made him leave the city under an escort of guards, and he was taken to the Buddha who was to decide his fate. He pretended to be repentant, but he had dipped his nails in a deadly poison, and as he lay prostrate before the Maser, he tried to scratch his ankle. The Master pushed him away with his toe; then the ground opened; fierce flames burst forth, and they swallowed up the infamous Devadatta.

13. Prasenajit and Ajatasatru

ALTHOUGH the Buddha had chastened Ajatasatru's spirit, there were times when the king still gave way to anger. One day, because of a quarrel between a man from Rajagriha and one from Cravasti, he declared war on King Prasenajit.

He collected a vast army. There were foot-soldiers and horsemen; there were some mounted on chariots, others enclosed in towers carried by elephants, and swords and lances flashed in the sun as they marched into battle.

King Prasenajit also assembled his troops. He too had chariots and horses and elephants, and he advanced to meet Ajatasatru.

It was a terrible battle. It lasted four days. The first day Prasenajit lost his elephants; the second day he lost his horses; on the third, his chariots were destroyed; and on the fourth, his foot-soldiers were killed or made prisoners; and Prasenajit himself, defeated and panic-stricken, fled in the only chariot that had been saved in the disaster and escaped to Cravasti. There, in a small, unlighted hall, he flung himself down on a low couch. He was silent, a prey to his melancholy thoughts. He never stirred; he appeared to be dead, except for the tears that coursed down his cheeks.

A man entered; it was the merchant Anathapindika.

"My lord," said he, "long may you live, and may the tide of victory turn!"

"My soldiers are dead," the king lamented, "all my soldiers are dead! My soldiers! My soldiers!"

"Grieve not, O king. Raise another army."

"I lost my fortune when I lost my army."

"King," said Anathapindika, "I shall give you the gold you need, and you will be victorious."

Prasenajit sprang to his feet.

"You have saved me, Anathapindika!" he exclaimed. "I am grateful."

With Anathapindika's gold, Prasenajit raised a formidable host. He marched against Ajatasatru.

When the two armies met, the din terrified the Gods themselves. Prasenajit used a battle array he had been taught by men from a distant land. He attacked swiftly; Ajatasatru had no defense. He, in turn, was defeated, and he was captured.

"Kill me," he cried to Prasenajit. "I shall spare your life," said Prasenajit. "I shall take you to the Blessed Master, and he will decide your fate."

The Master had recently arrived at Jeta's park. Prasenajit said to him:

"Behold, O Blessed One! King Ajatasatru is my prisoner. He hates me, though I bear him no ill will. He attacked me, for some trivial reason, and defeated me at first, but now he is at my mercy. I do not wish to kill him, O Blessed One. For the sake of his father, Vimbasara, who was my friend, I would like to set him free."

"Then set him free," said the Master. "Victory begets hatred; defeat begets suffering. They that are wise will forgo both victory and defeat. Insult is born of insult, anger of anger. They that are wise will forgo both victory and defeat. Every murderer is struck down by a murderer; every conqueror is struck down by a conqueror. They that are wise will forgo both victory and defeat."

In the presence of the Master, Ajatasatru promised to be a faithful friend to Prasenajit.

"And," he added, "let us be more than friends. I have a son, as you know, and you have a daughter, Kshema, who is still unmarried. Will you give your daughter to my son?"

"So be it," said Prasenajit. "And may this happy marriage be the earnest of our happy friendship."

The Master approved. The two kings ever after lived at peace with each other, and Ajatasatru became known for his gentleness.

14. The Buddha Teaches the Doctrine

THE Master was growing old. When he was in Rajagriha, he called the monks together, and he spoke to them at great length:

"Monks, do not forget the precepts I have given you. Observe them carefully. You will assemble twice a month, and you will confess your transgressions to one another. If you feel that you have done evil, and you keep it to yourself, you will be guilty of a lie. Admit your transgressions: the confession will bring you rest and peace. The four gravest sins a monk can commit are, as you know: to have intercourse with a woman; to steal anything whatsoever; to kill a human being or instigate a murder; and to pretend to possess a superhuman power that he knows he does not possess. A monk who has committed one of these four sins must be expelled from the community. Monks, do not bandy words with women, and do not corrupt them. Do not bear false witness against your brothers. Do not try to sow discord in the community. Do not strive to evade a reprimand. Never lie, and insult no one. Observe carefully, O monks, all the precepts I have given you."

He said further:

"Seriousness is the province of immortality; frivolity, the province of death. They that are serious do not die; they that are frivolous are always dead. Therefore would the wise be serious. The wise attain the supreme blessing, nirvana. He sees his glory increase who is energetic and can remember, who thinks honestly and acts deliberately, who is continent, who lives within the law, and who is serious. It is frivolity the fools and the weak-minded pursue; the wise treasure seriousness as a miser his gold. The monk who would be serious, who sees the danger of frivolity, shakes the evil law like the wind does the leaves; he tears asunder the bonds that bind him to the world; he is close to nirvana. Standing on the terrace of wisdom, released from all suffering, the serious man who has conquered frivolity looks out over the unhappy multitude, as, from the summit of a mountain, one might gaze upon the crowd in the plains below."

15. The Buddha and the Shepherd

BEFORE he died, the Blessed One decided to go on a long journey. He wanted to visit certain of his disciples and exhort them to observe his teachings with scrupulous care. With only Ananda for a companion, he left the city of Rajagriha.

One day, while he was resting in the corner of a field, he said to Ananda:

"There will come a time when men will wonder why I once entered a woman's womb. They will question the perfect purity of my birth, and they will doubt whether I ever had supreme power. These benighted men will never understand that, for him who devotes his life to works of holiness, the body is free from the impurity of birth. He who would seek supreme knowledge must enter a woman's womb; he must, out of pity for mankind, be born into the world of men. For if he were a God, how could he set in motion the wheel of the law? Imagine the Buddha as a God, Ananda; men would soon lose heart. They would say, 'The Buddha, who is a God, has happiness, holiness, perfection; but we, how can we hope to attain them?' And they would be in deep despair. Oh, let them keep still, these benighted creatures! Let them not try to steal the law, for they would use it ill. Rather, let them consider the Buddha's nature incomprehensible, these men who will never be able to gauge my eminence!"

A shepherd was crossing the field. He had the serenity of a man who is quietly performing a labor of joy.

"Who are you, shepherd?" the Master asked him.

"My name is Dhaniya," replied the shepherd.

"Where are you going?" asked the Master.

"I am going home to my wife and children."

"You seem to know pure happiness, shepherd?"

"I have boiled my rice, I have milked my cows," said the shepherd Dhaniya; "I live with my family on the banks of the river; my house is well roofed, my fire is lighted; so fall if you will, O rain of the sky.

"I am rid of anger, I am rid of stubbornness," said the Master; "I bide for a night on the banks of the river; my house has no roof, the fire of passions is quenched in my being; so fall if you will, O rain of the sky."

"The gadflies never torment my herd," said the shepherd Dhaniya; "my cows roam in the grassy meadows; they can abide the coming rain; so fall if you will, O rain of the sky." "I built a sturdy raft, I set sail for nirvana," said the Master; "I crossed the torrent of passions and I reached the saintly shores; I need the raft no longer; so fall if you will, O rain of the sky."

"My wife is obedient, she is chaste and good," said the shepherd Dhaniya; "she has lived with me these many years; she is pleasant and kindly, no one speaks ill of her; so fall if you will, O rain of the sky."

"My mind is obedient, it is loosed from all bonds," said the Master; "I have trained it these many years; it is quite docile, no evil is left in me; so fall if you will, O rain of the sky."

"I myself pay my servants their wages," said the shepherd Dhaniya; "my children receive wholesome food at my board; no one has ever tried to speak ill of them; so fall if you will, O rain of the sky."

"I am the servant of no one," said the Master; "with what I earn I travel the whole world; there is for me no need of a servant; so fall if you will, O rain of the sky."

"I have cows, I have calves, I have heifers," said the shepherd Dhaniya, "and I have a dog that is lord of my herd; so fall if you will, O rain of the s y.

"I have neither cows nor calves nor heifers," said the Master, "and I have no dog to be on guard; so fall if you will, O rain of the sky."

"The stakes are driven deep in the ground, nothing can move them," said the shepherd Dhaniya; the ropes are new and made of strong grasses; the cows will never break them now; so fall if you will, O rain of the sky."

"Like the dog that has broken his chain," said the Master, "like the elephant that has broken his shackles, never again will I enter a womb; so fall if you will, O rain of the sky."

The shepherd Dhaniya bowed before the Master and said:

"I know now who you are, O Blessed One; come with me to my home."

As they were about to enter the house, the rain fell in torrents and formed little streams that trickled over the ground. When Dhaniya heard the rain, he spoke these words:

"Verily, we have acquired great riches since we have seen the Buddha. O Master, you are our refuge, you who have looked at us with the eyes of wisdom. Be our protector, O Saint! We are obedient, my wife and I; if we lead a life of holiness, we shall conquer birth and death, and we shall have done with suffering."

Then a voice was heard, and Mara, the Evil One, stood before them. No one had seen him come.

"He who has sons is happy to see his sons," said Mara, the Evil One; "he who has cows is happy to see his cows; happy is the man of substance, and he who has no substance has no happiness."

"He who has sons is worried to see his sons," said the Master; "he who has cows is worried to see his cows; worried is the man of substance, and he who has no substance has no worries."

But Mara had fled. Dhaniya and his wife were listening to the Master speak.

16. The Buddha Instructs the Monks of Vaisali

THE Master came to the banks of the Ganges, to the place where the city of Pataliputra was being built. He bowed before the walls that were beginning to rise out of the ground, and he exclaimed:

"This city will one day have greatness and renown; many heroes will be born here, here will reign a famous king. A thriving city you will be, O Pataliputra, and down through the ages men will praise your name."

He crossed the river. He set out for Vaisali, but in the village of Bailva he became gravely ill. He suffered intense pain. Ananda wept, for he thought he was dying. But the Master remembered the many disciples he had still to visit; he did not wish to enter nirvana until he had given them final instructions. By the strength of his will, he overcame the sickness, and life did not leave him. He recovered.

When he was well again, he went outside the house that had given him shelter, and he took a seat that had been prepared for him near the door. Ananda came and sat down beside him. "My Lord," said he, "I see that you have recovered your health. When I found you so ill, my strength failed me; I was faint. There were times I could not realize that the Master was sick. And yet I was reassured, for I remembered that you had not disclosed your intentions regarding the community, and I knew you would not enter nirvana without first revealing them."

The Blessed One spoke these words:

"What more does the community want of me, Ananda? I have stated the doctrine, and I have taught it; there is not a single point I have not expounded! Let him who thinks, 'I want to rule over the community,' disclose his intentions regarding the community. The Blessed One, Ananda, never thought, 'I want to rule over the community.' Why then should he disclose his intentions? I am an old man, Ananda; my hair is white, and I have grown feeble. I am eighty years old; I have come to the end of the road. Be, now, each one of you, your own torch; look to no one to bring you light. He who is his own torch, after I have left the world, will show that he has understood the meaning of my words; he will be my true disciple, Ananda; he will know the right way to live."

He set out again, and presently he arrived at Vaisali. He went through the city, begging his food from door to door. Suddenly, he saw Mara standing before him.

"The hour has come," said the Evil One; "enter nirvana, O Blessed One."

"No," replied the Buddha. "I know when I must enter nirvana; I know better than you, Evil One. A few months more, and it will be time. Three months more, and the Blessed One will enter nirvana."

At these words the earth shook, and thunder rolled across the sky: the Blessed One had destroyed the will by which he still held to life; he had set the time for his entry into nirvana. The earth shook, and thunder rolled across the sky.

In the evening he assembled the monks of Vaisali, and he addressed them.

"O monks, preserve carefully, the knowledge I have acquired and that I have taught you, and walk in the right path, in order that the life of holiness may long endure, for the joy and salvation of the world, for the joy and salvation of the Gods, for the joy and salvation of mankind. A few months more, and my time will have come; three months more, and I shall enter nirvana. I go and you remain. But never cease to struggle, O monks. He who falters not in the path of truth avoids birth, avoids death, for ever and ever avoids suffering." The following day, he again wandered through the city, in quest of alms; then, with a few disciples, he set out on the road to Kusinagara, where he had decided to enter nirvana.

17. The Meal at Cunda's

THE Master and his disciples stopped at Pava, in the garden of Cunda, the blacksmith. Cunda came and paid homage to the Master, and said to him:

"My Lord, do me the honor of taking your meal at my home, to-morrow."

The Master accepted. The next day, Cunda had pork and other delicacies prepared for his guests. They arrived and took their seats. When the Master saw the pork, he pointed to it and said:

"No one but me could eat that, Cunda; you must keep it for me. My disciples will partake of the other delicacies."

When he had eaten, he said:

"Bury deep in the ground what I have left untouched; the Buddha alone can eat of such meat."

Then he left. The disciples followed.

They had gone only a short distance from Pava when the Master began to feel weary and sick. Ananda grieved, and he cursed Cunda, the blacksmith, for having offered the Master this fatal meal.

"Ananda," said the Master, "do not be angry with Cunda, the blacksmith. Great rewards are reserved to him for the food he gave me. Of all the meals I have ever had, two are most deserving of praise: the one that Sujata, and the other that Cunda, the blacksmith, served to me."

He overcame his weariness and presently he reached the banks of the Kakutstha. The river was peaceful and pure. The Master bathed in the limpid waters. After the bath, he drank, then went to a mango grove. There, he said to the monk Cundaka:

"Fold my cloak in four, that I may lie down and rest."

Cundaka cheerfully obeyed. He quickly folded the cloak

in four and spread it on the ground. The Master lay down, and Cundaka sat beside him.

The Master rested a few hours. Then he set out again, and he finally arrived at Kusinagara. There, on the banks of the Hiranyavati, stood a pleasant, peaceful little wood.

The Master said:

"Go, Ananda, and prepare a couch for me between two twin trees. Have the head to the north. I am ill, Ananda."

Ananda prepared the couch, and the Master went and reclined on it.

18. The Buddha Enters Nirvana

IT was not the season for trees to bloom, yet the two trees that sheltered the Master were covered with blossoms. The flowers fell gently upon his couch, and from the sky, sweet melodies slowly drifted down.

The Master said to pious Ananda:

"See: it is not the season for flowers, yet these trees have bloomed, and the blossoms are raining down upon me. Listen: the air is joyous with the songs that the happy Gods are singing in the sky in honor of the Buddha. But the Buddha is paid a more enduring honor than this. Monks, nuns, believers, all those who see the truth, all those who live within the law, they are the ones that do the Buddha supreme honor. Therefore you must live according to the law, Ananda, and, even in the most trivial matters, you must follow the sacred path of truth."

Ananda was weeping. He walked away, to hide his tears.

He thought, "For many misdeeds I have not yet been forgiven, and I shall be guilty of many more misdeeds. Oh, I am still far from the saintly goal, and he who took pity on me, the Master, is about to enter nirvana."

The Master called him back and said:

"Do not grieve, Ananda, do not despair. Remember my words: from all that delights us, from all that we love, we must one day be separated. How can that which is born be other than inconstant and perishable? How can that which is born, how can that which is created, endure for ever? Long have you honored me, Ananda; you have been a devoted friend. Yours was a happy friendship, and you were faithful to it in thought, in word and in deed. You have done great good, Ananda; continue in the right path, and you will be forgiven your former misdeeds."

Night came on. The inhabitants of Kusinagara had heard

that the Master was reclining under two twin trees, and they came in great crowds to pay him homage. An aged hermit, Subhadra, appeared, and bowing before the Master, professed his belief in the Buddha, in the law and in the community; and Subhadra was the last of the faithful to have the joy of seeing the Master face to face.

The night was beautiful. Ananda was seated beside the Master. The Master said:

"Perhaps, Ananda, you will think, 'We no longer have a Master.' But you must not think that. The law remains, the law that I taught you; let it be your guide, Ananda, when I shall no longer be with you."

He said again:

"Verily, O monks, all that is created must perish. Never cease to struggle."

He was no longer of this world. His face was of luminous gold. His spirit ascended to the realms of ecstasy. He entered nirvana. The earth shook, and thunder rolled across the sky.

Near the ramparts, at dawn, they of Kusinagara built a great funeral pile, as though for a king of the world, and there they burned the body of the Blessed One.

THE DHAMMAPADA

Translated by F. Max Müller

Chapter I

The Twin-Verses

1. All that we are is the result of what we have thought: it is founded on our thoughts, it is made up of our thoughts. If a man speaks or acts with an evil thought, pain follows him, as the wheel follows the foot of the ox that draws the carriage.
2. All that we are is the result of what we have thought: it is founded on our thoughts, it is made up of our thoughts. If a man speaks or acts with a pure thought, happiness follows him, like a shadow that never leaves him.
3. "{He abused me, he beat me, he defeated me, he robbed me,"{ — in those who harbour such thoughts hatred will never cease.
4. "{He abused me, he beat me, he defeated me, he robbed me,"{ — in those who do not harbour such thoughts hatred will cease.
5. For hatred does not cease by hatred at any time: hatred ceases by love, this is an old rule.
6. The world does not know that we must all come to an end here; — but those who know it, their quarrels cease at once.
7. He who lives looking for pleasures only, his senses uncontrolled, immoderate in his food, idle, and weak, Mara (the tempter) will certainly overthrow him, as the wind throws down a weak tree.
8. He who lives without looking for pleasures, his senses well controlled, moderate in his food, faithful and strong, him Mara will certainly not overthrow, any more than the wind throws down a rocky mountain.

9. He who wishes to put on the yellow dress without having cleansed himself from sin, who disregards temperance and truth, is unworthy of the yellow dress.

10. But he who has cleansed himself from sin, is well grounded in all virtues, and regards also temperance and truth, he is indeed worthy of the yellow dress.

11. They who imagine truth in untruth, and see untruth in truth, never arrive at truth, but follow vain desires.

12. They who know truth in truth, and untruth in untruth, arrive at truth, and follow true desires.

13. As rain breaks through an ill-thatched house, passion will break through an unreflecting mind.

14. As rain does not break through a well-thatched house, passion will not break through a well-reflecting mind.

15. The evil-doer mourns in this world, and he mourns in the next; he mourns in both. He mourns and suffers when he sees the evil of his own work.

16. The virtuous man delights in this world, and he delights in the next; he delights in both. He delights and rejoices, when he sees the purity of his own work.

17. The evil-doer suffers in this world, and he suffers in the next; he suffers in both. He suffers when he thinks of the evil he has done; he suffers more when going on the evil path.

18. The virtuous man is happy in this world, and he is happy in the next; he is happy in both. He is happy when he thinks of the good he has done; he is still more happy when going on the good path.

19. The thoughtless man, even if he can recite a large portion (of the law), but is not a doer of it, has no share in the priesthood, but is like a cowherd counting the cows of others.

20. The follower of the law, even if he can recite only a small portion (of the law), but, having forsaken passion and hatred and foolishness, possesses true knowledge and serenity of mind, he, caring for nothing in this world or that to come, has indeed a share in the priesthood.

Chapter II

On Earnestness

21. Earnestness is the path of immortality (Nirvana), thoughtlessness the path of death. Those who are in earnest do not die, those who are thoughtless are as if dead already.
22. Those who are advanced in earnestness, having understood this clearly, delight in earnestness, and rejoice in the knowledge of the Ariyas (the elect).
23. These wise people, meditative, steady, always possessed of strong powers, attain to Nirvana, the highest happiness.
24. If an earnest person has roused himself, if he is not forgetful, if his deeds are pure, if he acts with consideration, if he restrains himself, and lives according to law, — then his glory will increase.
25. By rousing himself, by earnestness, by restraint and control, the wise man may make for himself an island which no flood can overwhelm.
26. Fools follow after vanity, men of evil wisdom. The wise man keeps earnestness as his best jewel.
27. Follow not after vanity, nor after the enjoyment of love and lust! He who is earnest and meditative, obtains ample joy.
28. When the learned man drives away vanity by earnestness, he, the wise, climbing the terraced heights of wisdom, looks down upon the fools, serene he looks upon the toiling crowd, as one that stands on a mountain looks down upon them that stand upon the plain.
29. Earnest among the thoughtless, awake among the sleepers, the wise man advances like a racer, leaving behind the hack.

30. By earnestness did Maghavan (Indra) rise to the lordship of the gods. People praise earnestness; thoughtlessness is always blamed.

31. A Bhikshu (mendicant) who delights in earnestness, who looks with fear on thoughtlessness, moves about like fire, burning all his fetters, small or large.

32. A Bhikshu (mendicant) who delights in reflection, who looks with fear on thoughtlessness, cannot fall away (from his perfect state) — he is close upon Nirvana.

Chapter III

Thought

33. As a fletcher makes straight his arrow, a wise man makes straight his trembling and unsteady thought, which is difficult to guard, difficult to hold back.

34. As a fish taken from his watery home and thrown on dry ground, our thought trembles all over in order to escape the dominion of Mara (the tempter).

35. It is good to tame the mind, which is difficult to hold in and flighty, rushing wherever it listeth; a tamed mind brings happiness.

36. Let the wise man guard his thoughts, for they are difficult to perceive, very artful, and they rush wherever they list: thoughts well guarded bring happiness.

37. Those who bridle their mind which travels far, moves about alone, is without a body, and hides in the chamber (of the heart), will be free from the bonds of Mara (the tempter).

38. If a man's thoughts are unsteady, if he does not know the true law, if his peace of mind is troubled, his knowledge will never be perfect.

39. If a man's thoughts are not dissipated, if his mind is not perplexed, if he has ceased to think of good or evil, then there is no fear for him while he is watchful.

40. Knowing that this body is (fragile) like a jar, and making this thought firm like a fortress, one should attack Mara (the tempter) with the weapon of knowledge, one should watch him when conquered, and should never rest.

41. Before long, alas! this body will lie on the earth, despised, without understanding, like a useless log.

42. Whatever a hater may do to a hater, or an enemy to an enemy, a wrongly-directed mind will do us greater mischief.

43. Not a mother, not a father will do so much, nor any other relative; a well-directed mind will do us greater service.

Chapter IV

Flowers

44. Who shall overcome this earth, and the world of Yama (the lord of the departed), and the world of the gods? Who shall find out the plainly shown path of virtue, as a clever man finds out the (right) flower?

45. The disciple will overcome the earth, and the world of Yama, and the world of the gods. The disciple will find out the plainly shown path of virtue, as a clever man finds out the (right) flower.

46. He who knows that this body is like froth, and has learnt that it is as unsubstantial as a mirage, will break the flower-pointed arrow of Mara, and never see the king of death.

47. Death carries off a man who is gathering flowers and whose mind is distracted, as a flood carries off a sleeping village.

48. Death subdues a man who is gathering flowers, and whose mind is distracted, before he is satiated in his pleasures.

49. As the bee collects nectar and departs without injuring the flower, or its colour or scent, so let a sage dwell in his village.

50. Not the perversities of others, not their sins of commission or omission, but his own misdeeds and negligences should a sage take notice of.

51. Like a beautiful flower, full of colour, but without scent, are the fine but fruitless words of him who does not act accordingly.

52. But, like a beautiful flower, full of colour and full of scent, are the fine and fruitful words of him who acts accordingly.

53. As many kinds of wreaths can be made from a heap of flowers, so many good things may be achieved by a mortal when once he is born.

54. The scent of flowers does not travel against the wind, nor (that of) sandal-wood, or of Tagara and Mallika flowers; but the odour of good people travels even against the wind; a good man pervades every place.

55. Sandal-wood or Tagara, a lotus-flower, or a Vassiki, among these sorts of perfumes, the perfume of virtue is unsurpassed.

56. Mean is the scent that comes from Tagara and sandal-wood; — the perfume of those who possess virtue rises up to the gods as the highest.

57. Of the people who possess these virtues, who live without thoughtlessness, and who are emancipated through true knowledge, Mara, the tempter, never finds the way.

58, 59. As on a heap of rubbish cast upon the highway the lily will grow full of sweet perfume and delight, thus the disciple of the truly enlightened Buddha shines forth by his knowledge among those who are like rubbish, among the people that walk in darkness.

Chapter V

The Fool

60. Long is the night to him who is awake; long is a mile to him who is tired; long is life to the foolish who do not know the true law.
61. If a traveler does not meet with one who is his better, or his equal, let him firmly keep to his solitary journey; there is no companionship with a fool.
62. "{These sons belong to me, and this wealth belongs to me,"{ with such thoughts a fool is tormented. He himself does not belong to himself; how much less sons and wealth?
63. The fool who knows his foolishness, is wise at least so far. But a fool who thinks himself wise, he is called a fool indeed.
64. If a fool be associated with a wise man even all his life, he will perceive the truth as little as a spoon perceives the taste of soup.
65. If an intelligent man be associated for one minute only with a wise man, he will soon perceive the truth, as the tongue perceives the taste of soup.
66. Fools of little understanding have themselves for their greatest enemies, for they do evil deeds which must bear bitter fruits.
67. That deed is not well done of which a man must repent, and the reward of which he receives crying and with a tearful face.
68. No, that deed is well done of which a man does not repent, and the reward of which he receives gladly and cheerfully.
69. As long as the evil deed done does not bear fruit, the fool thinks it is like honey; but when it ripens, then the fool suffers grief.

70. Let a fool month after month eat his food (like an ascetic) with the tip of a blade of Kusa grass, yet he is not worth the sixteenth particle of those who have well weighed the law.

71. An evil deed, like newly-drawn milk, does not turn (suddenly); smouldering, like fire covered by ashes, it follows the fool.

72. And when the evil deed, after it has become known, brings sorrow to the fool, then it destroys his bright lot, nay, it cleaves his head.

73. Let the fool wish for a false reputation, for precedence among the Bhikshus, for lordship in the convents, for worship among other people!

74. "{May both the layman and he who has left the world think that this is done by me; may they be subject to me in everything which is to be done or is not to be done,"{ thus is the mind of the fool, and his desire and pride increase.

75. "{One is the road that leads to wealth, another the road that leads to Nirvana;"{ if the Bhikshu, the disciple of Buddha, has learnt this, he will not yearn for honour, he will strive after separation from the world.

Chapter VI

The Wise Man (Pandita)

76. If you see an intelligent man who tells you where true treasures are to be found, who shows what is to be avoided, and administers reproofs, follow that wise man; it will be better, not worse, for those who follow him.
77. Let him admonish, let him teach, let him forbid what is improper!- -he will be beloved of the good, by the bad he will be hated.
78. Do not have evil-doers for friends, do not have low people for friends: have virtuous people for friends, have for friends the best of men.
79. He who drinks in the law lives happily with a serene mind: the sage rejoices always in the law, as preached by the elect (Ariyas).
80. Well-makers lead the water (wherever they like); fletchers bend the arrow; carpenters bend a log of wood; wise people fashion themselves.
81. As a solid rock is not shaken by the wind, wise people falter not amidst blame and praise.
82. Wise people, after they have listened to the laws, become serene, like a deep, smooth, and still lake.
83. Good people walk on whatever befall, the good do not prattle, longing for pleasure; whether touched by happiness or sorrow wise people never appear elated or depressed.
84. If, whether for his own sake, or for the sake of others, a man wishes neither for a son, nor for wealth, nor for lordship, and if he does not wish for his own success by unfair means, then he is good, wise, and virtuous.

85. Few are there among men who arrive at the other shore (become Arhats); the other people here run up and down the shore.

86. But those who, when the law has been well preached to them, follow the law, will pass across the dominion of death, however difficult to overcome.

87, 88. A wise man should leave the dark state (of ordinary life), and follow the bright state (of the Bhikshu). After going from his home to a homeless state, he should in his retirement look for enjoyment where there seemed to be no enjoyment. Leaving all pleasures behind, and calling nothing his own, the wise man should purge himself from all the troubles of the mind.

89. Those whose mind is well grounded in the (seven) elements of knowledge, who without clinging to anything, rejoice in freedom from attachment, whose appetites have been conquered, and who are full of light, are free (even) in this world.

Chapter VII

The Venerable (Arhat)

90. There is no suffering for him who has finished his journey, and abandoned grief, who has freed himself on all sides, and thrown off all fetters.
91. They depart with their thoughts well-collected, they are not happy in their abode; like swans who have left their lake, they leave their house and home.
92. Men who have no riches, who live on recognized food, who have perceived void and unconditioned freedom (Nirvana), their path is difficult to understand, like that of birds in the air.
93. He whose appetites are stilled, who is not absorbed in enjoyment, who has perceived void and unconditioned freedom (Nirvana), his path is difficult to understand, like that of birds in the air.
94. The gods even envy him whose senses, like horses well broken in by the driver, have been subdued, who is free from pride, and free from appetites.
95. Such a one who does his duty is tolerant like the earth, like Indra's bolt; he is like a lake without mud; no new births are in store for him.
96. His thought is quiet, quiet are his word and deed, when he has obtained freedom by true knowledge, when he has thus become a quiet man.
97. The man who is free from credulity, but knows the uncreated, who has cut all ties, removed all temptations, renounced all desires, he is the greatest of men.

98. In a hamlet or in a forest, in the deep water or on the dry land, wherever venerable persons (Arhanta) dwell, that place is delightful.

99. Forests are delightful; where the world finds no delight, there the passionless will find delight, for they look not for pleasures.

Chapter VIII

The Thousands

100. Even though a speech be a thousand (of words), but made up of senseless words, one word of sense is better, which if a man hears, he becomes quiet.

101. Even though a Gatha (poem) be a thousand (of words), but made up of senseless words, one word of a Gatha is better, which if a man hears, he becomes quiet.

102. Though a man recite a hundred Gathas made up of senseless words, one word of the law is better, which if a man hears, he becomes quiet.

103. If one man conquer in battle a thousand times thousand men, and if another conquer himself, he is the greatest of conquerors.

104, 105. One's own self conquered is better than all other people; not even a god, a Gandharva, not Mara with Brahman could change into defeat the victory of a man who has vanquished himself, and always lives under restraint.

106. If a man for a hundred years sacrifice month after month with a thousand, and if he but for one moment pay homage to a man whose soul is grounded (in true knowledge), better is that homage than sacrifice for a hundred years.

107. If a man for a hundred years worship Agni (fire) in the forest, and if he but for one moment pay homage to a man whose soul is grounded (in true knowledge), better is that homage than sacrifice for a hundred years.

108. Whatever a man sacrifice in this world as an offering or as an oblation for a whole year in order to gain merit, the whole of it

is not worth a quarter (a farthing); reverence shown to the righteous is better.

109. He who always greets and constantly reveres the aged, four things will increase to him, viz. life, beauty, happiness, power.

110. But he who lives a hundred years, vicious and unrestrained, a life of one day is better if a man is virtuous and reflecting.

111. And he who lives a hundred years, ignorant and unrestrained, a life of one day is better if a man is wise and reflecting.

112. And he who lives a hundred years, idle and weak, a life of one day is better if a man has attained firm strength.

113. And he who lives a hundred years, not seeing beginning and end, a life of one day is better if a man sees beginning and end.

114. And he who lives a hundred years, not seeing the immortal place, a life of one day is better if a man sees the immortal place.

115. And he who lives a hundred years, not seeing the highest law, a life of one day is better if a man sees the highest law.

Chapter IX

Evil

116. If a man would hasten towards the good, he should keep his thought away from evil; if a man does what is good slothfully, his mind delights in evil.

117. If a man commits a sin, let him not do it again; let him not delight in sin: pain is the outcome of evil.

118. If a man does what is good, let him do it again; let him delight in it: happiness is the outcome of good.

119. Even an evil-doer sees happiness as long as his evil deed has not ripened; but when his evil deed has ripened, then does the evil-doer see evil.

120. Even a good man sees evil days, as long as his good deed has not ripened; but when his good deed has ripened, then does the good man see happy days.

121. Let no man think lightly of evil, saying in his heart, It will not come nigh unto me. Even by the falling of water-drops a water-pot is filled; the fool becomes full of evil, even if he gather it little by little.

122. Let no man think lightly of good, saying in his heart, It will not come nigh unto me. Even by the falling of water-drops a water-pot is filled; the wise man becomes full of good, even if he gather it little by little.

123. Let a man avoid evil deeds, as a merchant, if he has few companions and carries much wealth, avoids a dangerous road; as a man who loves life avoids poison.

124. He who has no wound on his hand, may touch poison with his hand; poison does not affect one who has no wound; nor is there evil for one who does not commit evil.

125. If a man offend a harmless, pure, and innocent person, the evil falls back upon that fool, like light dust thrown up against the wind.

126. Some people are born again; evil-doers go to hell; righteous people go to heaven; those who are free from all worldly desires attain Nirvana.

127. Not in the sky, not in the midst of the sea, not if we enter into the clefts of the mountains, is there known a spot in the whole world where death could not overcome (the mortal).

Chapter X

Punishment

129. All men tremble at punishment, all men fear death; remember that you are like unto them, and do not kill, nor cause slaughter.
130. All men tremble at punishment, all men love life; remember that thou art like unto them, and do not kill, nor cause slaughter.
131. He who seeking his own happiness punishes or kills beings who also long for happiness, will not find happiness after death.
132. He who seeking his own happiness does not punish or kill beings who also long for happiness, will find happiness after death.
133. Do not speak harshly to anybody; those who are spoken to will answer thee in the same way. Angry speech is painful, blows for blows will touch thee.
134. If, like a shattered metal plate (gong), thou utter not, then thou hast reached Nirvana; contention is not known to thee.
135. As a cowherd with his staff drives his cows into the stable, so do Age and Death drive the life of men.
136. A fool does not know when he commits his evil deeds: but the wicked man burns by his own deeds, as if burnt by fire.
137. He who inflicts pain on innocent and harmless persons, will soon come to one of these ten states:
138. He will have cruel suffering, loss, injury of the body, heavy affliction, or loss of mind,
139. Or a misfortune coming from the king, or a fearful accusation, or loss of relations, or destruction of treasures,
140. Or lightning-fire will burn his houses; and when his body is destroyed, the fool will go to hell.

141. Not nakedness, not platted hair, not dirt, not fasting, or lying on the earth, not rubbing with dust, not sitting motionless, can purify a mortal who has not overcome desires.

142. He who, though dressed in fine apparel, exercises tranquility, is quiet, subdued, restrained, chaste, and has ceased to find fault with all other beings, he indeed is a Brahmana, an ascetic (sramana), a friar (bhikshu).

143. Is there in this world any man so restrained by humility that he does not mind reproof, as a well-trained horse the whip?

144. Like a well-trained horse when touched by the whip, be ye active and lively, and by faith, by virtue, by energy, by meditation, by discernment of the law you will overcome this great pain (of reproof), perfect in knowledge and in behaviour, and never forgetful.

145. Well-makers lead the water (wherever they like); fletchers bend the arrow; carpenters bend a log of wood; good people fashion themselves.

Chapter XI

Old Age

146. How is there laughter, how is there joy, as this world is always burning? Why do you not seek a light, ye who are surrounded by darkness?
147. Look at this dressed-up lump, covered with wounds, joined together, sickly, full of many thoughts, which has no strength, no hold!
148. This body is wasted, full of sickness, and frail; this heap of corruption breaks to pieces, life indeed ends in death.
149. Those white bones, like gourds thrown away in the autumn, what pleasure is there in looking at them?
150. After a stronghold has been made of the bones, it is covered with flesh and blood, and there dwell in it old age and death, pride and deceit.
151. The brilliant chariots of kings are destroyed, the body also approaches destruction, but the virtue of good people never approaches destruction, — thus do the good say to the good.
152. A man who has learnt little, grows old like an ox; his flesh grows, but his knowledge does not grow.
153, 154. Looking for the maker of this tabernacle, I shall have to run through a course of many births, so long as I do not find (him); and painful is birth again and again. But now, maker of the tabernacle, thou hast been seen; thou shalt not make up this tabernacle again. All thy rafters are broken, thy ridge-pole is sundered; the mind, approaching the Eternal (visankhara, nirvana), has attained to the extinction of all desires.

155. Men who have not observed proper discipline, and have not gained treasure in their youth, perish like old herons in a lake without fish.

156. Men who have not observed proper discipline, and have not gained treasure in their youth, lie, like broken bows, sighing after the past.

Chapter XII

Self

157. If a man hold himself dear, let him watch himself carefully; during one at least out of the three watches a wise man should be watchful.

158. Let each man direct himself first to what is proper, then let him teach others; thus a wise man will not suffer.

159. If a man make himself as he teaches others to be, then, being himself well subdued, he may subdue (others); one's own self is indeed difficult to subdue.

160. Self is the lord of self, who else could be the lord? With self well subdued, a man finds a lord such as few can find.

161. The evil done by oneself, self-begotten, self-bred, crushes the foolish, as a diamond breaks a precious stone.

162. He whose wickedness is very great brings himself down to that state where his enemy wishes him to be, as a creeper does with the tree which it surrounds.

163. Bad deeds, and deeds hurtful to ourselves, are easy to do; what is beneficial and good, that is very difficult to do.

164. The foolish man who scorns the rule of the venerable (Arahat), of the elect (Ariya), of the virtuous, and follows false doctrine, he bears fruit to his own destruction, like the fruits of the Katthaka reed.

165. By oneself the evil is done, by oneself one suffers; by oneself evil is left undone, by oneself one is purified. Purity and impurity belong to oneself, no one can purify another.

166. Let no one forget his own duty for the sake of another's, however great; let a man, after he has discerned his own duty, be always attentive to his duty.

Chapter XIII

The World

167. Do not follow the evil law! Do not live on in thoughtlessness! Do not follow false doctrine! Be not a friend of the world.
168. Rouse thyself! do not be idle! Follow the law of virtue! The virtuous rests in bliss in this world and in the next.
169. Follow the law of virtue; do not follow that of sin. The virtuous rests in bliss in this world and in the next.
170. Look upon the world as a bubble, look upon it as a mirage: the king of death does not see him who thus looks down upon the world.
171. Come, look at this glittering world, like unto a royal chariot; the foolish are immersed in it, but the wise do not touch it.
172. He who formerly was reckless and afterwards became sober, brightens up this world, like the moon when freed from clouds.
173. He whose evil deeds are covered by good deeds, brightens up this world, like the moon when freed from clouds.
174. This world is dark, few only can see here; a few only go to heaven, like birds escaped from the net.
175. The swans go on the path of the sun, they go through the ether by means of their miraculous power; the wise are led out of this world, when they have conquered Mara and his train.
176. If a man has transgressed one law, and speaks lies, and scoffs at another world, there is no evil he will not do.
177. The uncharitable do not go to the world of the gods; fools only do not praise liberality; a wise man rejoices in liberality, and through it becomes blessed in the other world.

178. Better than sovereignty over the earth, better than going to heaven, better than lordship over all worlds, is the reward of the first step in holiness.

Chapter XIV

The Buddha (The Awakened)

179. He whose conquest is not conquered again, into whose conquest no one in this world enters, by what track can you lead him, the Awakened, the Omniscient, the trackless?
180. He whom no desire with its snares and poisons can lead astray, by what track can you lead him, the Awakened, the Omniscient, the trackless?
181. Even the gods envy those who are awakened and not forgetful, who are given to meditation, who are wise, and who delight in the repose of retirement (from the world).
182. Difficult (to obtain) is the conception of men, difficult is the life of mortals, difficult is the hearing of the True Law, difficult is the birth of the Awakened (the attainment of Buddhahood).
183. Not to commit any sin, to do good, and to purify one's mind, that is the teaching of (all) the Awakened.
184. The Awakened call patience the highest penance, long-suffering the highest Nirvana; for he is not an anchorite (pravragita) who strikes others, he is not an ascetic (sramana) who insults others.
185. Not to blame, not to strike, to live restrained under the law, to be moderate in eating, to sleep and sit alone, and to dwell on the highest thoughts, — this is the teaching of the Awakened.
186. There is no satisfying lusts, even by a shower of gold pieces; he who knows that lusts have a short taste and cause pain, he is wise;

187. Even in heavenly pleasures he finds no satisfaction, the disciple who is fully awakened delights only in the destruction of all desires.

188. Men, driven by fear, go to many a refuge, to mountains and forests, to groves and sacred trees.

189. But that is not a safe refuge, that is not the best refuge; a man is not delivered from all pains after having gone to that refuge.

190. He who takes refuge with Buddha, the Law, and the Church; he who, with clear understanding, sees the four holy truths: —

191. Viz. pain, the origin of pain, the destruction of pain, and the eightfold holy way that leads to the quieting of pain; —

192. That is the safe refuge, that is the best refuge; having gone to that refuge, a man is delivered from all pain.

193. A supernatural person (a Buddha) is not easily found, he is not born everywhere. Wherever such a sage is born, that race prospers.

194. Happy is the arising of the awakened, happy is the teaching of the True Law, happy is peace in the church, happy is the devotion of those who are at peace.

195, 196. He who pays homage to those who deserve homage, whether the awakened (Buddha) or their disciples, those who have overcome the host (of evils), and crossed the flood of sorrow, he who pays homage to such as have found deliverance and know no fear, his merit can never be measured by anybody.

Chapter XV

Happiness

197. Let us live happily then, not hating those who hate us! among men who hate us let us dwell free from hatred!

198. Let us live happily then, free from ailments among the ailing! among men who are ailing let us dwell free from ailments!

199. Let us live happily then, free from greed among the greedy! among men who are greedy let us dwell free from greed!

200. Let us live happily then, though we call nothing our own! We shall be like the bright gods, feeding on happiness!

201. Victory breeds hatred, for the conquered is unhappy. He who has given up both victory and defeat, he, the contented, is happy.

202. There is no fire like passion; there is no losing throw like hatred; there is no pain like this body; there is no happiness higher than rest.

203. Hunger is the worst of diseases, the body the greatest of pains; if one knows this truly, that is Nirvana, the highest happiness.

204. Health is the greatest of gifts, contentedness the best riches; trust is the best of relationships, Nirvana the highest happiness.

205. He who has tasted the sweetness of solitude and tranquility, is free from fear and free from sin, while he tastes the sweetness of drinking in the law.

206. The sight of the elect (Arya) is good, to live with them is always happiness; if a man does not see fools, he will be truly happy.

207. He who walks in the company of fools suffers a long way; company with fools, as with an enemy, is always painful; company with the wise is pleasure, like meeting with kinsfolk.

208. Therefore, one ought to follow the wise, the intelligent, the learned, the much enduring, the dutiful, the elect; one ought to follow a good and wise man, as the moon follows the path of the stars.

Chapter XVI

Pleasure

209. He who gives himself to vanity, and does not give himself to meditation, forgetting the real aim (of life) and grasping at pleasure, will in time envy him who has exerted himself in meditation.

210. Let no man ever look for what is pleasant, or what is unpleasant. Not to see what is pleasant is pain, and it is pain to see what is unpleasant.

211. Let, therefore, no man love anything; loss of the beloved is evil. Those who love nothing and hate nothing, have no fetters.

212. From pleasure comes grief, from pleasure comes fear; he who is free from pleasure knows neither grief nor fear.

213. From affection comes grief, from affection comes fear; he who is free from affection knows neither grief nor fear.

214. From lust comes grief, from lust comes fear; he who is free from lust knows neither grief nor fear.

215. From love comes grief, from love comes fear; he who is free from love knows neither grief nor fear.

216. From greed comes grief, from greed comes fear; he who is free from greed knows neither grief nor fear.

217. He who possesses virtue and intelligence, who is just, speaks the truth, and does what is his own business, him the world will hold dear.

218. He in whom a desire for the Ineffable (Nirvana) has sprung up, who is satisfied in his mind, and whose thoughts are not bewildered by love, he is called urdhvamsrotas (carried upwards by the stream).

219. Kinsmen, friends, and lovers salute a man who has been long away, and returns safe from afar.

220. In like manner his good works receive him who has done good, and has gone from this world to the other; — as kinsmen receive a friend on his return.

Chapter XVII

Anger

221. Let a man leave anger, let him forsake pride, let him overcome all bondage! No sufferings befall the man who is not attached to name and form, and who calls nothing his own.

222. He who holds back rising anger like a rolling chariot, him I call a real driver; other people are but holding the reins.

223. Let a man overcome anger by love, let him overcome evil by good; let him overcome the greedy by liberality, the liar by truth!

224. Speak the truth, do not yield to anger; give, if thou art asked for little; by these three steps thou wilt go near the gods.

225. The sages who injure nobody, and who always control their body, they will go to the unchangeable place (Nirvana), where, if they have gone, they will suffer no more.

226. Those who are ever watchful, who study day and night, and who strive after Nirvana, their passions will come to an end.

227. This is an old saying, O Atula, this is not only of to-day: 'They blame him who sits silent, they blame him who speaks much, they also blame him who says little; there is no one on earth who is not blamed.'

228. There never was, there never will be, nor is there now, a man who is always blamed, or a man who is always praised.

229, 230. But he whom those who discriminate praise continually day after day, as without blemish, wise, rich in knowledge and virtue, who would dare to blame him, like a coin made of gold from the Gambu river? Even the gods praise him, he is praised even by Brahman.

231. Beware of bodily anger, and control thy body! Leave the sins of the body, and with thy body practice virtue!

232. Beware of the anger of the tongue, and control thy tongue! Leave the sins of the tongue, and practice virtue with thy tongue!
233. Beware of the anger of the mind, and control thy mind! Leave the sins of the mind, and practice virtue with thy mind!
234. The wise who control their body, who control their tongue, the wise who control their mind, are indeed well controlled.

Chapter XVIII

Impurity

235. Thou art now like a sear leaf, the messengers of death (Yama) have come near to thee; thou standest at the door of thy departure, and thou hast no provision for thy journey.

236. Make thyself an island, work hard, be wise! When thy impurities are blown away, and thou art free from guilt, thou wilt enter into the heavenly world of the elect (Ariya).

237. Thy life has come to an end, thou art come near to death (Yama), there is no resting-place for thee on the road, and thou hast no provision for thy journey.

238. Make thyself an island, work hard, be wise! When thy impurities are blown away, and thou art free from guilt, thou wilt not enter again into birth and decay.

239. Let a wise man blow off the impurities of his self, as a smith blows off the impurities of silver one by one, little by little, and from time to time.

240. As the impurity which springs from the iron, when it springs from it, destroys it; thus do a transgressor's own works lead him to the evil path.

241. The taint of prayers is non-repetition; the taint of houses, non- repair; the taint of the body is sloth; the taint of a watchman, thoughtlessness.

242. Bad conduct is the taint of woman, greediness the taint of a benefactor; tainted are all evil ways in this world and in the next.

243. But there is a taint worse than all taints, — ignorance is the greatest taint. O mendicants! throw off that taint, and become taintless!

244. Life is easy to live for a man who is without shame, a crow hero, a mischief-maker, an insulting, bold, and wretched fellow.

245. But life is hard to live for a modest man, who always looks for what is pure, who is disinterested, quiet, spotless, and intelligent.

246. He who destroys life, who speaks untruth, who in this world takes what is not given him, who goes to another man's wife;

247. And the man who gives himself to drinking intoxicating liquors, he, even in this world, digs up his own root.

248. O man, know this, that the unrestrained are in a bad state; take care that greediness and vice do not bring thee to grief for a long time!

249. The world gives according to their faith or according to their pleasure: if a man frets about the food and the drink given to others, he will find no rest either by day or by night.

250. He in whom that feeling is destroyed, and taken out with the very root, finds rest by day and by night.

251. There is no fire like passion, there is no shark like hatred, there is no snare like folly, there is no torrent like greed.

252. The fault of others is easily perceived, but that of oneself is difficult to perceive; a man winnows his neighbour's faults like chaff, but his own fault he hides, as a cheat hides the bad die from the gambler.

253. If a man looks after the faults of others, and is always inclined to be offended, his own passions will grow, and he is far from the destruction of passions.

254. There is no path through the air, a man is not a Samana by outward acts. The world delights in vanity, the Tathagatas (the Buddhas) are free from vanity.

255. There is no path through the air, a man is not a Samana by outward acts. No creatures are eternal; but the awakened (Buddha) are never shaken.

Chapter XIX

The Just

256, 257. A man is not just if he carries a matter by violence; no, he who distinguishes both right and wrong, who is learned and leads others, not by violence, but by law and equity, and who is guarded by the law and intelligent, he is called just.

258. A man is not learned because he talks much; he who is patient, free from hatred and fear, he is called learned.

259. A man is not a supporter of the law because he talks much; even if a man has learnt little, but sees the law bodily, he is a supporter of the law, a man who never neglects the law.

260. A man is not an elder because his head is grey; his age may be ripe, but he is called 'Old-in-vain.'

261. He in whom there is truth, virtue, love, restraint, moderation, he who is free from impurity and is wise, he is called an elder.

262. An envious greedy, dishonest man does not become respectable by means of much talking only, or by the beauty of his complexion.

263. He in whom all this is destroyed, and taken out with the very root, he, when freed from hatred and wise, is called respectable.

264. Not by tonsure does an undisciplined man who speaks falsehood become a Samana; can a man be a Samana who is still held captive by desire and greediness?

265. He who always quiets the evil, whether small or large, he is called a Samana (a quiet man), because he has quieted all evil.

266. A man is not a mendicant (Bhikshu) simply because he asks others for alms; he who adopts the whole law is a Bhikshu, not he who only begs.

267. He who is above good and evil, who is chaste, who with knowledge passes through the world, he indeed is called a Bhikshu.

268, 269. A man is not a Muni because he observes silence (mona, i.e. mauna), if he is foolish and ignorant; but the wise who, taking the balance, chooses the good and avoids evil, he is a Muni, and is a Muni thereby; he who in this world weighs both sides is called a Muni.

270. A man is not an elect (Ariya) because he injures living creatures; because he has pity on all living creatures, therefore is a man called Ariya.

271, 272. Not only by discipline and vows, not only by much learning, not by entering into a trance, not by sleeping alone, do I earn the happiness of release which no worldling can know. Bhikshu, be not confident as long as thou hast not attained the extinction of desires.

Chapter XX

The Way

273. The best of ways is the eightfold; the best of truths the four words; the best of virtues passionlessness; the best of men he who has eyes to see.
274. This is the way, there is no other that leads to the purifying of intelligence. Go on this way! Everything else is the deceit of Mara (the tempter).
275. If you go on this way, you will make an end of pain! The way was preached by me, when I had understood the removal of the thorns (in the flesh).
276. You yourself must make an effort. The Tathagatas (Buddhas) are only preachers. The thoughtful who enter the way are freed from the bondage of Mara.
277. 'All created things perish,' he who knows and sees this becomes passive in pain; this is the way to purity.
278. 'All created things are grief and pain,' he who knows and sees this becomes passive in pain; this is the way that leads to purity.
279. 'All forms are unreal,' he who knows and sees this becomes passive in pain; this is the way that leads to purity.
280. He who does not rouse himself when it is time to rise, who, though young and strong, is full of sloth, whose will and thought are weak, that lazy and idle man will never find the way to knowledge.
281. Watching his speech, well restrained in mind, let a man never commit any wrong with his body! Let a man but keep these three roads of action clear, and he will achieve the way which is taught by the wise.

282. Through zeal knowledge is gotten, through lack of zeal knowledge is lost; let a man who knows this double path of gain and loss thus place himself that knowledge may grow.

283. Cut down the whole forest (of lust), not a tree only! Danger comes out of the forest (of lust). When you have cut down both the forest (of lust) and its undergrowth, then, Bhikshus, you will be rid of the forest and free!

284. So long as the love of man towards women, even the smallest, is not destroyed, so long is his mind in bondage, as the calf that drinks milk is to its mother.

285. Cut out the love of self, like an autumn lotus, with thy hand! Cherish the road of peace. Nirvana has been shown by Sugata (Buddha).

286. 'Here I shall dwell in the rain, here in winter and summer,' thus the fool meditates, and does not think of his death.

287. Death comes and carries off that man, praised for his children and flocks, his mind distracted, as a flood carries off a sleeping village.

288. Sons are no help, nor a father, nor relations; there is no help from kinsfolk for one whom death has seized.

289. A wise and good man who knows the meaning of this, should quickly clear the way that leads to Nirvana.

Chapter XXI

Miscellaneous

290. If by leaving a small pleasure one sees a great pleasure, let a wise man leave the small pleasure, and look to the great.

291. He who, by causing pain to others, wishes to obtain pleasure for himself, he, entangled in the bonds of hatred, will never be free from hatred.

292. What ought to be done is neglected, what ought not to be done is done; the desires of unruly, thoughtless people are always increasing.

293. But they whose whole watchfulness is always directed to their body, who do not follow what ought not to be done, and who steadfastly do what ought to be done, the desires of such watchful and wise people will come to an end.

294. A true Brahmana goes scatheless, though he have killed father and mother, and two valiant kings, though he has destroyed a kingdom with all its subjects.

295. A true Brahmana goes scatheless, though he have killed father and mother, and two holy kings, and an eminent man besides.

296. The disciples of Gotama (Buddha) are always well awake, and their thoughts day and night are always set on Buddha.

297. The disciples of Gotama are always well awake, and their thoughts day and night are always set on the law.

298. The disciples of Gotama are always well awake, and their thoughts day and night are always set on the church.

299. The disciples of Gotama are always well awake, and their thoughts day and night are always set on their body.

300. The disciples of Gotama are always well awake, and their mind day and night always delights in compassion.

301. The disciples of Gotama are always well awake, and their mind day and night always delights in meditation.

302. It is hard to leave the world (to become a friar), it is hard to enjoy the world; hard is the monastery, painful are the houses; painful it is to dwell with equals (to share everything in common) and the itinerant mendicant is beset with pain. Therefore let no man be an itinerant mendicant and he will not be beset with pain.

303. Whatever place a faithful, virtuous, celebrated, and wealthy man chooses, there he is respected.

304. Good people shine from afar, like the snowy mountains; bad people are not seen, like arrows shot by night.

305. He alone who, without ceasing, practices the duty of sitting alone and sleeping alone, he, subduing himself, will rejoice in the destruction of all desires alone, as if living in a forest.

Chapter XXII

The Downward Course

306. He who says what is not, goes to hell; he also who, having done a thing, says I have not done it. After death both are equal, they are men with evil deeds in the next world.
307. Many men whose shoulders are covered with the yellow gown are ill-conditioned and unrestrained; such evil-doers by their evil deeds go to hell.
308. Better it would be to swallow a heated iron ball, like flaring fire, than that a bad unrestrained fellow should live on the charity of the land.
309. Four things does a wreckless man gain who covets his neighbour's wife, — a bad reputation, an uncomfortable bed, thirdly, punishment, and lastly, hell.
310. There is bad reputation, and the evil way (to hell), there is the short pleasure of the frightened in the arms of the frightened, and the king imposes heavy punishment; therefore let no man think of his neighbour's wife.
311. As a grass-blade, if badly grasped, cuts the arm, badly-practiced asceticism leads to hell.
312. An act carelessly performed, a broken vow, and hesitating obedience to discipline, all this brings no great reward.
313. If anything is to be done, let a man do it, let him attack it vigorously! A careless pilgrim only scatters the dust of his passions more widely.
314. An evil deed is better left undone, for a man repents of it afterwards; a good deed is better done, for having done it, one does not repent.

315. Like a well-guarded frontier fort, with defences within and without, so let a man guard himself. Not a moment should escape, for they who allow the right moment to pass, suffer pain when they are in hell.

316. They who are ashamed of what they ought not to be ashamed of, and are not ashamed of what they ought to be ashamed of, such men, embracing false doctrines enter the evil path.

317. They who fear when they ought not to fear, and fear not when they ought to fear, such men, embracing false doctrines, enter the evil path.

318. They who forbid when there is nothing to be forbidden, and forbid not when there is something to be forbidden, such men, embracing false doctrines, enter the evil path.

319. They who know what is forbidden as forbidden, and what is not forbidden as not forbidden, such men, embracing the true doctrine, enter the good path.

Chapter XXIII

The Elephant

320. Silently shall I endure abuse as the elephant in battle endures the arrow sent from the bow: for the world is ill-natured.

321. They lead a tamed elephant to battle, the king mounts a tamed elephant; the tamed is the best among men, he who silently endures abuse.

322. Mules are good, if tamed, and noble Sindhu horses, and elephants with large tusks; but he who tames himself is better still.

323. For with these animals does no man reach the untrodden country (Nirvana), where a tamed man goes on a tamed animal, viz. on his own well-tamed self.

324. The elephant called Dhanapalaka, his temples running with sap, and difficult to hold, does not eat a morsel when bound; the elephant longs for the elephant grove.

325. If a man becomes fat and a great eater, if he is sleepy and rolls himself about, that fool, like a hog fed on wash, is born again and again.

326. This mind of mine went formerly wandering about as it liked, as it listed, as it pleased; but I shall now hold it in thoroughly, as the rider who holds the hook holds in the furious elephant.

327. Be not thoughtless, watch your thoughts! Draw yourself out of the evil way, like an elephant sunk in mud.

328. If a man find a prudent companion who walks with him, is wise, and lives soberly, he may walk with him, overcoming all dangers, happy, but considerate.

329. If a man find no prudent companion who walks with him, is wise, and lives soberly, let him walk alone, like a king who has left his conquered country behind, — like an elephant in the forest.

330. It is better to live alone, there is no companionship with a fool; let a man walk alone, let him commit no sin, with few wishes, like an elephant in the forest.

331. If an occasion arises, friends are pleasant; enjoyment is pleasant, whatever be the cause; a good work is pleasant in the hour of death; the giving up of all grief is pleasant.

332. Pleasant in the world is the state of a mother, pleasant the state of a father, pleasant the state of a Samana, pleasant the state of a Brahmana.

333. Pleasant is virtue lasting to old age, pleasant is a faith firmly rooted; pleasant is attainment of intelligence, pleasant is avoiding of sins.

Chapter XXIV

Thirst

334. The thirst of a thoughtless man grows like a creeper; he runs from life to life, like a monkey seeking fruit in the forest.

335. Whomsoever this fierce thirst overcomes, full of poison, in this world, his sufferings increase like the abounding Birana grass.

336. He who overcomes this fierce thirst, difficult to be conquered in this world, sufferings fall off from him, like water-drops from a lotus leaf.

337. This salutary word I tell you, 'Do ye, as many as are here assembled, dig up the root of thirst, as he who wants the sweet-scented Usira root must dig up the Birana grass, that Mara (the tempter) may not crush you again and again, as the stream crushes the reeds.'

338. As a tree, even though it has been cut down, is firm so long as its root is safe, and grows again, thus, unless the feeders of thirst are destroyed, the pain (of life) will return again and again.

339. He whose thirst running towards pleasure is exceeding strong in the thirty-six channels, the waves will carry away that misguided man, viz. his desires which are set on passion.

340. The channels run everywhere, the creeper (of passion) stands sprouting; if you see the creeper springing up, cut its root by means of knowledge.

341. A creature's pleasures are extravagant and luxurious; sunk in lust and looking for pleasure, men undergo (again and again) birth and decay.

342. Men, driven on by thirst, run about like a snared hare; held in fetters and bonds, they undergo pain for a long time, again and again.

343. Men, driven on by thirst, run about like a snared hare; let therefore the mendicant drive out thirst, by striving after passionlessness for himself.

344. He who having got rid of the forest (of lust) (i.e. after having reached Nirvana) gives himself over to forest-life (i.e. to lust), and who, when removed from the forest (i.e. from lust), runs to the forest (i.e. to lust), look at that man! though free, he runs into bondage.

345. Wise people do not call that a strong fetter which is made of iron, wood, or hemp; far stronger is the care for precious stones and rings, for sons and a wife.

346. That fetter wise people call strong which drags down, yields, but is difficult to undo; after having cut this at last, people leave the world, free from cares, and leaving desires and pleasures behind.

347. Those who are slaves to passions, run down with the stream (of desires), as a spider runs down the web which he has made himself; when they have cut this, at last, wise people leave the world free from cares, leaving all affection behind.

348. Give up what is before, give up what is behind, give up what is in the middle, when thou goest to the other shore of existence; if thy mind is altogether free, thou wilt not again enter into birth and decay.

349. If a man is tossed about by doubts, full of strong passions, and yearning only for what is delightful, his thirst will grow more and more, and he will indeed make his fetters strong.

350. If a man delights in quieting doubts, and, always reflecting, dwells on what is not delightful (the impurity of the body, &c.), he certainly will remove, nay, he will cut the fetter of Mara.

351. He who has reached the consummation, who does not tremble, who is without thirst and without sin, he has broken all the thorns of life: this will be his last body.

352. He who is without thirst and without affection, who understands the words and their interpretation, who knows the order of letters (those which are before and which are after), he

has received his last body, he is called the great sage, the great man.

353. 'I have conquered all, I know all, in all conditions of life I am free from taint; I have left all, and through the destruction of thirst I am free; having learnt myself, whom shall I teach?'

354. The gift of the law exceeds all gifts; the sweetness of the law exceeds all sweetness; the delight in the law exceeds all delights; the extinction of thirst overcomes all pain.

355. Pleasures destroy the foolish, if they look not for the other shore; the foolish by his thirst for pleasures destroys himself, as if he were his own enemy.

356. The fields are damaged by weeds, mankind is damaged by passion: therefore a gift bestowed on the passionless brings great reward.

357. The fields are damaged by weeds, mankind is damaged by hatred: therefore a gift bestowed on those who do not hate brings great reward.

358. The fields are damaged by weeds, mankind is damaged by vanity: therefore a gift bestowed on those who are free from vanity brings great reward.

359. The fields are damaged by weeds, mankind is damaged by lust: therefore a gift bestowed on those who are free from lust brings great reward.

Chapter XXV

The Bhikshu (Mendicant)

360. Restraint in the eye is good, good is restraint in the ear, in the nose restraint is good, good is restraint in the tongue.

361. In the body restraint is good, good is restraint in speech, in thought restraint is good, good is restraint in all things. A Bhikshu, restrained in all things, is freed from all pain.

362. He who controls his hand, he who controls his feet, he who controls his speech, he who is well controlled, he who delights inwardly, who is collected, who is solitary and content, him they call Bhikshu.

363. The Bhikshu who controls his mouth, who speaks wisely and calmly, who teaches the meaning and the law, his word is sweet.

364. He who dwells in the law, delights in the law, meditates on the law, follows the law, that Bhikshu will never fall away from the true law.

365. Let him not despise what he has received, nor ever envy others: a mendicant who envies others does not obtain peace of mind.

366. A Bhikshu who, though he receives little, does not despise what he has received, even the gods will praise him, if his life is pure, and if he is not slothful.

367. He who never identifies himself with name and form, and does not grieve over what is no more, he indeed is called a Bhikshu.

368. The Bhikshu who acts with kindness, who is calm in the doctrine of Buddha, will reach the quiet place (Nirvana), cessation of natural desires, and happiness.

369. O Bhikshu, empty this boat! if emptied, it will go quickly; having cut off passion and hatred thou wilt go to Nirvana.

370. Cut off the five (senses), leave the five, rise above the five. A Bhikshu, who has escaped from the five fetters, he is called Oghatinna, 'saved from the flood.'

371. Meditate, O Bhikshu, and be not heedless! Do not direct thy thought to what gives pleasure that thou mayest not for thy heedlessness have to swallow the iron ball (in hell), and that thou mayest not cry out when burning, 'This is pain.'

372. Without knowledge there is no meditation, without meditation there is no knowledge: he who has knowledge and meditation is near unto Nirvana.

373. A Bhikshu who has entered his empty house, and whose mind is tranquil, feels a more than human delight when he sees the law clearly.

374. As soon as he has considered the origin and destruction of the elements (khandha) of the body, he finds happiness and joy which belong to those who know the immortal (Nirvana).

375. And this is the beginning here for a wise Bhikshu: watchfulness over the senses, contentedness, restraint under the law; keep noble friends whose life is pure, and who are not slothful.

376. Let him live in charity, let him be perfect in his duties; then in the fullness of delight he will make an end of suffering.

377. As the Vassika plant sheds its withered flowers, men should shed passion and hatred, O ye Bhikshus!

378. The Bhikshu whose body and tongue and mind are quieted, who is collected, and has rejected the baits of the world, he is called quiet.

379. Rouse thyself by thyself, examine thyself by thyself, thus self- protected and attentive wilt thou live happily, O Bhikshu!

380. For self is the lord of self, self is the refuge of self; therefore curb thyself as the merchant curbs a good horse.

381. The Bhikshu, full of delight, who is calm in the doctrine of Buddha will reach the quiet place (Nirvana), cessation of natural desires, and happiness.

382. He who, even as a young Bhikshu, applies himself to the doctrine of Buddha, brightens up this world, like the moon when free from clouds.

Chapter XXVI

The Brahmana (Arhat)

383. Stop the stream valiantly, drive away the desires, O Brahmana! When you have understood the destruction of all that was made, you will understand that which was not made.

384. If the Brahmana has reached the other shore in both laws (in restraint and contemplation), all bonds vanish from him who has obtained knowledge.

385. He for whom there is neither this nor that shore, nor both, him, the fearless and unshackled, I call indeed a Brahmana.

386. He who is thoughtful, blameless, settled, dutiful, without passions, and who has attained the highest end, him I call indeed a Brahmana.

387. The sun is bright by day, the moon shines by night, the warrior is bright in his armour, the Brahmana is bright in his meditation; but Buddha, the Awakened, is bright with splendour day and night.

388. Because a man is rid of evil, therefore he is called Brahmana; because he walks quietly, therefore he is called Samana; because he has sent away his own impurities, therefore he is called Pravragita (Pabbagita, a pilgrim).

389. No one should attack a Brahmana, but no Brahmana (if attacked) should let himself fly at his aggressor! Woe to him who strikes a Brahmana, more woe to him who flies at his aggressor!

390. It advantages a Brahmana not a little if he holds his mind back from the pleasures of life; when all wish to injure has vanished, pain will cease.

391. Him I call indeed a Brahmana who does not offend by body, word, or thought, and is controlled on these three points.

392. After a man has once understood the law as taught by the Well- awakened (Buddha), let him worship it carefully, as the Brahmana worships the sacrificial fire.

393. A man does not become a Brahmana by his platted hair, by his family, or by birth; in whom there is truth and righteousness, he is blessed, he is a Brahmana.

394. What is the use of platted hair, O fool! what of the raiment of goat-skins? Within thee there is ravening, but the outside thou makest clean.

395. The man who wears dirty raiments, who is emaciated and covered with veins, who lives alone in the forest, and meditates, him I call indeed a Brahmana.

396. I do not call a man a Brahmana because of his origin or of his mother. He is indeed arrogant, and he is wealthy: but the poor, who is free from all attachments, him I call indeed a Brahmana.

397. Him I call indeed a Brahmana who has cut all fetters, who never trembles, is independent and unshackled.

398. Him I call indeed a Brahmana who has cut the strap and the thong, the chain with all that pertains to it, who has burst the bar, and is awakened.

399. Him I call indeed a Brahmana who, though he has committed no offence, endures reproach, bonds, and stripes, who has endurance for his force, and strength for his army.

400. Him I call indeed a Brahmana who is free from anger, dutiful, virtuous, without appetite, who is subdued, and has received his last body.

401. Him I call indeed a Brahmana who does not cling to pleasures, like water on a lotus leaf, like a mustard seed on the point of a needle.

402. Him I call indeed a Brahmana who, even here, knows the end of his suffering, has put down his burden, and is unshackled.

403. Him I call indeed a Brahmana whose knowledge is deep, who possesses wisdom, who knows the right way and the wrong, and has attained the highest end.

404. Him I call indeed a Brahmana who keeps aloof both from laymen and from mendicants, who frequents no houses, and has but few desires.

405. Him I call indeed a Brahmana who finds no fault with other beings, whether feeble or strong, and does not kill nor cause slaughter.

406. Him I call indeed a Brahmana who is tolerant with the intolerant, mild with fault-finders, and free from passion among the passionate.

407. Him I call indeed a Brahmana from whom anger and hatred, pride and envy have dropt like a mustard seed from the point of a needle.

408. Him I call indeed a Brahmana who utters true speech, instructive and free from harshness, so that he offend no one.

409. Him I call indeed a Brahmana who takes nothing in the world that is not given him, be it long or short, small or large, good or bad.

410. Him I call indeed a Brahmana who fosters no desires for this world or for the next, has no inclinations, and is unshackled.

411. Him I call indeed a Brahmana who has no interests, and when he has understood (the truth), does not say How, how? and who has reached the depth of the Immortal.

412. Him I call indeed a Brahmana who in this world is above good and evil, above the bondage of both, free from grief from sin, and from impurity.

413. Him I call indeed a Brahmana who is bright like the moon, pure, serene, undisturbed, and in whom all gaiety is extinct.

414. Him I call indeed a Brahmana who has traversed this miry road, the impassable world and its vanity, who has gone through, and reached the other shore, is thoughtful, guileless, free from doubts, free from attachment, and content.

415. Him I call indeed a Brahmana who in this world, leaving all desires, travels about without a home, and in whom all concupiscence is extinct.

416. Him I call indeed a Brahmana who, leaving all longings, travels about without a home, and in whom all covetousness is extinct.

417. Him I call indeed a Brahmana who, after leaving all bondage to men, has risen above all bondage to the gods, and is free from all and every bondage.

418. Him I call indeed a Brahmana who has left what gives pleasure and what gives pain, who is cold, and free from all germs (of renewed life), the hero who has conquered all the worlds.

419. Him I call indeed a Brahmana who knows the destruction and the return of beings everywhere, who is free from bondage, welfaring (Sugata), and awakened (Buddha).

420. Him I call indeed a Brahmana whose path the gods do not know, nor spirits (Gandharvas), nor men, whose passions are extinct, and who is an Arhat (venerable).

421. Him I call indeed a Brahmana who calls nothing his own, whether it be before, behind, or between, who is poor, and free from the love of the world.

422. Him I call indeed a Brahmana, the manly, the noble, the hero, the great sage, the conqueror, the impassible, the accomplished, the awakened.

423. Him I call indeed a Brahmana who knows his former abodes, who sees heaven and hell, has reached the end of births, is perfect in knowledge, a sage, and whose perfections are all perfect.

THE SUTTA-NIPÂTA
Translated by V. Fausböll

I URAGAVAGGA

I URAGASUTTA

1. He who restrains his anger when it has arisen, as (they) by medicines (restrain) the poison of the snake spreading (in the body), that Bhikkhu leaves this and the further shore, as a snake (quits its) old worn out skin.
2. He who has cut off passion entirely, as (they cut off) the lotus-flower growing in a lake, after diving (into the water), that Bhikkhu leaves this and the further shore, as a snake (quits its) old worn out skin.
3. He who has cut off desire entirely, the flowing, the quickly running, after drying it up, that Bhikkhu leaves this and the further shore, as a snake (quits its) old worn out skin.
4. He who has destroyed arrogance entirely, as the flood (destroys) a very frail bridge of reeds, that Bhikkhu leaves this and the further shore, as a snake (quits its) old worn out skin.
5. He who has not found any essence in the existences, like one that looks for flowers on fig-trees, that Bhikkhu leaves this and the further shore, as a snake (quits its) old worn out skin.
6. He in whose breast there are no feelings of anger, who has thus overcome reiterated existence, that Bhikkhu leaves this and the further shore, as a snake (quits its) old worn out skin.
7. He whose doubts are scattered, cut off entirely inwardly, that Bhikkhu leaves this and the further shore, as a snake (quits its) old worn out skin.
8. He who did not go too fast forward, nor was left behind, who overcame all this (world of) delusion, that Bhikkhu leaves this and the further shore, as a snake (quits its) old worn out skin.
9. He who did not go too fast forward, nor was left behind,

having seen that all this in the world is false, that Bhikkhu leaves this and the further shore, as a snake (quits its) old worn out skin.
10. He who did not go too fast forward, nor was left behind, being free from covetousness, (seeing) that all this is false, that Bhikkhu leaves this and the further shore, as a snake (quits its) old worn out skin.
11. He who did not go too fast forward, nor was left behind, being free from passion, (seeing) that all this is false, that Bhikkhu leaves this and the further shore, as a snake (quits its) old worn out skin.
12. He who did not go too fast forward, nor was left behind, being free from hatred, (seeing) that all this is false, that Bhikkhu leaves this and the further shore, as a snake (quits its) old worn out skin.
13. He who did not go too fast forward, nor was left behind, being free from folly, (seeing) that all this is false, that Bhikkhu leaves his and the further shore, as a snake (quits its) old worn out skin.
14. He to whom there are no affections whatsoever, whose sins are extirpated from the root, that Bhikkhu leaves this and the further shore, as a snake (quits its) old worn out skin.
15. He to whom there are no (sins) whatsoever originating in fear, which are the causes of coming back to this shore, that Bhikkhu leaves this and the further shore, as a snake (quits its) old worn out skin.
16. He to whom there are no (sins) whatsoever originating in desire, which are the causes of binding (men) to existence, that Bhikkhu leaves this and the further shore, as a snake (quits its) old worn out skin.
17. He who, having left the five obstacles, is free from suffering, has overcome doubt, and is without pain, that Bhikkhu leaves this and the further shore. as a snake (quits its) old worn out skin.
Uragasutta is ended.

2 DHANIYASUTTA

1. 'I have boiled (my) rice, I have milked (my cows),' — so said the herdsman Dhaniya, — 'I am living together with my fellows near the banks of the Mahî (river), (my) house is covered, the fire is kindled: therefore, if thou like, rain, O sky!'
2. 'I am free from anger, free from stubbornness,' — so said Bhagavat, — 'I am abiding for one night near the banks of the Mahî (river), my house is uncovered, the fire (of passions) is extinguished: therefore, if thou like, rain, O sky!'
3. 'Gad-flies are not to be found (with me),' — so said the herdsman Dhaniya, — 'in meadows abounding with grass the cows are roaming, and they can endure rain when it comes: therefore, if thou like, rain, O sky!'
4. '(By me) is made a well-constructed raft,' — so said Bhagavat, — 'I have passed over (to Nibbâna), I have reached the further bank, having overcome the torrent (of passions); there is no (further) use for a raft: therefore, if thou like, rain, O sky!'
5. 'My wife is obedient, not wanton,' — so said the herdsman Dhaniya, — 'for a long time she has been living together (with me), she is winning, and I hear nothing wicked of her: therefore, if thou like, rain, O sky!'
6. 'My mind is obedient, delivered (from all worldliness),' — so said Bhagavat, — 'it has for a long time been highly cultivated and well-subdued, there is no longer anything wicked in me: therefore, if thou like, rain, O sky!'
7. 'I support myself by my own earnings,' — so said the herdsman Dhaniya, — 'and my children are (all) about me, healthy; I hear nothing wicked of them: therefore, if thou like, rain, O sky!'
8. 'I am no one's servant,' — so said Bhagavat, — 'with what I

have gained I wander about in all the world, there is no need (for me) to serve: therefore, if thou like, rain, O sky!'

9. 'I have cows, I have calves,' — so said the herdsman Dhaniya; — 'I have cows in calf and heifers, and I have also a bull as lord over the cows: therefore, if thou like, rain, O sky!'

10. 'I have no cows, I have no calves,' — so said Bhagavat, — 'I have no cows in calf and no heifers, and I have no bull as a lord over the cows: therefore, if thou like, rain, O sky!

11. 'The stakes are driven in, and cannot be shaken,' — so said the herdsman Dhaniya, — 'the ropes are made of muñga grass, new and well-made, the cows will not be able to break them: therefore, if thou like, rain, O sky!'

12. 'Having, like a bull, rent the bonds; having, like an elephant, broken through the galu*kkhi* creeper, I shall not again enter into a womb: therefore, if thou like, rain, O sky!'

Then at once a shower poured down, filling both sea and land. Hearing the sky raining, Dhaniya spoke thus:

13. 'No small gain indeed (has accrued) to us since we have seen Bhagavat; we take refuge in thee, O (thou who art) endowed with the eye (of wisdom); be thou our master, O great Muni!'

14. 'Both my wife and myself are obedient; (if) we lead a holy life before Sugata, we shall conquer birth and death, and put an end to pain.'

15. 'He who has sons has delight in sons,' — so said the wicked Mâra, — 'he who has cows has delight likewise in cows; for upadhi (substance) is the delight of man, but he who has no upadhi has no delight.'

16. 'He who has sons has care with (his) sons,' — so said Bhagavat, — 'he who has cows has likewise care with (his) cows; for upadhi (is the cause of) people's cares, but he who has no upadhi has no care.'

Dhaniyasutta is ended.

3 KHAGGA VISÂNASUTTA

Family life and intercourse with others should be avoided, for society has all vices in its train; therefore one should leave the corrupted state of society and lead a solitary life.

1. Having laid aside the rod against all beings, and not hurting any of them, let no one wish for a son, much less for a companion, let him wander alone like a rhinoceros.
2. In him who has intercourse (with others) affections arise, (and then) the pain which follows affection; considering the misery that originates in affection let one wander alone like a rhinoceros.
3. He who has compassion on his friends and confidential (companions) loses (his own) advantage, having a fettered mind; seeing this danger in friendship let one wander alone like a rhinoceros.
4. Just as a large bamboo tree (with its branches) entangled (in each other, such is) the care one has with children and wife; (but) like the shoot of a bamboo not clinging (to anything) let one wander alone like a rhinoceros.
5. As a beast unbound in the forest goes feeding at pleasure, so let the wise man, considering (only his) own will, wander alone like a rhinoceros.
6. There is (a constant) calling in the midst of company, both when sitting, standing, walking, and going away; (but) let one, looking (only) for freedom from desire and for following his own will, wander alone like a rhinoceros.
7. There is sport and amusement in the midst of
8. He who is at home in (all) the four regions and is not hostile (to any one), being content with this or that, overcoming (all) dangers fearlessly, let him wander alone like a rhinoceros.

9. Discontented are some pabba*g*itas (ascetics), also some gaha*tth*as (householders) dwelling in houses; let one, caring little about other people's children, wander alone like a rhinoceros.

10. Removing the marks of a gihin (a householder) like a Kovilâra tree whose leaves are fallen, let one, after cutting off heroically the ties of a gihin, wander alone like a rhinoceros.

11. If one acquires a clever companion, an associate righteous and wise, let him, overcoming all dangers, wander about with him glad and, thoughtful.

12. If one does not acquire a clever companion, an associate righteous and wise, then as a king abandoning (his) conquered kingdom, let him wander alone like a rhinoceros.

13. Surely we ought to praise the good luck of having companions, the best (and such as are our) equals ought to be sought for; not having acquired such friends let one, enjoying (only) allowable things, wander alone like a rhinoceros.

14. Seeing bright golden (bracelets), well-wrought by the goldsmith, striking (against each other when there are) two on one arm, let one wander alone like a rhinoceros.

16. The sensual pleasures indeed, which are various, sweet, and charming, under their different shapes agitate the mind; seeing the misery (originating) in sensual pleasures, let one wander alone like a rhinoceros.

17. These (pleasures are) to me calamities, boils, misfortunes, diseases, sharp pains, and dangers; seeing this danger (originating) in sensual pleasures, let one wander alone like a rhinoceros.

18. Both cold and heat, hunger and thirst, wind and a burning sun, and gad-flies and snakes — having overcome all these things, let one wander alone like a rhinoceros.

19. As the elephant, the strong, the spotted, the large, after leaving the herd walks at pleasure in the forest, even so let one wander alone like a rhinoceros.

20. For him who delights in intercourse (with others, even) that is inconvenient which tends to temporary deliverance; reflecting on the words of (Buddha) the kinsman of the Âdi*kk*a family, let one wander alone like a rhinoceros.

21. The harshness of the (philosophical) views I have overcome, I have acquired self-command, I have attained to the way (leading to perfection), I am in possession of knowledge, and not to be led by others; so speaking, let one wander alone like a rhinoceros.

22. Without covetousness, without deceit, without

23. Let one avoid a wicked companion who teaches what is useless and has gone into what is wrong, let him not cultivate (the society of) one who is devoted (to and) lost in sensual pleasures, let one wander alone like a rhinoceros.

24. Let one cultivate (the society of) a friend who is learned and keeps the Dhamma, who is magnanimous and wise; knowing the meaning (of things and) subduing his doubts, let one wander alone like a rhinoceros.

25. Not adorning himself, not looking out for sport, amusement, and the delight of pleasure in the world, (on the contrary) being loath of a life of dressing, speaking the truth, let one wander alone like a rhinoceros.

26. Having left son and wife, father and mother, wealth, and corn, and relatives, the different objects of desire, let one wander alone like a rhinoceros.

27. 'This is a tie, in this there is little happiness, little enjoyment, but more of pain, this is a fish-hook,' so having understood, let a thoughtful man wander alone like a rhinoceros.

28: Having torn the ties, having broken the net as a fish in the water, being like a fire not returning to the burnt place, let one wander alone like a rhinoceros.

29. With downcast eyes, and not prying, with his senses guarded, with his mind protected free from

30. Removing the characteristics of a gihin (householder), like a Pâri*kh*atta tree whose leaves are cut off, clothed in a yellow robe after wandering away (from his house), let one wander alone like a rhinoceros.

31. Not being greedy of sweet things, not being unsteady, not supporting others, going begging from house to house, having a mind which is not fettered to any household, let one wander alone like a rhinoceros.

32. Having left the five obstacles of the mind, having dispelled all sin, being independent, having cut off the sin of desire, let one wander alone like a rhinoceros.

33. Having thrown behind (himself bodily) pleasure and pain, and previously (mental) joy and distress, having acquired equanimity, tranquillity, purity, let one wander alone like a rhinoceros.

34. Strenuous for obtaining the supreme good (i.e. Nibbâna), with a mind free from attachment, not living in idleness, being firm, endowed with bodily and mental strength, let one wander alone like a rhinoceros.

35. Not abandoning seclusion and meditation, always wandering in (accordance with) the Dhammas, seeing misery in the existences, let one wander alone like a rhinoceros.

36. Wishing for the destruction of desire (i.e. Nibbâna), being careful, no fool, learned, strenuous, considerate, restrained, energetic, let one wander alone like a rhinoceros.

38. As a lion strong by his teeth, after overcoming (all animals), wanders victorious as the king of the animals, and haunts distant dwelling-places, (even so) let one wander alone like a rhinoceros.

39. Cultivating in (due) time kindness, equanimity, compassion, deliverance, and rejoicing (with others), unobstructed by the whole world, let one wander alone like a rhinoceros.

40. Having abandoned both passion and hatred and folly, having rent the ties, not trembling in the loss of life, let one wander alone like a rhinoceros.

41. They cultivate (the society of others) and serve them for the sake of advantage; friends without a motive are now difficult to get, men know their own profit and are impure; (therefore) let one wander alone like a rhinoceros.

Khaggavisânasutta is ended.

4 KASIBHÂRADVÂGASUTTA

So it was heard by me:
At one time Bhagavat dwelt in Magadha at Dakkhinâgiri in the Brâmana village Ekanalâ. And at that time the Brâmana Kasibhâradvâga's five hundred ploughs were tied (to the yokes) in the sowing season. Then Bhagavat, in the morning, having put on his raiment and taken his bowl and robes, went to the place where the Brâmana Kasibhâradvâga's work (was going on). At that time the Brâmana Kasibhâradvâga's distribution of food took place. Then Bhagavat went to the place where the distribution of food took place, and having gone there, he stood apart. The Brâmana Kasibhâradvâga saw Bhagavat standing there to get alms, and having seen him, he said this to Bhagavat:
'I, O Samana, both plough and sow, and having ploughed and sown, I eat; thou also, O Samana, shouldst plough and sow, and having ploughed and sown, thou shouldst eat.'
'I also, O Brâmana, both plough and sow, and having ploughed and sown, I eat,' so said Bhagavat.
'Yet we do not see the yoke, or the plough, or the ploughshare, or the goad, or the oxen of the venerable Gotama.'
And then the venerable Gotama spoke in this way:
'I also, O Brâmana, both plough and sow, and having ploughed and sown, I eat,' so said Bhagavat.
Then the Brâmana Kasibhâradvâga addressed Bhagavat in a stanza:
1. 'Thou professest to be a ploughman, and yet we do not see thy ploughing; asked about (thy) ploughing, tell us (of it), that we may know thy ploughing.'
2. Bhagavat answered: 'Faith is the seed, penance the rain, understanding my yoke and plough, modesty the pole of the

plough, mind the tie, thoughtfulness my ploughshare and goad.

3. 'I am guarded in respect of the body, I am guarded in respect of speech, temperate in food; I make truth to cut away (weeds), tenderness is my deliverance.

4. 'Exertion is my beast of burden; carrying (me) to Nibbâna he goes without turning back to the place where having gone one does not grieve.

5. 'So this ploughing is ploughed, it bears the fruit of immortality; having ploughed this ploughing one is freed from all pain.'

Then the Brâma*n*a Kasibhâradvâ*g*a, having poured rice-milk into a golden bowl, offered it to Bhagavat, saying, 'Let the venerable Bhagavat eat of the rice-milk; the venerable is a ploughman, for the venerable Gotama ploughs a ploughing that bears the fruit of immortality.'

6. Bhagavat said: 'What is acquired by reciting stanzas is not to be eaten by me; this is, O Brâma*n*a, not the Dhamma of those that see rightly; Buddha rejects what is acquired by reciting stanzas, this is the conduct (of Buddhas) as long as the Dhamma exists.

7. 'One who is an accomplished great Isi, whose passions are destroyed and whose misbehaviour has ceased, thou shouldst serve with other food and drink, for this is the field for one who looks for good works.'

'To whom then, O Gotama, shall I give this rice-milk?' so said Kasibhâradvâ*g*a.

'I do not see, O Brâma*n*a, in the world (of men)

Then the Brâma*n*a Kasibhâradvâ*g*a threw the rice-milk into some water with no worms. Then the rice-milk thrown into the water splashed, hissed, smoked in volumes; for as a ploughshare that has got hot during the day when thrown into the water splashes, hisses, and smokes in volumes, even so the rice-milk (when) thrown into the water splashed, hissed, and smoked in volumes.

Then the Brâma*n*a Kasibhâradvâ*g*a alarmed and terrified went up to Bhagavat, and after having approached and fallen with his head at Bhagavat's feet, he said this to Bhagavat:

'It is excellent, O venerable Gotama! It is excellent, O venerable

Gotama! As one raises what has been overthrown, or reveals what has been hidden, or tells the way to him who has gone astray, or holds out an oil lamp in the dark that those who have eyes may see the objects, even so by the venerable Gotama in manifold ways the Dhamma (has been) illustrated. I take refuge in the venerable Gotama and in the Dhamma and in the Assembly of Bhikkhus; I wish to receive the pabbaggâ, I wish to receive the upasampadâ (the robe and the orders) from the venerable Gotama,' so said Kasibhâradvâga.

Then the Brâmana Kasibhâradvâga received the pabbaggâ from Bhagavat, and he received also the upasampadâ; and the venerable Bhâradvâaga having lately received the upasampadâ, leading a solitary, retired, strenuous, ardent, energetic life, lived after having in a short time in this existence by his own understanding ascertained and possessed himself of that highest perfection of a religious life for the sake of which men of good family rightly wander, away from their houses to houseless state. 'Birth had been destroyed, a religious life had been led, what was to be done had been done, there was nothing else (to be done) for this existence,' so he perceived, and the venerable Bhâradvâaga became one of the arahats (saints).

Kasibhâradvâgasutta is ended.

5 KUNDASUTTA

Buddha describes the four different kinds of Samaṅas to Kunda, the smith.

1. 'I ask the Muni of great understanding,' — so said Kunda, the smith, — 'Buddha, the lord of the Dhamma, who is free from desire, the best of bipeds, the most excellent of charioteers, how many (kinds of) Samaṅas are there in the world; pray tell me that?'

2. 'There are four (kinds of) Samaṅas, (there is) not a fifth, O Kunda,' — so said Bhagavat, — 'these I will reveal to thee, being asked in person; (they are) Maggaginas and Maggadesakas, Maggaĝîvins and Maggadûsins.'

3. 'Whom do the Buddhas call a Maggagina?' — so said Kunda, the smith, — 'How is a Maggagghâyin unequalled? Being asked, describe to me a Maggaĝîvin, and reveal to me a Maggadûsin.'

4. Bhagavat said: 'He who has overcome doubt, is without pain, delights in Nibbâna, is free from greed, a leader of the world of men and gods, such a one the Buddhas call a maggagina (that is, victorious by the way).

5. 'He who in this world having known the best (i.e. Nibbâna) as the best, expounds and explains here the Dhamma, him, the doubt-cutting Muni, without desire, the second of the Bhikkhus they call a maggadesin (that is, teaching the way).

6. 'He who lives in the way that has so well been taught in the Dhammapada, and is restrained, attentive, cultivating blameless words, him the third of the Bhikshus they call a maggaĝîvin (that is, living in the way).

7. 'He who although counterfeiting the virtuous is forward, disgraces families, is impudent, deceitful, unrestrained, a babbler,

walking in disguise, such a one is a maggadûsin (that is, defiling the way).

8. 'He who has penetrated these (four Samaṇas), who is a householder, possessed of knowledge, a pupil of the venerable ones, wise, having known that they all are such, — having seen so, his faith is not lost; for how could he make the undepraved equal to the depraved and the pure equal to the impure?'

*K*undasutta is ended.

6 PARÂBHAVASUTTA

So it was heard by me:
At one time Bhagavat dwelt at Sâvatthî, in Getavana, in the park of Anâthapindika. Then when the night had gone, a certain deity of a beautiful appearance, having illuminated the whole Getavana, went up to Bhagavat, and having approached and saluted him, he stood apart, and standing apart that deity addressed Bhagavat in stanzas:
1. 'We ask (thee), Gotama, about a man that suffers loss; having come to ask, Bhagavat, (tell us) what is the cause (of loss) to the losing (man).'
2. Bhagavat: 'The winner is easily known, easily known (is also) the loser: he who loves Dhamma is the winner, he who hates Dhamma is the loser.'
3. Deity: 'We know this to be so, this is the first loser; tell (us) the second, O Bhagavat, what is the cause (of loss) to the losing (man).'
4. Bhagavat: 'Wicked men are dear to him, he does not do anything that is dear to the good, he approves of the Dhamma of the wicked, — that is the cause (of loss) to the losing (man).'
5. Deity: 'We know this to be so, this is the second loser; tell us the third, O Bhagavat, what is the cause (of loss) to the losing (man).'
6. Bhagavat: 'The man who is drowsy, fond of society and without energy, lazy, given to anger, — that is the cause (of loss) to the losing (man).'
7. Deity: 'We know this to be so, this is the third loser; tell us the fourth, O Bhagavat, what is the cause (of loss) to the losing (man).'
8. Bhagavat: 'He who being rich does not support mother or

father who are old or past their youth, — that is the cause (of loss) to the losing (man).'

9. Deity: 'We know this to be so, this is the fourth loser; tell us the fifth, O Bhagavat, what is the cause (of loss) to the losing (man).'

10. Bhagavat: 'He who by falsehood deceives either a Brâmaṇa or a Samaṇa or any other mendicant, — that is the cause (of loss) to the losing (man).'

11. Deity: 'We know this to be so, this is the fifth loser; tell us the sixth, O Bhagavat, what is the cause (of loss) to the losing (man).'

12. Bhagavat: 'The man who is possessed of much property, who has gold and food, (and still) enjoys alone his sweet things, — that is the cause (of loss) to the losing (man).'

13. Deity: 'We know this to be so, this is the sixth loser; tell us the seventh, O Bhagavat, what is the cause (of loss) to the losing (man).'

14. Bhagavat: 'The man who proud of his birth, of his wealth, and of his family, despises his relatives, — that is the cause (of loss) to the losing (man).'

15. Deity: 'We know this to be so, this is the seventh loser; tell us the eighth, O Bhagavat, what is the cause (of loss) to the losing (man).'

16. Bhagavat: 'The man who given to women, to strong drink, and to dice, wastes whatever he has gained, — that is the cause (of loss) to the losing (man).'

17. Deity: 'We know this to be so, this is the eighth loser; tell us the ninth, O Bhagavat, what is the cause (of loss) to the losing (man).'

18. Bhagavat: 'He who, not satisfied with his own wife, is seen with harlots and the wives of others, — that is the cause (of loss) to the losing (man).'

19. Deity: 'We know this to be so, this is the ninth loser; tell us the tenth, O Bhagavat, what (is) the cause (of loss) to the losing (man).'

20. Bhagavat: 'The man who, past his youth, brings home a

woman with breasts like the timbaru fruit, and for jealousy of her cannot sleep, — that is the cause (of loss) to the losing (man).'

21. Deity: 'We know this to be so, this is the tenth loser; tell us the eleventh, O Bhagavat, what is the cause (of loss) to the losing (man).'

22. Bhagavat: 'He who places in supremacy a woman given to drink and squandering, or a man of the same kind, — that is the cause (of loss) to the losing (man).'

23. Deity: 'We know this to be so, this is the eleventh loser; tell us the twelfth, O Bhagavat, what is the cause (of loss) to the losing (man).'

24. Bhagavat: 'He who has little property, (but) great desire, is born in a Khattiya family and wishes for the kingdom in this world, — that is the cause (of loss) to the losing (man).'

25. Having taken into consideration these losses in the world, the wise, venerable man, who is endowed with insight, cultivates the happy world (of the gods).'

Parâbhavasutta is ended.

7 VASALASUTTA

The Brâmaṇa Aggikabhâradvâga is converted by Buddha, after hearing his definition of an outcast, illustrated by the story of Mâtaṅga, told in the Mâtaṅgagâtaka. Comp. Sp. Hardy, The Legends and Theories of the Buddhists,
. — Text and translation in Alwis's Buddhist Nirvâṇa,

So it was heard by me: At one time Bhagavat dwelt at Sâvatthî, in Getavana, in the park of Anâthapiṇḍika. Then Bhagavat having put on his raiment in the morning, and having taken his bowl and his robes, entered Sâvatthî for alms. Now at that time in the house of the Brâmaṇa Aggikabhâradvâga the fire was blazing, the offering brought forth. Then Bhagavat going for alms from house to house in Sâvatthî went to the house of the Brâmaṇa Aggikabhâradvâga. The Brâmaṇa Aggikabhâradvâga saw Bhagavat coming at a distance, and seeing him he said this: 'Stay there, O Shaveling; (stay) there, O Samaṇaka (i.e. wretched Samaṇa); (stay) there, O Vasalaka (i.e. outcast)!'
This having been said, Bhagavat replied to the Brâmaṇa Aggikabhâradvâga: 'Dost thou know, O Brâmaṇa, an outcast, or the things that make an outcast?'
'No, O venerable Gotama, I do not know an outcast, or the things that make an outcast; let the venerable Gotama teach me this so well that I may know an outcast, or the things that make an outcast."
'Listen then, O Brâmaṇa, attend carefully, I will tell (thee).'
'Even so, O venerable one,' so the Brâmaṇa Aggikabhâradvâga replied to Bhagavat. Then Bhagavat said this:
1. 'The man who is angry and bears hatred, who is wicked and hypocritical, who has embraced wrong views, who is deceitful, let

one know him as an outcast.

2. 'Whosoever in this world harms living beings, whether once or twice born, and in whom there is no compassion for living beings, let one know him as an outcast.

3. 'Whosoever destroys or lays siege to villages and towns, and is known as an enemy, let one know him as an outcast.

4. 'Be it in the village or in the wood, whosoever appropriates by theft what is the property of others and what has not been given, let one know him as an outcast.

5. 'Whosoever, having really contracted a debt, runs away when called upon (to pay), saying, "There is no debt (that I owe) thee," let one know him as an outcast.

6. 'Whosoever for love of a trifle having killed a man going along the road, takes the trifle, let one know him as an outcast.

7. 'The man who for his own sake or for that of others or for the sake of wealth speaks falsely when asked as a witness, let one know him as an outcast.

8. 'Whosoever is seen with the wives of relatives or of friends either by force or with their consent, let one know him as an outcast.

9. 'Whosoever being rich does not support mother or father when old and past their youth, let one know him as an outcast.

10. 'Whosoever strikes or by words annoys mother or father, brother, sister, or mother-in-law, let one know him as an outcast.

11. 'Whosoever, being asked about what is good, teaches what is bad and advises (another, while) concealing (something from him), let one know him as an outcast.

12. 'Whosoever, having committed a bad deed, hopes (saying), "Let no one know me" (as having done it, who is) a dissembler, let one know him as an outcast.

13. 'Whosoever, having gone to another's house and partaken of his good food, does not in return honour him when he comes, let one know him as an outcast.

14. 'Whosoever by falsehood deceives either a Brâhmana or a Samana or any other mendicant, let one know him as an outcast.

15. 'Whosoever by words annoys either a Brâhmana or a Samana

when meal-time has come and does not give (him anything), let one know him as an outcast.

16. 'Whosoever enveloped in ignorance in this world predicts what is not (to take place), coveting a trifle, let one know him as an outcast.

17. 'Whosoever exalts himself and despises others, being mean by his pride, let one know him as an outcast.

18. 'Whosoever is a provoker and is avaricious, has sinful desires, is envious, wicked, shameless, and fearless of sinning, let one know him as an outcast.

19. 'Whosoever reviles Buddha or his disciple, be he a wandering mendicant (paribbâga) or a householder (gahattha), let one know him as an outcast.

20. 'Whosoever without being a saint (arahat) pretends to be a saint, (and is) a thief in all the worlds including that of Brahman, he is indeed the lowest outcast; (all) these who have been described by me to you are indeed called outcasts.

21. 'Not by birth does one become an outcast, not by birth does one become a Brâmana; by deeds one becomes an outcast, by deeds one becomes a Brâmana.

22. 'Know ye this in the way that this example of mine (shows): There was a Kandâla of the Sopâka caste, well known as Mâtanga.

23. 'This Mâtanga reached the highest fame, such as was very difficult to obtain, and many Khattiyas and Brâmanas went to serve him.

24. 'He having mounted the vehicle of the gods, (and entered) the high road (that is) free from dust, having abandoned sensual desires, went to the Brahma world.

25. 'His birth did not prevent him from being re-born in the Brahma world; (on the other hand) there are Brâmanas, born in the family of preceptors, friends of the hymns (of the Vedas),

26. 'But they are continually caught in sinful deeds, and are to be blamed in this world, while in the coming (world) hell (awaits them); birth does not save them from hell nor from blame.

27. '(Therefore) not by birth does one become an outcast, not by birth does one become a Brâmana, by deeds one becomes an

outcast, by deeds one becomes a Brâmaṇa.'

This having been said, the Brâmaṇa Aggikabhâradvâga answered Bhagavat as follows:

'Excellent, O venerable Gotama! Excellent, O venerable Gotama! As one, O venerable Gotama, raises what has been overthrown, or reveals what has been hidden, or tells the way to him who has gone astray, or holds out an oil lamp in the dark that those who have eyes may see the objects, even so by the venerable Gotama in manifold ways the Dhamma has been illustrated; I take refuge in the venerable Gotama and in the Dhamma and in the Assembly of Bhikkhus. Let the venerable Gotama accept me as an upâsaka (a follower, me) who henceforth for all my life have taken refuge (in him).'

Vasalasutta is ended.

8 METTASUTTA

A peaceful mind and goodwill towards all beings are praised. — Text by Grimblot in Journal Asiatique, t. xviii I), , and by Childers in Khuddaka Pâ*th*a, ; translation (?) by Gogerly in the Ceylon Friend, 1839, , by Childers in Kh. Pâ*th*a and by L. Feer in Journal Asiatique, t. xviii I), .

1. Whatever is to be done by one who is skilful in seeking (what is) good, having attained that tranquil state (of Nibbâna): — Let him be able and upright and conscientious and of soft speech, gentle, not proud,
2. And contented and easily supported and having few cares, unburdened and with his senses calmed and wise, not arrogant, without (showing) greediness (when going his round) in families.
3. And let him not do anything mean for which others who are wise might reprove (him); may all beings be happy and secure, may they be happy-minded.
4. Whatever living beings there are, either feeble or strong, all either long or great, middle-sized, short, small or large,
5. Either seen or which are not seen, and which live far (or) near, either born or seeking birth, may all creatures be happy-minded.
6. Let no one deceive another, let him not despise (another) in any place, let him not out of anger or resentment wish harm to another.
7. As a mother at the risk of her life watches over her own child, her only child, so also let every one cultivate a boundless (friendly) mind towards all beings.
8. And let him cultivate goodwill towards all the world, a boundless (friendly) mind, above and below and across, unobstructed, without hatred, without enmity.

9. Standing, walking or sitting or lying, as long as he be awake, let him devote himself to this mind; this (way of) living they say is the best in this world.

10. He who, not having embraced (philosophical) views, is virtuous, endowed with (perfect) vision, after subduing greediness for sensual pleasures, will never again go to a mother's womb.

Mettasutta is ended.

9 HEMAVATASUTTA

A dialogue between two Yakkhas on the qualities of Buddha. They go to Buddha, and after having their questions answered they, together with ten hundred Yakkhas, become the followers of Buddha.

1. 'To-day is the fifteenth, a fast day; a lovely night has come,' — so said the Yakkha Sâtâgira, — 'let us (go and) see the renowned Master Gotama.'
2. 'Is the mind of such a one well disposed towards all beings?' — so said the Yakkha Hemavata, — 'are his thoughts restrained as to things wished for or not wished for?'
3. 'His mind is well disposed towards all beings, (the mind) of such a one,' — so said the Yakkha Sâtâgira, — 'and his thoughts are restrained as to things wished for or not wished for.'
4. 'Does he not take what has not been given (to him)?' — so said the Yakkha Hemavata, — 'is he self-controlled (in his behaviour) to living beings? is he far from (a state of) carelessness? does he not abandon meditation?'
5. 'He does not take what has not been given (to him),' — so said the Yakkha Sâtâgira, — 'and he is self-controlled (in his behaviour) to living beings, and he is far from (a state of) carelessness; Buddha does not abandon meditation.'
6. 'Does he not speak falsely?' — so said the Yakkha Hemavata, — 'is he not harsh-spoken? does he not utter slander? does he not talk nonsense?'
7. 'He does not speak falsely,' — so said the Yakkha Sâtâgira, — 'he is not harsh-spoken, he does not utter slander, with judgment he utters what is good sense.'
8. 'Is he not given to sensual pleasures?' — so said the Yakkha

Hemavata, — 'is his mind undisturbed? has he overcome folly? does he see clearly in (all) things (dhammas)?'

9. 'He is not given to sensual pleasures,' — so said the Yakkha Sâtâgira, — 'and his mind is undisturbed; he has overcome all folly; Buddha sees clearly in (all) things.'

10. 'Is he endowed with knowledge?' — so said the Yakkha Hemavata, — 'is his conduct pure? have his passions been destroyed? is there no new birth (for him)?'

11. 'He is endowed with knowledge,' — so said the Yakkha Sâtâgira, — 'and his conduct is pure; all his passions have been destroyed; there is no new birth for him.

12. 'The mind of the Muni is accomplished in deed and word; Gotama, who is accomplished by his knowledge and conduct, let us (go and) see.

13. 'Come, let us (go and) see Gotama, who has legs like an antelope, who is thin, who is wise, living on little food, not covetous, the Muni who is meditating in the forest.

14. 'Having gone to him who is a lion amongst those that wander alone and does not look for sensual pleasures, let us ask about the (means of) deliverance from the snares of death.

15. 'Let us ask Gotama, the preacher, the expounder, who has penetrated all things, Buddha who has overcome hatred and fear.'

16. 'In what has the world originated?' — so said the Yakkha Hemavata, — 'with what is the world intimate? by what is the world afflicted, after having grasped at what?'

17. 'In six the world has originated, O Hemavata,' — so said Bhagavat, — 'with six it is intimate, by six the world is afflicted, after having grasped at six.'

18. Hemavata said: 'What is the grasping by which the world is afflicted? Asked about salvation, tell (me) how one is released from pain?'

19. Bhagavat said: 'Five pleasures of sense are said to be in the world, with (the pleasure of) the mind as the sixth; having divested oneself of desire for these, one is thus released from pain.

20. 'This salvation of the world has been told to you truly, this I tell you: thus one is released from pain.'

21. Hemavata said: 'Who in this world crosses the stream (of existence)? who in this world crosses the sea? who does not sink into the deep, where there is no footing and no support?'

22. Bhagavat said: 'He who is always endowed with virtue, possessed of understanding, well composed, reflecting within himself, and thoughtful, crosses the stream that is difficult to cross.

23. 'He who is disgusted with sensual pleasures, who has overcome all bonds and destroyed joy, such a one does not sink into the deep.'

24. Hemavata said: 'He who is endowed with a profound understanding, seeing what is subtle, possessing nothing, not clinging to sensual pleasures, behold him who is in every respect liberated, the great Isi, walking in the divine path.

25. 'He who has got a great name, sees what is subtle, imparts understanding; and does not cling to the abode of sensual pleasures, behold him, the all-knowing, the wise, the great Isi, walking in the noble path.

26. 'A good sight indeed (has met) us to-day, a good daybreak, a beautiful rising, (for) we have seen the perfectly enlightened (sambuddham), who has crossed the stream, and is free from passion.

27. 'These ten hundred Yakkhas, possessed of supernatural power and of fame, they all take refuge in thee, thou art our incomparable Master.

28. 'We will wander about from village to village, from mountain to mountain, worshipping the perfectly enlightened and the perfection of the Dhamma.'

Hemavatasutta is ended.

10 ÂLAVAKASUTTA

The Yakkha Âlavaka first threatens Buddha, then puts some questions to him which Buddha answers, whereupon Âlavaka is converted.

So it was heard by me:
At one time Bhagavat dwelt at Âlavî, in the realm of the Yakkha Âlavaka. Then the Yakkha Âlavaka went to the place where Bhagavat dwelt, and having gone there he said this to Bhagavat:
'Come out, O Samana!'
'Yes, O friend!' so saying Bhagavat came out.
'Enter, O Samana!'
'Yes, O friend!' so saying Bhagavat entered.
A second time the Yakkha Âlavaka said this to Bhagavat: 'Come out, O Samana!'
'Yes, O friend!' so saying Bhagavat came out.
'Enter, O Samana!'
'Yes, O friend!' so saying Bhagavat entered.
A third time the Yakkha Âlavaka said this Bhagavat: 'Come out, O Samana!'
' Yes, O friend!' so saying Bhagavat came out.
'Enter, O Samana!'
'Yes, O friend!' so saying Bhagavat entered.
A fourth time the Yakkha Âlavaka said this to Bhagavat: 'Come out, O Samana!'
'I shall not come out to thee, O friend, do what thou pleasest.'
'I shall ask thee a question, O Samana, if thou canst not answer it, I will either scatter thy thoughts or cleave thy heart, or take thee by thy feet and throw thee over to the other shore of the Gangâ.'
'I do not see, O friend, any one in this world nor in the world of

gods, Mâras, Brahmans, amongst the beings comprising gods, men, Samaṇas, and Brâhmaṇas, who can either scatter my thoughts or cleave my heart, or take me by the feet and throw me over to the other shore of the Ganġâ; however, O friend, ask what thou pleasest.'

Then the Yakkha Âḷavaka addressed Bhagavat in stanzas:

1. 'What in this world is the best property for a man? what, being well done, conveys happiness? what is indeed the sweetest of sweet things? how lived do they call life the best?'

2. Bhagavat said: 'Faith is in this world the best property for a man; Dhamma, well observed, conveys happiness; truth indeed is the sweetest of things; and that life they call the best which is lived with understanding.'

3. Âḷavaka said: 'How does one cross the stream (of existence)? how does one cross the sea? how does one conquer pain? how is one purified?'

4. Bhagavat said: 'By faith one crosses the stream, by zeal the sea, by exertion one conquers pain, by understanding one is purified.'

5. Âḷavaka said: 'How does one obtain understanding? how does one acquire wealth? how does one obtain fame? how does one bind friends (to himself)? how does one not grieve passing away from this world to the other?'

6. Bhagavat said: 'He who believes in the Dhamma of the venerable ones as to the acquisition of Nibbâna, will obtain understanding from his desire to hear, being zealous and discerning.

7. 'He who does what is proper, who takes the yoke (upon him and) exerts himself, will acquire wealth, by truth he will obtain fame, and being charitable he will bind friends (to himself).

8. 'He who is faithful and leads the life of a householder, and possesses the following four Dhammas (virtues), truth, justice (dhamma), firmness, and liberality, — such a one indeed does not grieve when passing away.

9. 'Pray, ask also other Samaṇas and Brâhmaṇas far and wide, whether there is found in this world anything greater than truth, self-restraint, liberality, and forbearance.'

10. Âlavaka said: 'Why should I now ask Samanas and Brâhmanas far and wide? I now know what is my future good.

11. 'For my good Buddha came to live at Âlavî; now I know where (i.e. on whom bestowed) a gift will bear great fruit.

12. 'I will wander about from village to village, from town to town, worshipping the perfectly enlightened (sambuddha) and the perfection of the Dhamma.'

Âlavakasutta is ended.

11 VIGAYASUTTA

A reflection on the worthlessness of the human body; a follower of Buddha only sees the body as it really is, and consequently goes to Nibbâna. — Comp. Gâtaka I,

1. If either walking or standing, sitting or lying, any one contracts (or) stretches (his body, then) this is the motion of the body.
2. The body which is put together with bones and sinews, plastered with membrane and flesh, and covered with skin, is not seen as it really is.
3. It is filled with the intestines, the stomach, the lump of the liver, the abdomen, the heart, the lungs, the kidneys, the spleen.
4. With mucus, saliva, perspiration, lymph, blood, the fluid that lubricates the joints, bile, and fat.
5. Then in nine streams impurity flows always from it; from the eye the eye-excrement, from the ear the ear-excrement,
6. Mucus from the nose, through the mouth it ejects at one time bile and (at other times) it ejects phlegm, and from (all) the body come sweat and dirt.
7. Then its hollow head is filled with the brain. A fool led by ignorance thinks it a fine thing.
8. And when it lies dead, swollen and livid, discarded in the cemetery, relatives do not care (for it).
9. Dogs eat it and jackals, wolves and worms; crows and vultures eat it, and what other living creatures there are.
10. The Bhikkhu possessed of understanding in this world, having listened to Buddha's words, he certainly knows it (i.e. the body) thoroughly, for he sees it as it really is.
11. "As this (living body is) so is that (dead one), as this is so that (will be); let one put away desire for the body, both as to its

interior and as to its exterior."

12. Such a Bhikkhu who has turned away from desire and attachment, and is possessed of understanding in this world, has (already) gone to the immortal peace, the unchangeable state of Nibbâna.

13. This (body) with two feet is cherished (although) impure, ill-smelling, filled with various kinds of stench, and trickling here and there.

14. He who with such a body thinks to exalt himself or despises others — what else (is this) but blindness?

Vigayasutta is ended.

12 MUNISUTTA

Definition of a Muni.

1. From acquaintanceship arises fear, from house-life arises defilement; the houseless state, freedom from acquaintanceship — this is indeed the view of a Muni.
2. Whosoever, after cutting down the (sin that has) arisen, does not let (it again) take root and does not give way to it while springing up towards him, him the solitarily wandering they call a Muni; such a great Isi has seen the state of peace.
3. Having considered the causes (of sin, and) killed the seed, let him not give way to desire for it; such a Muni who sees the end of birth and destruction (i.e. Nibbâna), after leaving reasoning behind, does not enter the number (of living beings).
4. He who has penetrated all the resting-places (of the mind, and) does not wish for any of them, — such a Muni indeed, free from covetousness and free from greediness, does not gather up (resting-places), for he has reached the other shore.
5. The man who has overcome everything, who knows everything, who is possessed of a good understanding, undefiled in all things (dhamma), abandoning everything, liberated in the destruction of desire (i.e. Nibbâna), him the wise style a Muni.
6. The man who has the strength of understanding, is endowed with virtue and (holy) works, is composed, delights in meditation, is thoughtful, free from ties, free from harshness (akhila), and free from passion, him the wise style a Muni.
7. The Muni that wanders solitarily, the zealous,
8. Whosoever becomes firm as the post in a bathing-place, in whom others acknowledge propriety of speech, who is free from passion, and (endowed) with well-composed senses, such a one

the wise style a Muni.

9. Whosoever is firm, like a straight shuttle, and is disgusted with evil actions, reflecting on what is just and unjust, him the wise style a Muni.

10. Whosoever is self-restrained and does not do evil, is a young or middle-aged Muni, self-subdued, one that should not be provoked (as) he does not provoke any, him the wise style a Muni.

11. Whosoever, living upon what is given by others, receives a lump of rice from the top, from the middle or from the rest (of the vessel, and) does not praise (the giver) nor speak harsh words, him the wise style a Muni.

12. The Muni that wanders about abstaining from sexual intercourse, who in his youth is not fettered in any case, is abstaining from the insanity of pride, liberated, him the wise style a Muni.

13. The man who, having penetrated the world, sees the highest truth, such a one, after crossing the stream and sea (of existence), who has cut off all ties, is independent, free from passion, him indeed the wise style a Muni.

14. Two whose mode of life and occupation are quite different, are not equal: a householder maintaining a wife, and an unselfish virtuous man. A householder (is intent) upon the destruction of other living creatures, being unrestrained; but a Muni always protects living creatures, being restrained.

15. As the crested bird with the blue neck (the peacock) never attains the swiftness of the swan, even so a householder does not equal a Bhikkhu, a secluded Muni meditating in the wood.

II KÛLAVAGGA

I RATANASUTTA

For all beings salvation is only to be found in Buddha, Dhamma, and Sa<u>n</u>gha. — Text and translation in Childers' Khuddaka Pâ<u>t</u>ha,

1. Whatever spirits have come together here, either belonging to the earth or living in the air, let all spirits be happy, and then listen attentively to what is said.
2. Therefore, O spirits, do ye all pay attention, show kindness to the human race who both day and night bring their offerings; therefore protect them strenuously.
3. Whatever wealth there be here or in the other world, or whatever excellent jewel in the heavens, it is certainly not equal to Tathâgata. This excellent jewel (is found) in Buddha, by this truth may there be salvation.
4. The destruction (of passion), the freedom from passion, the excellent immortality which Sakyamuni attained (being) composed, — there is nothing equal to that Dhamma. This excellent jewel (is found) in the Dhamma, by this truth may there be salvation.
5. The purity which the best of Buddhas praised, the meditation which they call uninterrupted, there is no meditation like this. This excellent jewel (is found) in the Dhamma, by this truth may there be salvation.
6. The eight persons that are praised by the righteous, and make these four pairs, they are worthy of offerings, (being) Sugata's disciples; what is given to these will bear great fruit. This excellent jewel (is found) in the Assembly (sa<u>n</u>gha), by this truth may there

be salvation.

7. Those who have applied themselves studiously with a firm mind and free from desire to the commandments of Gotama, have obtained the highest gain, having merged into immortality, and enjoying happiness after getting it for nothing. This excellent jewel (is found) in the Assembly, by this truth may there be salvation.

8. As a post in the front of a city gate is firm in the earth and cannot be shaken by the four winds, like that I declare the righteous man to be who, having penetrated the noble truths, sees (them clearly). This excellent jewel (is found) in the Assembly, by this truth may there be salvation.

9. Those who understand the noble truths well taught by the profoundly wise (i.e. Buddha), though they be greatly distracted, will not (have to) take the eighth birth. This excellent jewel (is found) in the Assembly, by this truth may there be salvation.

10. On his (attaining the) bliss of (the right) view three things (dhammas) are left behind (by him): conceit and doubt and whatever he has got of virtue and (holy) works. He is released also from the four hells, and he is incapable of committing the six

11. Even if he commit a sinful deed by his body, or in word or in thought, he is incapable of concealing it, (for) to conceal is said to be impossible for one that has seen the state (of Nibbâna). This excellent jewel (is found) in the Assembly, by this truth may there be salvation.

12. As in a clump of trees with their tops in bloom in the first heat of the hot month, so (Buddha) taught the excellent Dhamma leading to Nibbâna to the greatest benefit (for all). This excellent jewel (is found) in Buddha, by this truth may there be salvation.

13. The excellent one who knows what is excellent, who gives what is excellent, and who brings what is excellent, the incomparable one taught the excellent Dhamma. This excellent jewel (is found) in Buddha, by this truth may there be salvation.

14. The old is destroyed, the new has not arisen, those whose minds are disgusted with a future existence, the wise who have destroyed their seeds (of existence, and) whose desires do not

increase, go out like this lamp. This excellent jewel (is found) in the Assembly, by this truth may there be salvation.

15. Whatever spirits have come together here, either belonging to the earth or living in the air, let us worship the perfect (tathâgata) Buddha, revered by gods and men; may there be salvation.

16. Whatever spirits have come together here, either belonging to the earth or living in the air, let us worship the perfect (tathâgata) Dhamma, revered by gods and men; may there be salvatlon.

17. Whatever spirits have come together here, either belonging to the earth or living in the air, let us worship the perfect (tathâgata) Sa<u>n</u>gha, revered by gods and men; may there be salvation.

Ratanasutta is ended.

2 ÂMAGANDHASUTTA

A bad mind and wicked deeds are what defiles a man; no outward observances can purify him.

1. Âmagandhabrâhmana: 'Those who eat sâmâka, kingûlaka, and kînaka, pattaphala, mûlaphala, and gaviphala (different sorts of grass, leaves, roots, &c.), justly obtained of the just, do not speak falsehood, (nor are they) desirous of sensual pleasures.
2. 'He who eats what has been well prepared, well dressed, what is pure and excellent, given by others, he who enjoys food made of rice, eats, O Kassapa, Âmagandha (what defiles one).
3. '(The charge of) Âmagandha does not apply to me,' so thou sayest, 'O Brahman (brahmabandhu, although) enjoying food (made) of rice together with the well-prepared flesh of birds. I ask thee, O Kassapa, the meaning of this, of what description (is then) thy Âmagandha?'
4. Kassapabuddha: 'Destroying living beings, killing, cutting, binding, stealing, speaking falsehood, fraud and deception, worthless reading, intercourse with another's wife; — this is Âmagandha, but not the eating of flesh.
6. 'Those who are rough, harsh, backbiting, treacherous, merciless, arrogant, and (who being) illiberal do not give anything to any one; — this is Âmagandha, but not the eating of flesh.
7. 'Anger, intoxication, obstinacy, bigotry, deceit, envy, grandiloquence, pride and conceit, intimacy with the unjust; — this is Âmagandha, but not the eating of flesh.
8. 'Those who in this world are wicked, and such as do not pay their debts, are slanderers, false in their dealings, counterfeiters, those who in this world being the lowest of men commit sin; — this is Âmagandha, but not the eating of flesh.

9. 'Those persons who in this world are unrestrained (in their behaviour) towards living creatures, who are bent upon injuring after taking others' (goods), wicked, cruel, harsh, disrespectful; — this is Âmagandha, but not the eating of flesh.

10. 'Those creatures who are greedy of these (living beings, who are) hostile, offending; always bent upon (evil) and therefore, when dead, go to darkness and fall with their heads downwards into hell; — this is Âmagandha, but not the eating of flesh.

11. 'Neither the flesh of fish, nor fasting, nor nakedness, nor tonsure, nor matted hair, nor dirt, nor rough skins, nor the worshipping of the fire, nor the many immortal penances in the world, nor hymns, nor oblations, nor sacrifice, nor observance of the seasons, purify a mortal who has not conquered his doubt.

12. 'The wise man wanders about with his organs of sense guarded, and his senses conquered, standing firm in the Dhamma, delighting in what is right and mild; having overcome all ties and left behind all pain, he does not cling to what is seen and heard.'

13. Thus Bhagavat preached this subject again and again, (and the Brâhmana) who was accomplished in the hymns (of the Vedas) understood it; the Muni who is free from defilement, independent, and difficult to follow, made it clear in various stanzas.

14. Having heard Buddha's well-spoken words, which are free from defilement and send away all pain, he worshipped Tathâgata's (feet) in humility, and took orders at once.

Âmagandhasutta is ended.

3 HIRISUTTA

On true frendship.

1. He who transgresses and despises modesty, who says, 'I am a friend,' but does not undertake any work that can be done, know (about) him: 'he is not my (friend).'
2. Whosoever uses pleasing words to friends without effect, him the wise know as one that (only) talks, but does not do anything.
3. He is not a friend who always eagerly suspects a breach and looks out for faults; but he with whom he dwells as a son at the breast (of his mother),
4. He who hopes for fruit, cultivates the energy that produces joy and the pleasure that brings praise, (while) carrying the human yoke.
5. Having tasted the sweetness of seclusion and tranquillity one becomes free from fear and free from sin, drinking in the sweetness of the Dhamma.

Hirisutta is ended.

4 MAHÂMANGALASUTTA

Buddha defines the highest blessing to a deity. — Text by Grimblot in Journal Asiatique, t. xviii I), , and by Childers in Kh. Pâ*th*a, ; translation by Gogerly in the Ceylon Friend, 1839, ; by Childers in Kh. Pâ*th*a, ; and by L. Feer in Journal Asiatique, t. xviii I),

So it was heard by me:
At one time Bhagavat dwelt at Sâvatthî, in Getavana, in the park of Anâthapi*nd*ika. Then, when the night had gone, a deity of beautiful appearance, having illuminated the whole Getavana, approached Bhagavat, and having approached and saluted him, he stood apart, and standing apart that deity addressed Bhagavat in a stanza:
1. 'Many gods and men have devised blessings, longing for happiness, tell thou (me) the highest blessing.'
2. Buddha said: 'Not cultivating (the society of)
3. 'To live in a suitable country, to have done good deeds in a former (existence), and a thorough study of one's self, this is the highest blessing.
4. 'Great learning and skill, well-learnt discipline, and well-spoken words, this is the highest blessing.
5. 'Waiting on mother and father, protecting child and wife, and a quiet calling, this is the highest blessing.
6. 'Giving alms, living religiously, protecting relatives, blameless deeds, this is the highest blessing.
7. 'Ceasing and abstaining from sin, refraining from intoxicating drink, perseverance in the Dhammas, this is the highest blessing.
8. 'Reverence and humility, contentment and gratitude, the hearing of the Dhamma at due seasons, this is the highest

blessing.

9. 'Patience and pleasant speech, intercourse with Samaṇas, religious conversation at due seasons, this is the highest blessing.

10. 'Penance and chastity, discernment of the noble truths, and the realisation of Nibbâna, this is the highest blessing.

11. 'He whose mind is not shaken (when he is) touched by the things of the world (lokadhamma), (but remains) free from sorrow, free from defilement, and secure, this is the highest blessing.

12. 'Those who, having done such (things), are undefeated in every respect, walk in safety everywhere, theirs is the highest blessing.'

Mahâmaṅgala is ended.

5 SÛKILOMASUTTA

The Yakkha Sûkiloma threatens to harm Buddha, if he cannot answer his questions. Buddha answers that all passions proceed from the body.

So it was heard by me:
At one time Bhagavat dwelt at Gayâ (seated) on a stone seat in the realm of the Yakkha Sûkiloma. And at that time the Yakkha Khara and the Yakkha Sûkiloma passed by, not far from Bhagavat. And then the Yakkha Khara said this to the Yakkha Sûkiloma: 'Is this man a Samana?'
Sûkiloma answered: 'He is no Samana, he is a Samanaka (a wretched Samana); however I will ascertain whether he is a Samana or a Samanaka.'
Then the Yakkha Sûkiloma went up to Bhagavat, and having gone up to him, he brushed against Bhagavat's body. Then Bhagavat took away his body. Then the Yakkha Sûkiloma said this to Bhagavat: 'O Samana, art thou afraid of me?'
Bhagavat answered: 'No, friend, I am not afraid of thee, but thy touching me is sinful.'
Sûkiloma said: 'I will ask thee a question, O Samana; if thou canst not answer it I will either scatter thy thoughts or cleave thy heart, or take thee by the feet and throw thee over to the other shore of the Gangâ.'
Bhagavat answered: 'I do not see, O friend, neither in this world together with the world of the Devas, Mâras, Brahmans, nor amongst the generation of Samana and Brâhmanas, gods and men, the one who can either scatter my thoughts or cleave my heart, or take me by the feet and throw me over to the other shore of the Gangâ. However ask, O friend, what thou pleasest.' Then the

Yakkha Sûkiloma addressed Bhagavat in a stanza:

1. ' What origin have passion and hatred, disgust, delight, and horror? wherefrom do they arise? whence arising do doubts vex the mind, as boys vex a crow?'

2. Buddha said: 'Passion and hatred have their origin from this (body), disgust, delight, and horror arise from this body; arising from this (body) doubts vex the mind, as boys vex a crow.

3. 'They originate in desire, they arise in self, like the shoots of the banyan tree; far and wide they are connected, with sensual pleasures, like the mâluvâ creeper spread in the wood.

4. 'Those who know whence it (sin) arises, drive it away. Listen, O Yakkha! They cross over this stream that is difficult to cross, and has not been crossed before, with a view to not being born again.'

Sûkilomasutta is ended.

6 DHAMMAKARIYASUTTA OR KAPILASUTTA

The Bhikkhus are admonished to rid themselves of sinful persons and advised to lead a pure life.

1. A just life, a religious life, this they call the best gem, if any one has gone forth from house-life to a houseless life.
2. But if he be harsh-spoken, and like a beast delighting in injuring (others), then the life of such a one is very wicked, and he increases his own pollution.
3. A Bhikkhu who delights in quarrelling and is shrouded in folly, does not understand the Dhamma that is preached and taught by Buddha.
4. Injuring his own cultivated mind, and led by ignorance, he does not understand that sin is the way leading to hell.
5. Having gone to calamity, from womb to womb, from darkness to darkness, such a Bhikkhu verily, after passing away, goes to pain.
6. As when there is a pit of excrement (that has become) full during a number of years, — he who should be such a one full of sin is difficult to purify.
7. Whom you know to be such a one, O Bhikkhus, (a man) dependent on a house, having sinful desires, sinful thoughts, and being with sinful deeds and objects,
8. Him do avoid, being all in concord; blow him away as sweepings, put him away as rubbish.
9. Then remove as chaff those that are no Samanas, (but only) think themselves, blowing away those that have sinful desires and those with sinful deeds and objects.
10. Be pure and live together with the pure, being thoughtful; then agreeing (and) wise you will put an end to pain.
Dhammakariyasutta is ended.

7 BRÂHMAṆADMAMMIKASUTTA

Wealthy Brâhmaṇas come to Buddha, asking about the customs of the ancient Brâhmaṇas. Buddha describes their mode of life and the change wrought in them by seeing the king's riches, and furthermore, how they induced the king to commit the sin of having living creatures slain at sacrifices. On hearing Buddha's enlightened discourse the wealthy Brâhmaṇas are converted. Compare Sp. Hardy's Legends,

So it was heard by me:
At one time Bhagavat dwelt at Sâvatthî, in Getavana, in the park of Anâthapiṇḍika. Then many wealthy Brâhmaṇas of Kosala, decrepit, elderly, old, advanced in age, or arrived at extreme old age, went to Bhagavat, and having gone to him they talked pleasantly with him, and after having had some pleasant and remarkable talk with him, they sat down apart. Sitting down apart these wealthy Brâhmaṇas said this to Bhagavat: 'O venerable Gotama, are the Brâhmaṇas now-a-days seen (engaged) in the Brâhmanical customs (dhamma) of the ancient Brâhmaṇas?'
Bhagavat answered: 'The Brâhmaṇas now-a-days, O Brâhmaṇas, are not seen (engaged) in the Brâhmanical customs of the ancient Brâhmaṇas.'
The Brâhmaṇas said: 'Let the venerable Gotama tell us the Brâhmanical customs of the ancient Brâhmaṇas, if it is not inconvenient to the venerable Gotama.'
Bhagavat answered: 'Then listen, O Brâhmaṇas, pay great attention, I will speak.'
'Yes,' so saying the wealthy Brâhmaṇas listened to Bhagavat. Bhagavat said this:
1. The old sages (isayo) were self-restrained, penitent; having

abandoned the objects of the five senses, they studied their own welfare.

2. There were no cattle for the Brâhmaṇas, nor gold, nor corn, (but) the riches and corn of meditation were for them, and theey kept watch over the best treasure.

3. What was prepared for them and placed as food at the door, they thought was to be given to those that seek for what has been prepared by faith.

4. With garments variously coloured, with beds and abodes, prosperous people from the provinces and the whole country worshipped those Brâhmaṇas.

5. Inviolable were the Brâhmaṇas, invincible, protected by the Dhamma, no one opposed them (while standing) at the doors of the houses anywhere.

6. For forty-eight years they practised juvenile chastity, the Brâhmaṇas formerly went in search of science and exemplary conduct.

7. The Brâhmaṇas did not marry (a woman belonging to) another (caste), nor did they buy a wife; they chose living together in mutual love after having come together.

8. Excepting from the time about the cessation of the menstruation else the Brâhmaṇas did not indulge in sexual intercourse.

9. They praised chastity and virtue, rectitude, mildness, penance, tenderness, compassion, and patience.

10. He who was the best of them, a strong Brâhmaṇa, did not (even) in sleep indulge in sexual intercourse.

11. Imitating his practices some wise men in this world praised chastity and patience.

12. Having asked for rice, beds, garments, butter. and oil, and gathered them justly, they made sacrifices

13. Like unto a mother, a father, a brother, and other relatives the cows are our best friends, in which medicines are produced.

14. They give food, and they give strength, they likewise give (a good) complexion and happiness; knowing the real state of this, they did not kill cows.

15. They were graceful, large, handsome, renowned, Brâhmaṇas by nature, zealous for their several works; as long as they lived in the world, this race prospered.

16. But there was a change in them: after gradually seeing the king's prosperity and adorned women,

17. Well-made chariots drawn by noble horses, carpets in variegated colours, palaces and houses, divided into compartments and measured out,

18. The great human wealth, attended with a number of cows, and combined with a flock of beautiful women, the Brâhmaṇas became covetous.

19. They then, in this matter, having composed hymns, went to Okkâka, and said: 'Thou hast much wealth and corn, sacrifice thy great property, sacrifice thy great wealth.'

20. And then the king, the lord of chariots, instructed by the Brâhmaṇas, brought about assamedha, purisamedha, sammâpâsa, and vâkâpeyya without any hinderance, and having offered these sacrifices he gave the Brâhmaṇas wealth:

21. Cows, beds, garments, and adorned women, and well-made chariots, drawn by noble horses, carpets in variegated colours,

22. Beautiful palaces, well divided into compartments; and having filled these with different (sorts of) corn, he gave this wealth to the Brâhmaṇas.

23. And they having thus received wealth wished for a store, and the desire of those who had given way to (their) wishes increased still more; they then, in this matter, having composed hymns, went again to Okkâka, and said:

24. 'As water, earth, gold, wealth, and corn, even so are there cows for men, for this is a requisite for living beings; sacrifice thy great property, sacrifice thy wealth.'

25. And then the king, the lord of chariots, instructed by the Brâhmaṇas, caused many hundred thousand cows to be slain in offerings.

26. The cows, that are like goats, do not hurt any one with their feet or with either of their horns, they are tender, and yield vessels (of milk), — seizing them by the horns the king caused them to

be slain with a weapon.

27. Then the gods, the forefathers, Inda, the Asuras, and the Rakkhasas cried out: 'This is injustice,' because of the weapon falling on the cows.

28. There were formerly three diseases: desire, hunger, and decay, but from the slaying of cattle there came ninety-eight.

29. This injustice of (using) violence that has come down (to us), was old; innocent (cows) are slain, the sacrificing (priests) have fallen off from the Dhamma.

30. So this old and mean Dhamma is blamed by the wise; where people see such a one, they blame the sacrificing priest.

31. So Dhamma being lost, the Suddas and the Vessikas disagreed, the Khattiyas disagreed in manifold ways, the wife despised her husband.

32. The Khattiyas and the Brâhmanas and those others who had been protected by their castes, after doing away with their disputes on descent, fell into the power of sensual pleasures.

This having been said, those wealthy Brâhmanas said to Bhagavat as follows:

'It is excellent, O venerable Gotama! It is excellent, O venerable Gotama! As one raises what has been overthrown, or reveals what has been hidden, or tells the way to him who has gone astray, or holds out an oil lamp in the dark that those who have eyes may see the objects, even so by the venerable Gotama in manifold ways the Dhamma has been illustrated; we take refuge in the venerable Gotama, in the Dhamma, and in the Assembly of Bhikkhus; may the venerable Gotama receive us as followers (upâsaka), who from this day for life have taken refuge (in him).'

Brâhmanadhammikasutta is ended.

8 NÂVÂSUTTA

On choosing a good and learned teacher.

1. A man should worship him from whom he learns the Dhamma, as the gods (worship) Inda; the learned man being worshipped and pleased with him, makes the (highest) Dhamma manifest.
2. Having heard and considered that (Dhamma), the wise man practising the Dhamma that is in accordance with the (highest) Dhamma, becomes learned, expert, and skilful, strenuously associating with such a (learned teacher).
3. He who serves a low (teacher), a fool who has not understood the meaning, and who is envious, goes to death, not having overcome doubt, and not having understood the Dhamma.
4. As a man, after descending into a river, a turgid water with a rapid current, is borne along following the current, — how will he be able to put others across?
5. Even so how will a man, not having understood the Dhamma, and not attending to the explanation of the learned and not knowing it himself, not having overcome doubt, be able to make others understand it?
6. As one, having gone on board a strong ship, provided with oars and rudder, carries across in it many others, knowing the way to do it, and being expert and thoughtful,
7. So also he who is accomplished, of a cultivated mind, learned, intrepid, makes others endowed with attention and assiduity understand it, knowing (it himself).
8. Therefore indeed one should cultivate (the society of) a good man, who is intelligent and learned; he who leads a regular life, having understood what is good and penetrated the Dhamma, will obtain happiness.

Nâvâsutta is ended.

9 KIMSÎLASUTTA

How to obtain the highest good.

1. By what virtue, by what conduct, and performing what works, will a man be perfectly established (in the commandments) and obtain the highest good?
2. Let him honour old people, not be envious, let him know the (right) time for seeing his teachers, let him know the (right) moment for listening to their religious discourses, let him assiduously hearken to their well-spoken (words).
3. Let him in due time go to the presence of his teachers, let him be humble after casting away obstinacy, let him remember and practise what is good, the Dhamma, self-restraint, and chastity.
4. Let his pleasure be the Dhamma, let him delight in the Dhamma, let him stand fast in the Dhamma, let him know how to enquire into the Dhamma, let him not raise any dispute that pollutes the Dhamma, and let him spend his time in (speaking) well-spoken truths.
5. Having abandoned ridiculous talk, lamentation, corruption, deceit, hypocrisy, greediness and haughtiness, clamour and harshness, depravity and foolishness, let him live free from infatuation, with a steady mind.
6. The words, the essence of which is understood, are well spoken, and what is heard, if understood, contains the essence of meditation; but the understanding and learning of the man who is hasty and careless, does not increase.

Kimsîlasutta is ended.

10 U*TTH*ÂNASUTTA

Advice not to be lukewarm and slothful.

1. Rise, sit up, what is the use of your sleeping; to those who are sick, pierced by the arrow (of pain), and suffering, what sleep is there?
2. Rise, sit up, learn steadfastly for the sake of peace, let not the king of death, knowing you to be indolent (pamatta), befool you and lead you into his power.
3. Conquer this desire which gods and men stand wishing for and are dependent upon, let not the (right) moment pass by you; for those who have let the (right) moment pass, will grieve when they have been consigned to hell.
4. Indolence (pamâda) is defilement, continued indolence is defilement; by earnestness (appamâda) and knowledge let one pull out his arrow.

U*tth*ânasutta is ended.

II RÂHULASUTTA

Buddha recommends the life of a recluse to Râhula, and admonishes him to turn his mind away from the world and to be moderate.

1. Bhagavat said: 'Dost thou not despise the wise man, from living with him constantly? Is he who holds up a torch to mankind honoured by thee?'
2. Râhula: 'I do not despise the wise man, from living with him constantly; he who holds up a torch to mankind is always honoured by me.'
Vatthugâthâ.
3. Bhagavat: 'Having abandoned the objects of the five senses, the beautiful, the charming, and gone out from thy house with faith, do thou put an end to pain.
4. 'Cultivate (the society of) virtuous friends and a distant dwelling-place, secluded and quiet; be moderate in food.
5. 'Robes, alms (in bowl), requisites (for the sick), a dwelling-place, — do not thirst after these (things), that thou mayest not go back to the world again.
6. 'Be subdued according to the precepts, and as to the five senses, be attentive as regards thy body, and be full of disgust (with the world).
7. 'Avoid signs, what is pleasant and is accompanied with passion, turn thy mind undisturbed and well composed to what is not pleasant.
8. 'Cherish what is signless, leave the inclinations for pride; then by destroying pride thou shalt wander calm.'
So Bhagavat repeatedly admomshed the venerable Râhula with these stanzas.

Râhulasutta is ended.

12 VANGÎSASUTTA

Vangîsa desires to know the fate of Nigrodhakappa, whether he has been completely extinguished, or whether he is still with some elements of existence left behind. He is answered by Buddha.

So it was heard by me:
At one time Bhagavat dwelt at Aḷavî, in the temple of Aggâḷava. At that time the teacher of the venerable Vangîsa, the Thera, by name Nigrodhakappa, had attained bliss not long before (aḱiraparinibbuta). Then this reflection occurred to the venerable Vangîsa, while retired and meditating:
Whether my teacher be blessed (parinibbuta) or whether he be not blessed. Then the venerable Vangîsa, at the evening time, coming forth from his retirement went to Bhagavat, and having gone to him he sat down apart after saluting him, and sitting down apart the venerable Vangîsa said this to Bhagavat:
'Lord, while retired and meditating, this reflection occurred to me here: Whether my teacher be blessed or whether he be not blessed.'
Then the venerable Vangîsa, rising from his seat, throwing his robe over one shoulder and bending his joined hands towards Bhagavat, addressed him in stanzas:
1. 'We ask the Master of excellent understanding: he who in this world had cut off doubt, died at Aggâḷava, a Bhikkhu, well known, famous, and of a calm mind.
2. 'The name "Nigrodhakappa" was given to that Brâhmaṇa by thee, O Bhagavat; he wandered about worshipping thee, having liberation in view, strong, and seeing Nibbâna.
3. 'O Sakka, thou all-seeing, we all wish to learn (something about) this disciple; our ears are ready to hear, thou art our

Master, thou art incomparable.

4. 'Cut off our doubt, tell me of him, inform us of the blessed, O thou of great understanding; speak in the midst of us, O thou all-seeing, as the thousand-eyed Sakka (speaks in the midst) of the gods.

5. 'Whatever ties there are in this world (constituting) the way to folly, combined with ignorance, forming the seat of doubt, they do not exist before Tathâgata, for he is the best eye of men.

6. 'If a man does not for ever dispel the sin as the wind (dispels) a mass of clouds, all the world will be enveloped in darkness, not even illustrious men will shine.

7. 'Wise men are light-bringers, therefore, O wise man, I consider thee as such a one; we have come to him who beholds meditation, reveal Kappa to us in the assembly.

8. 'Uplift quickly, O thou beautiful one, thy beautiful voice, like the swans drawing up (their necks) sing softly with a rich and well-modulated voice; we will all listen to thee attentively.

9. 'Having earnestly called upon him who has completely left birth and death behind and shaken off (sin), I will make him proclaim the Dhamma, for ordinary people cannot do what they want, but the Tathâgatas act with a purpose.

11. ' Having perfectly comprehended the Dhamma of the venerable ones, do not delude (us), O thou of unsurpassed strength, knowing (everything); as one in the hot season pained by the heat (longs for) water, so I long for thy words; send a shower of learning.

12. 'The rich religious life which Kappâyana led, has not that been in vain (to him), has he been (completely) extinguished; or is he still with some elements of existence (left behind)? How he was liberated, that we want to hear.'

13. Bhagavat: 'He cut off the desire for name and form in this world,' — so said Bhagavat, — 'Ka*n*ha's (i.e. Mâra's) stream, adhered to for a long time, he crossed completely birth and death,' so said Bhagavat, the best of the five (Brâhma*n*as, pañkavaggiyâ).

14. Va*ng*îsa: 'Having heard thy word, O thou the best of the Isis,

311

I am pleased; not in vain have I asked, the Brâhmaṇa did not deceive me.

15. 'As he talked so he acted, he was a (true) disciple of Buddha, he cut asunder the outspread strong net of deceitful death.

16. 'Kappiya (Kappâyana) saw, O Bhagavat, the beginning of attachment, Kappâyana verily crossed the realm of death, which is very difficult to cross.'

Vangîsasutta is ended.

13 SAMMÂPARIBBÂGANIYASUTTA

The right path for a Bhikkhu.

1. 'We will ask the Muni of great understanding, who has crossed, gone to the other shore, is blessed (parinibbuta), and of a firm mind: How does a Bhikkhu wander rightly in the world, after having gone out from his house and driven away desire?'
2. 'He whose (ideas of) omens, meteors, dreams and signs are destroyed,' — so said Bhagavat, — 'such a Bhikkhu who has abandoned the sinful omens, wanders rightly in the world.
3. 'Let the Bhikkhu subdue his passion for human and divine pleasures, then after conquering existence and understanding the Dhamma, such a one will wander rightly in the world.
4. 'Let the Bhikkhu, after casting behind him slander and anger, abandon avarice and be free from compliance and opposition, then such a one will wander rightly in the world.
5. 'He who having left behind both what is agreeable and what is disagreeable, not seizing upon anything, is independent in every respect and liberated from bonds, such a one will wander rightly in the world.
6. 'He does not see any essence in the Upadhis, having subdued his wish and passion for attachments, he is independent and not to be led by others, such a one will wander rightly in the world.
7. 'He who is not opposed (to any one) in word, thought or deed, who, after having understood the Dhamma perfectly, longs for the state of Nibbâna, such a one will wander rightly in the world.
8. 'He who thinking "he salutes me" is not elated, the Bhikkhu who, although abused, does not reflect (upon it, and) having received food from others does not get intoxicated (with pride), such a one will wander rightly in the world.

9. 'The Bhikkhu who, after leaving behind covetousness and existence, is disgusted with cutting and binding (others), he who has overcome doubt, and is without pain, such a one will wander rightly in the world.

10. 'And knowing what becomes him, the Bhikkhu will not harm any one in the world, understanding the Dhamma thoroughly, such a one will wander rightly in the world.

11. 'He to whom there are no affections whatsoever, whose sins are extirpated from the root, he free from desire and not longing (for anything), such a one will wander rightly in the world.

12. 'He whose passions have been destroyed, who is free from pride, who has overcome all the path of passion, is subdued, perfectly happy (parinibbuta), and of a firm mind, such a one will wander rightly in the world.

13. 'The believer, possessed of knowledge, seeing

14. 'He who is pure and victorious, who has removed the veil (of the world), who is subdued in the Dhammas, has gone to the other shore, is without desire, and skilled in the knowledge of the cessation of the Samkhâras, such a one will wander rightly in the world.

15. 'He who has overcome time (kappâtîta) in the past and in the future, is of an exceedingly pure understanding, liberated from all the dwelling-places (of the mind), such a one will wander rightly in the world.

16. 'Knowing the step (of the four truths), understanding the Dhamma, seeing clearly the abandonment of the passions, destroying all the elements of existence (upadhî), such a one will wander rightly in the world.'

17. 'Certainly, O Bhagavat, it is so: whichever Bhikkhu lives in this way, subdued and having overcome all bonds, such a one will wander rightly in the world.'

Sammâparibbâganiyasutta is ended.

14 DHAMMIKASUTTA

Buddha shows Dhammika what the life of a Bhikkhu and what the life of a householder ought to be.

So it was heard by me:
At one time Bhagavat dwelt at Sâvatthî, in Getavana, in the park of Anâthapindika. Then the follower (upâsaka) Dhammika, together with five hundred followers, went to Bhagavat, and having gone to Bhagavat and saluted him, he sat down apart; sitting down apart the follower Dhammika addressed Bhagavat in stanzas:

1. 'I ask thee, O Gotama of great understanding, How is a Sâvaka (disciple) to act to be a good one? is it the one who goes from his house to the wilderness, or the followers with a house?

2. 'For thou knowest the doings of this world and that of the gods, and the final end; there is nobody like thee seeing the subtle meaning (of things); they call thee the excellent Buddha.

3. 'Knowing all knowledge thou hast revealed the Dhamma, having compassion on creatures; thou hast removed the veil (of the world), thou art all-seeing, thou shinest spotless in all the world.

4. 'The king of elephants, Erâvana by name, hearing that thou wert Gina (the Conqueror), came to thy presence, and having conversed with thee he went away delighted, after listening (to thee, and saying), "Very good!"

5. 'Also king Vessavana Kuvera came to ask thee about the Dhamma; him, too, thou, O wise man, answeredst when asked, and he also after listening was delighted.

6. 'All these disputatious Titthiyas and Âgivikas and Niganthas do not any of them overcome thee in understanding, as a man

standing (does not overcome) the one that is walking quickly.

7. 'All these disputatious Brâhmanas, and there are even some old Brâhmanas, all are bound by thy opinion, and others also that are considered disputants.

8. 'This subtle and pleasant Dhamma that has been well proclaimed by thee, O Bhagavat, and which we all long to hear, do thou, O thou best of Buddhas, speak to us when asked.

9. 'Let all these Bhikkhus and also Upâsakas that have sat down to listen, hear the Dhamma learnt (anubuddha) by the stainless (Buddha), as the gods (hear) the well-spoken (words) of Vâsava.'

10. Bhagavat: 'Listen to me, O Bhikkhus, I will teach you the Dhamma that destroys sin, do ye keep it, all of you; let him who looks for what is salutary, the thoughtful, cultivate the mode of life suitable for Pabbagitas.

11. 'Let not the Bhikkhu walk about at a wrong time, let him go to the village for alms at the right time; for ties ensnare the one that goes at a wrong time, therefore Buddhas do not go at a wrong time.

12. 'Form, sound, taste, smell, and touch which intoxicate creatures, having subdued the desire for (all) these things (dhammas), let him in due time go in for his breakfast.

13. 'And let the Bhikkhu, after having obtained his food at the right time and returned, sit down alone and privately; reflecting within himself let him not turn his mind to outward things, (but be) self-collected.

14. 'If he speak with a Sâvaka or with anybody else, or with a Bhikkhu, let him talk about the excellent Dhamma, (but let him) not (utter) slander, nor blaming words against others.

15. 'For some utter language contradicting others; those narrow-minded ones we do not praise. Ties

16. 'Let a Sâvaka of him with the excellent understanding (Buddha), after hearing the Dhamma taught by Sugata, discriminately seek for food, a monastery, a bed and a chair, and water for taking away the dirt of his clothes.

17. 'But without clinging to these things, to food, to bed and chair, to water for taking away the dirt of his clothes, let a

Bhikkhu be like a waterdrop on a lotus.

18. 'A householder's work I will also tell you, how a Sâvaka is to act to be a good one; for that complete Bhikkhu-dhamma cannot be carried out by one who is taken up by (worldly) occupations.

19. 'Let him not kill, nor cause to be killed any living being, nor let him approve of others killing, after having refrained from hurting all creatures, both those that are strong and those that tremble in the world.

20. 'Then let the Sâvaka abstain from (taking) anything in any place that has not been given (to him), knowing (it to belong to another), let him not cause any one to take, nor approve of those that take, let him avoid all (sort of) theft.

21. ' Let the wise man avoid an unchaste life as a burning heap of coals; not being able to live a life of chastity, let him not transgress with another man's wife.

22. 'Let no one speak falsely to another in the hall of justice or in the hall of the assembly, let him not cause (any one) to speak (falsely), nor approve of those that speak (falsely), let him avoid all (sort of) untruth.

23. 'Let the householder who approves of this Dhamma, not give himself to intoxicating drinks; let him not cause others to drink, nor approve of those that drink, knowing it to end in madness.

24. 'For through intoxication the stupid commit sins and make other people intoxicated; let him avoid this seat of sin, this madness, this folly, delightful to the stupid.

25. 'Let him not kill any living being, let him not take what has not been given (to him), let him not speak falsely, and let him not drink intoxicating drinks, let him refrain from unchaste sexual intercourse, and let him not at night eat untimely food.

26. 'Let him not wear wreaths nor use perfumes, let him lie on a couch spread on the earth: — this they call the eightfold abstinence (uposatha), proclaimed by Buddha, who has overcome pain.

27. 'Then having with a believing mind kept abstinence (uposatha) on the fourteenth, fifteenth, and the eighth days of the half-month, and (having kept) the complete Pâṅhârakapakkha

consisting of eight parts,

28. 'And then in the morning, after having kept abstinence, let a wise man with a believing mind, gladdening the assembly of Bhikkhus with food and drink, make distributions according to his ability.

29. 'Let him dutifully maintain his parents, and practise an honourable trade; the householder who observes this strenuously goes to the gods by name, Sayampabhas.'

II MAHÂVAGGA

I PABBA*GGÂ*SUTTA

King Bimbisâra feeling interested in Buddha tries to tempt him with wealth, but is mildly rebuked by Buddha.

1. I will praise an ascetic life such as the clearly-seeing (Buddha) led, such as he thinking (over it) approved of as an ascetic life.
2. ' This house-life is pain, the seat of impurity,' and 'an ascetic life is an open-air life,' so considering he embraced an ascetic life.
3. Leading an ascetic life, he avoided with his body sinful deeds, and having (also) abandoned sin in words, he cleansed his life.
4. Buddha went to Râgagaha, he entered the Giribbaga in Magadha for alms with a profusion of excellent signs.
5. Bimbisâra standing in his palace saw him, and seeing him endowed with these signs, he spoke these words:
6. 'Attend ye to this man, he is handsome, great, clean, he is both endowed with good conduct, and he does not look before him further than a yuga (the distance of a plough).
7. 'With downcast eyes, thoughtful, this one is not like those of low caste; let the king's messengers run off, (and ask): "Where is the Bhikkhu going?"'
8. The king's messengers followed after (him, and said): 'Where is the Bhikkhu going, where will he reside?
9. 'Going begging from house to house, watching the door (of the senses), well restrained, he quickly filled his bowl, conscious, thoughtful.
10. 'Wandering about in search of alms, having gone out of town, the Muni repaired to (the mountain) Pa*nd*ava; it must be there he lives.'

11. Seeing that he had entered his dwelling, the messengers then sat down, and one messenger having returned announced it to the king.

12. 'This Bhikkhu, O great king, is sitting on the east side of Pan*d*ava, like a tiger, like a bull, like a lion in a mountain cave.'

13. Having heard the messenger's words, the Khattiya in a fine chariot hastening went out to the Pan*d*ava mountain.

14. Having gone as far as the ground was practicable for a chariot, the Khattiya, after alighting from the chariot, and approaching on foot, having come up (to him), seated himself.

15. Having sat down the king then exchanged the usual ceremonious greetings with him, and after the complimentary talk he spoke these words:

16. 'Thou art both young and delicate, a lad in his first youth, possessed of a fine complexion, like a high-born Khattiya.

17. 'I will ornament the army-house, and at the head of the assembly of chiefs (nâga) give (thee) wealth; enjoy it and tell me thy birth, when asked.'

18. Buddha: 'Just beside Himavanta, O king, there lives a people endowed with the power of wealth, the inhabitants of Kosala.

19. 'They are Âdi*kk*as by family, Sâkiyas by birth; from that family I have wandered out, not longing for sensual pleasures.

20. 'Seeing misery in sensual pleasures, and considering the forsaking of the world as happiness, I will go and exert myself; in this my mind delights.'

Pabba*gg*âsutta is ended.

2 PADHÂNASUTTA

Mâra tries to tempt Buddha, but disappointed is obliged to withdraw. Comp. Gospel of S. Matthew iv.

1. To me, whose mind was intent upon exertion near the river Nerañgarâ, having exerted myself, and given myself to meditation for the sake of acquiring Nibbâna (yogakkhema),
2. Came Namuki speaking words full of compassion: 'Thou art lean, ill-favoured, death is in thy neighbourhood.
3. 'A thousandth part of thee (is the property) of death, (only) one part (belongs to) life; living life, O thou venerable one, is better; living thou wilt be able to do good works.
4. 'When thou livest a religious life, and feedest the sacrificial fire, manifold good works are woven to thee; what dost thou want with exertion?
5. 'Difficult is the way of exertion, difficult to pass, difficult to enter upon;' saying these verses Mâra stood near Buddha.
6. To Mâra thus speaking Bhagavat said this: 'O thou friend of the indolent, thou wicked one, for what purpose hast thou come here?
7. 'Even the least good work is of no use to me; and what good works are required, Mâra ought to tell.
8. 'I have faith and power, and understanding is found in me; while thus exerting myself, why do you ask me to live?
9. 'This (burning) wind will dry up even the currents of the rivers; should it not by degrees dry up my blood, while I am exerting myself?
10. 'While the blood is drying up, the bile and the phlegm are dried up; while the flesh is wasting away, the mind gets more tranquil, and my attention, understanding, and meditation get

more steadfast.

11. 'While I am living thus, after having felt the extreme sensations, my mind does not look for sensual pleasures; behold a being's purity.

12. 'Lust thy first army is called, discontent thy second, thy third is called hunger and thirst, thy fourth desire.

13. 'Thy fifth is called sloth and drowsiness, thy sixth cowardice, thy seventh doubt, thy eighth hypocrisy and stupor,

14. 'Gain, fame, honour, and what celebrity has

15. 'This, O Namuki, is thine, the black one's, fighting army; none but a hero conquers it, and after conquering it obtains joy.

16. 'Woe upon life in this world! death in battle is better for me than that I should live defeated.

17. 'Plunged into this world some Samanas and Brâmanas are not seen, and they do not know the way in which the virtuous walk.

18. 'Seeing on all sides an army arrayed, and Mâra on his elephant, I am going out to do battle, that he may not drive me away from my place.

19. 'This army of thine, which the world of men and gods cannot conquer, I will crush with understanding as (one crushes) an unbaked earthen pot with a stone.

20. 'Having made my thought subject to me and my attention firm, I shall wander about from kingdom to kingdom, training disciples extensively.

21. 'They (will be) zealous and energetic, executing my orders, (the orders) of one free from lust, and they will go (to the place) where, having gone, they will not mourn.'

22. Mâra: 'For seven years I followed Bhagavat step by step; I found no fault in the perfectly enlightened, thoughtful (Buddha).

24. 'Having obtained nothing sweet there, the crow went away from that spot. Thus like the crow approaching the rock, being disgusted, we shall go away from Gotama.'

25. While overcome with sorrow the string of his lute slipped down; then that evil-minded Yakkha disappeared there.

Padhânasutta is ended.

3 SUBHÂSITASUTTA

On well-spoken language.

So it was heard by me:
At one time Bhagavat dwelt at Sâvatthî in *G*etavana. Bhagavat said this: 'O Bhikkhus, the speech that is provided with four requisites is well-spoken, not ill-spoken, both faultless and blameless to the wise.'
'Which four?'
'O Bhikkhus, the Bhikkhu speaks well-spoken (language), not ill-spoken; he speaks what is right (dhamma), not what is unrighteous (adhamma); he speaks what is pleasing, not what is unpleasing; he speaks what is true, not what is false. O Bhikkhus, the speech that is provided with these four requisites, is well-spoken, not ill-spoken, both faultless

4 SUNDARIKABHÂRADVÂGASUTTA

Buddha shows to Sundarikabhâradvâga on whom to bestow oblations, and the Brâma*n*a is finally converted.

So it was heard by me:
At one time Bhagavat dwelt in Kosala on the bank of the river Sundarikâ. And during that time the Brâma*n*a Sundarikabhâradvâga made offerings to the fire and worshipped the fire. Then the Brâma*n*a Sundarikabhâradvâga, having made offerings to the fire and worshipped the fire, and having risen from his seat, looked about him on all sides towards the four quarters of the globe, saying: 'Who is to enjoy the rest of this oblation?' The Brâma*n*a Sundarikabhâradvâga saw Bhagavat sitting not far off at the root of a tree, wrapped up head and body; and seeing him he, after taking the rest of the oblation with his left hand and the waterpot with his right hand, went up to Bhagavat. Then Bhagavat, on hearing the footsteps of Sundarikabhâradvâga, the Brâma*n*a, uncovered his head. Then the Brâhma*n*a Sundarikabhâradvâga thought: 'This man is shaved, this man is a shaveling,' and he wished to return again from there. Then this came to the mind of Sundarikabhâradvâga, the Brâma*n*a: 'Some Brâma*n*as also here are shaved, I think I shall go up and ask him about his descent.' Then the Brâhma*n*a Sundarikabhâradvâga went up to Bhagavat, and having gone up he said this: 'Of what family art thou?'
Then Bhagavat answered Sundarikabhâradvâga, the Brâma*n*a, in stanzas:

1. 'No Brâma*n*a am I, nor a king's son, nor any Vessa; having thoroughly observed the class of common people, I wander about the world reflectingly, possessing nothing.

2. 'Dressed in a sanghâṭi and houseless I wander about, with my hair cut off, calm, not intermixing with people in this world. Thou askest me an unseasonable question about (my) family, O Brâhmaṇa!'

3. Sundarikabhâradvâga: 'Sir, Brâmaṇas together with Brâmaṇas ask truly, Art thou a Brâhmaṇa?'

Bhagavat: 'If thou sayest, I am a Brâmaṇa, and callest me no Brâmaṇa, then I ask thee about the Sâvitti that consists of three padas and twenty-four syllables.'

4. Sundarikabhâradvâga: 'For what (reason) did the Isis, men, Khattiyas, Brâmaṇas make offerings to the gods abundantly in this world?'

Bhagavat: 'He who, perfect and accomplished at the time of offering, obtains the ear of one or the other (god), he will succeed, so I say.'

5. 'Surely his offering will bear fruit,' — so said the Brâmaṇa, — 'because we saw such an accomplished man; for by not seeing such as you, somebody else will enjoy the oblation.'

6. Bhagavat: 'Therefore, O Brâmaṇa, as you have come here to ask for something, ask; perhaps thou mightest here find one that is calm, without anger, free from pain, free from desire, one with a good understanding.'

8. Bhagavat: 'Therefore, O Brâmaṇa, lend me thy ear, I will teach thee the Dhamma.

9. 'Do not ask about descent, but ask about conduct; from wood, it is true, fire is born; (likewise) a firm Muni, although belonging to a low family, may become noble, when restrained (from sinning) by humility.

10. 'He who is subdued by truth, endowed with temperance, accomplished, leading a religious life, on such a one in due time people should bestow oblations; let the Brâmaṇa who has good works in view, offer.

11. 'Those who, after leaving sensual pleasures, wander about houseless, well restrained, being like a straight shuttle, on such in due time people should bestow oblations; let the Brâmaṇa who has good works in view, offer.

12. 'Those whose passions are gone, whose senses are well composed, who are liberated like the moon out of the grasp of Râhu, on such in due time people should bestow oblations; let the Brâmana who has good works in view, offer.

13. 'Those who wander about in the world without clinging (to anything), always thoughtful, having left selfishness, on such in due time people should bestow oblations; let the Brâmana who has good works in view, offer.

14. 'He who, after leaving sensual pleasures, wanders about victorious, he who knows the end of birth and death, who is perfectly happy (parinibbuta), calm like a deep water, Tathâgata deserves the oblation.

15. 'Just with the just and far from the unjust, Tathâgata is possessed of infinite understanding; undefiled both in this world and in the other, Tathâgata deserves the oblation.

16. 'He in whom there lives no deceit, no arrogance, he who is free from cupidity, free from selfishness, free from desire, who has banished anger, who is calm, the Brâmana who has removed the taint of grief, Tathâgata deserves the oblation.

17. 'He who has banished (every) resting-place of the mind, he for whom there is no grasping, he who covets nothing either in this world or in the other, Tathâgata deserves the oblation.

18. 'He who is composed, who has crossed over the stream (of existence) and knows the Dhamma by (taking) the highest view (of it), he whose passions are destroyed, who is wearing the last body, Tathâgata deserves the oblation.

19. 'He whose passion for existence and whose harsh talk are destroyed, are perished, (and therefore) exist not, he the accomplished and in every respect liberated Tathâgata deserves the oblation.

20. 'He who has shaken off all ties, for whom there are no ties, who amongst arrogant beings is free from arrogance, having penetrated pain together with its domain and subject, Tathâgata deserves the oblation.

21. 'He who, without giving himself up to desire, sees seclusion (i.e. Nibbâna), who has overcome the view that is to be taught by

others, to whom there

22. 'He to whom all Dhammas of every description, after he has penetrated them, are destroyed, are perished, (and therefore) exist not, he who is calm, liberated in the destruction of attachment (i.e. Nibbâna), Tathâgata deserves the oblation.

23. 'He who sees the destruction of bond and birth, who has totally evaded the path of passion, (who is) pure, faultless, spotless, undepraved, Tathâgata deserves the oblation.

24. 'He who does not measure himself by himself, who is composed, upright, firm, without desire, free from harshness (akhila), free from doubt, Tathâgata deserves the oblation.

25. 'He to whom there is no cause of folly, who has a supernatural insight in all Dhammas, who wears the last body, and who has acquired perfect enlightenment, the highest, the blessed, (for him) thus a Yakkha's purification (takes place).'

26. Sundarikabhâradvâga: 'May my offering be a true offering, because I met with such a one out of the accomplished; Brahman is my witness, may Bhagavat accept me, may Bhagavat enjoy my oblation.'

27. Bhagavat: 'What is obtained by stanzas is not to be enjoyed by me, this is not the custom of the clearly-seeing, O Brâmana; Buddhas reject what is obtained by stanzas. While the Dhamma

28. 'With other food and drink must thou serve one that is perfect, a great Isi, whose passions are destroyed, and whose misbehaviour has ceased, for this is a field for one who looks for good works.'

29. Sundarikabhâradvâga: 'Good, O Bhagavat, then I should like to know, who will enjoy a gift from one like me, and whom I shall seek at the time of sacrifice (as one worthy of offerings) after having accepted thy doctrine.'

30. Bhagavat: 'Whosoever has no quarrels, whose mind is untroubled, and who has freed himself from lusts, whose sloth is driven away,

31. 'Whosoever conquers his sins, knows birth and death, the Muni who is endowed with wisdom, such a one who has resorted to offering,

32. 'Him you should worship and honour with food and drink; so the gifts will prosper.'

33. Sundarikabhâradvâga: 'Thou Buddha deservest the oblation, (thou art) the best field for good works, the object of offering to all the world; what is given to thee will bear great fruit.'

Then the Brâmaṅa Sundarikabhâradvâga said this to Bhagavat: 'It is excellent, O venerable Gotama! It is excellent, O venerable Gotama! As one raises what has been overthrown, or reveals what has been hidden, or tells the way to him who has gone astray, or holds out an oil lamp in the dark that those who have eyes may see the objects, even so by the venerable Gotama in manifold ways the Dhamma has been illustrated; I take refuge in

The Brâmaṅa Sundarikabhâradvâga received the pabbaggâ from Bhagavat, and he received also the upasampadâ; and the venerable Bhâradvâga, having lately received the upasampadâ, leading a solitary, retired, strenuous, ardent, energetic life, lived after having in a short time in this existence by his own understanding ascertained and possessed himself of that highest perfection of a religious life for the sake of which men of good family rightly wander away from their houses to a houseless state. 'Birth had been destroyed, a religious life had been led, what was to be done had been done, there was nothing else (to be done) for this existence,' so he perceived, and the venerable Bhâradvâga became one of the arahats.

Sundarikabhâradvâgasutta is ended.

5 MÂGHASUTTA

Buddha on being asked tells Mâgha of those worthy of offerings and the blessing of offering.

So it was heard by me:
At one time Bhagavat dwelt at Râgagaha, in the mountain (called) the Vulture's Peak (Gigghakûta).
Then the young man Mâgha went to Bhagavat, and having gone to him he talked pleasantly with him, and after having had some pleasant, remarkable conversation with him he sat down apart; sitting down apart the young man Mâgha spoke this to Bhagavat: 'O venerable Gotama, I am a liberal giver, bountiful, suitable to beg of; justly I seek for riches, and having sought for riches justly, I give out of the justly obtained and justly acquired riches to one, to two, to three, to four, to five, to six, to seven, to eight, to nine, to ten, to twenty, to thirty, to forty, to fifty, to a hundred, I give still more. (I should like to know), O venerable Gotama, whether I, while so giving, so offering, produce much good.'
'Certainly, O young man, dost thou in so offering produce much good; he, O young man, who is a liberal giver, bountiful, suitable to beg of, and who justly seeks for riches, and having sought for riches justly, gives out of his justly obtained and justly acquired riches to one, to two, to three, to four, to five, to six, to seven, to eight, to nine, to ten, to twenty, to thirty, to forty, to fifty, to a hundred, and gives still more, produces much good.'
Then the young man Mâgha addressed Bhagavat in stanzas:
1. 'I ask the venerable Gotama, the bountiful,' — so said the young man Mâgha, — 'wearing the yellow robe, wandering about houseless:' 'He who is a householder, suitable to beg of, a donor, who, desirous of good, offers having what is good in view, and

giving to others in this world food and drink, — where (i.e. on whom bestowed) will the oblation of such an offerer prosper?'

2. 'He who is a householder, suitable to beg of, a donor, O Mâgha,' — so said Bhagavat, — 'who, desirous of good, offers having what is good in view, and giving to others in this world food and drink, such a one will prosper with those worthy of offerings.'

3. 'He who is a householder, suitable to beg of, a donor,' — so said the young man, — 'who, desirous of good, offers having what is good in view, and giving to others in this world food and drink, — tell me (I being such a one), O Bhagavat, of those worthy of offerings.'

4. Bhagavat: 'Those indeed who wander about in the world without clinging to anything and without possessing anything, perfect, self-restrained, on such in due time people should bestow oblations; let the Brâhma*n*a who has good (works) in view, offer.

5. 'Those who have cut through all bonds and fetters, who are subdued, liberated, free from pain, and free from desire, on such in due time people should bestow oblations; let the Brâma*n*a who has good (works) in view, offer.

6. 'Those who are released from all bonds, who are subdued, liberated, free from pain, and free from desire on such in due time people should bestow oblations; let the Brâma*n*a who has good (works) in view, offer.

7. 'Those who, having forsaken both passion and hatred and folly, have destroyed their desires and lead a religious life, on such in due time people should bestow oblations; let the Brâhma*n*a who has good (works) in view, offer.

8. 'Those in whom there lives no deceit, no arrogance, who are free from cupidity, free from selfishness, free from desire, on such in due time people should bestew oblations; let the Brâma*n*a who has good (works) in view, offer.

9. 'Those indeed who without being lost in desire,

10. 'Those in whom there is no desire for anything in the world, nor for existence after existence here or in the other world, on such in due time people should bestow oblations; let the Brâma*n*a

who has good (works) in view, offer.

11. 'Those who, after leaving sensual pleasures, wander about houseless, well restrained, being like a straight shuttle, on such in due time people should bestow oblations; let the Brâmana who has good (works) in view, offer.

12. 'Those whose passions are gone, whose senses are well composed, who are liberated like the moon out of the grasp of Râhu, on such in due time people should bestow oblations; let the Brâhmana who has good (works) in view, offer.

13. 'Those who are calm, whose passions are gone, who are without anger, and for whom there is no transmigration after having left here, on such in due time people should bestow oblations; let the Brâhmana who has good (works) in view, offer.

14. 'Those who, after leaving birth and death altogether, have conquered all doubt, on such in due time people should bestow oblations; let the Brâmana who has good (works) in view, offer.

15. 'Those who wander about in the world with themselves for a light, not possessed of anything, in every respect liberated, on such in due time people should bestow oblations; let the Brâmana who has good (works) in view, offer.

16. 'Those who in this world rightly understand this: "This is the last (birth), there is no re-birth," on such in due time people should bestow oblations; let the Brâmana who has good (works) in view, offer.

17. 'He who is accomplished, and delights in meditation, thoughtful, possessed of thorough enlightenment, a refuge for many, on such a one in due time people should bestow oblations; let the Brâhmana who has good (works) in view, offer.'

18. 'Certainly my question was not in vain, Bhagavat has told me of those worthy of offerings; for thou truly knowest this in this world, as surely to thee this Dhamma is known.

19. 'He who is a householder, suitable to beg of, a donor,' — so said the young man Mâgha, — 'who, desirous of good, offers having what is good in view, and giving to others in this world food and drink, — tell me (I being such a one), O Bhagavat, of the blessing of offering.'

20. 'Offer, O Mâgha,' — so said Bhagavat, — 'and while offering make calm thy mind in all things; the object of the one that offers is the oblation, standing fast in this he leaves hatred behind.

21. 'Such a one whose passion is gone will repress hatred, cultivating an unbounded friendly mind; continually strenuous night and day he will spread infinite goodness through all regions.'

22. Mâgha: 'Who prospers? who is liberated and who is bound? In which way can one by himself go to Brahmaloka? Tell this to me who does not know, O Muni, when asked. Bhagavat is indeed my witness that Brahman is seen by me to-day, for thou art to us equal to Brahman, this is the truth; how can one attain Brahmaloka, O thou glorious one?'

23. 'He who offers the threefold blessing of oblation, O Mâgha,' — so said Bhagavat, — 'such a one will prosper with those worthy of offerings; so, having offered properly, he who is suitable to beg of attains Brahmaloka, so I say.'

This having been said, Mâgha the young man spoke as follows to Bhagavat: 'Excellent, O venerable Gotama! Excellent, O venerable Gotama! As one raises what has been overthrown, or reveals what has been hidden, or tells the way to him who has gone astray, or holds out an oil lamp in the dark that those who have eyes may see the objects, even so by the venerable Gotama in manifold ways the Dhamma has been illustrated; I take refuge in the venerable Gotama and in the Dhamma and in the Assembly of Bhikkhus. Let the venerable Gotama accept me as an upâsaka (a follower, me), who henceforth for all my life have taken refuge (in him).'

Mâghasutta is ended.

6 SABHIYASUTTA

Sabhiya, the Paribbâgaka, goes to the six famous teachers of his time to have his questions answered, but not having his doubts solved, he repairs to Gotama and asks him how one is to behave to become a Brâmana, a Samana, a Nahâtaka, a Khettagina, a Kusala, a Pandita, a Muni, a Vedagû, an Anuvidita, a Dhîra, an Âgâniya, a Sottiya, an Ariya, a Karanavat, a Paribbâgaka. Bhagavat answers his questions, and Sabhiya finally receives the robe and the orders from Buddha.

So it was heard by me:
At one time Bhagavat dwelt at Râgagaha, in Veluvana, in Kalandakanivâpa. And at that time questions were recited to Sabhiya, the Paribbâgaka (wandering mendicant), by an old benevolent deity: 'He who, O Sabhiya, be it a Samana or a Brâmana, explains these questions to thee when asked, near him thou shouldst live a religious life.'
Then Sabhiya, the Paribbâgaka, having learnt the questions from that deity, went to whatever Samanas and Brâmanas there were that had an assembly (of Bhikkhus), a crowd (of followers), and were well-known teachers, famous leaders, considered excellent by the multitude, as Pûrana-Kassapa, Makkhali-Gosâla, Agita-Kesakambali, Pakudha-Kakkâyana, Sañgaya-Belatthiputta, and Nigantha-Nâtaputta. Those he went to, and after going to them, he asked the questions. They, being asked the questions by Sabhiya, the Paribbâgaka, did not succeed (in answering them), and not succeeding, they showed wrath and hatred and discontent, and they also in return put questions to Sabhiya, the Paribbâgaka.
Then this came to the mind of Sabhiya, the Paribbâgaka:

'Whatever Samaṇas and Brāmaṇas there are that have an assembly (of Bhikkhus), a crowd (of followers), and are well-known teachers, famous leaders, considered excellent by the multitude, as Pûraṇa-Kassapa, Makkhali-Gosâla, Agita-Kesakambali, Pakudha-Kakkâyana, Sañgaya-Belaṭṭhiputta, and Nigaṇṭha-Nâtaputta, they, being asked questions by me, did not succeed (in answering them), and not succeeding they showed wrath and hatred and discontent, and they also in return put questions to me in this matter; surely I think I shall go back to what I have left, and enjoy sensual pleasures.'

Then this came to the mind of Sabhiya, the Paribbâgaka: 'This Samaṇa Gotama has both an assembly (of Bhikkhus) and a crowd (of followers), and is a well-known teacher, a famous leader, considered excellent by the multitude, surely I think I shall go to Samaṇa Gotama and ask these questions.' Then this came to the mind of Sabhiya, the Paribbâgaka: 'Whatever Samaṇas and Brâhmaṇas there are that are decayed, old, aged, advanced in years, having reached old age, experienced elders, long ordained, having assemblies (of Bhikkhus), crowds (of followers), being teachers well-known, famous leaders, considered excellent by the multitude, as Pûraṇa-Kassapa, Makkhali-Gosâla, Agita-Kesakambali, Pakudha-Kakkâyana, Sañgaya-Belaṭṭhiputta, and Nigaṇṭha-Nâtaputta, they, being asked questions by me, did not succeed (in answering them), and not succeeding they showed wrath and hatred and discontent, and they also in return put questions to me in this matter; (I should like to know) whether Samaṇa Gotama being asked these questions will be able to explain them to me, for Samaṇa Gotama is both young by birth and new in ascetic life.'

Then this came to the mind of Sabhiya, the Paribbâgaka: 'Samaṇa Gotama is not to be slighted because he is young; even if the Samaṇa is young, yet he is mighty and powerful; surely I think I shall go to Samaṇa Gotama and ask these questions.' Then Sabhiya, the Paribbâgaka, went on a journey to Râgagaha, and wandering on his journey in regular order he came to Râgagaha, Veḷuvana, Kalandakanivâpa, to Bhagavat, and having come to

Bhagavat he talked pleasantly with him, and after having had some pleasant and remarkable conversation with him he sat down apart; sitting down apart Sabhiya, the Paribbâgaka, spoke to Bhagavat in stanzas:

1. 'Anxious and doubtful I have come,' — so said Sabhiya, — 'longing to ask questions. Do thou put an end to these (doubts when) asked these questions by me, in regular order, and rightly explain them to me.'

2. 'Thou hast come from afar, O Sabhiya,' — so said Bhagavat, — 'longing to ask questions; I shall put an end to those (doubts when) asked those questions by thee, in regular order, and rightly I shall explain them to thee.

3. 'Ask me, O Sabhiya, a question; whatsoever thou wishest in thy mind that question I (will explain, and) put an end to (thy doubt).'

Then this came to the mind of Sabhiya, the Paribbâgaka: 'It is marvellous, it is wonderful indeed, the reception which I did not get from other Samaṇas and Brâhmaṇas has been given me by Gotama,' so saying he glad, rejoicing, delighted, and highly elated asked Bhagavat a question:

4. 'What should a man (necessarily) have obtained that people may call him a Bhikkhu?' — so said Sabhiya, — 'how may they call him compassionate, and how subdued? how can he be called enlightened (buddha)? Asked (about this) do thou, Bhagavat, explain it to me.'

5. 'He who by the path he has himself made, O Sabhiya,' — so said Bhagavat, — 'has attained to perfect happiness, who has conquered doubt, who lives after having left behind both gain and goods, who has destroyed re-birth, he is a Bhikkhu.

6. 'Always resigned and attentive, he will not hurt any one in all the world, the Samaṇa who has crossed the stream (of existence, and is) untroubled; for whom there are no desires (ussada), he is compassionate.

7. 'He whose senses are trained internally and externally in all the world, he who after penetrating this and the other world longs for death, being trained, he is subdued.

8. 'Whosoever, after having considered all times (kappa), the revolution (saṃsâra), both the vanishing and re-appearance (of beings), is free from defilement, free from sin, is pure, and has obtained destruction of birth, him they call enlightened (buddha).'

Then Sabhiya, the Paribbâgaka, having approved of and rejoiced at the words of Bhagavat, glad, rejoicing, delighted, highly elated, asked Bhagavat another question:

9. 'What should a man (necessarily) have obtained that people may call him a Brâmaṇa?' — so said Sabhiya, — 'and how (may they call him) a Samaṇa? and how a Nahâtaka? how can he be called a Nâga? Asked (about this) do thou Bhagavat explain it to me.'

10. 'He who, after removing all sins, O Sabhiya,' — so said Bhagavat, — 'is immaculate, well composed, firm-minded, perfect after crossing the Saṃsâra, such an independent one is called a Brâmaṇa.

11. 'He who is calm, having left behind good and evil, free from defilement, having understood this and the other world, and conquered birth and death, such a one is called a Samaṇa by being so.'

12. 'Whosoever, after having washed away all sins internally and externally in all the world, does

13. 'He who does not commit any crime in the world, who, after abandoning all bonds and fetters, clings to nothing, being liberated, such a one is called a Nâga (sinless) by being so.'

Then Sabhiya, the Paribbâgaka, having approved of and rejoiced at the words of Bhagavat, glad, rejoicing, delighted, highly elated, further asked Bhagavat a question:

14. 'Whom do the Buddhas call a Khettagina?' — so said Sabhiya, — 'how (can they call any one) a Kusala? and how a Paṇḍita? how can he be called a Muni? Asked (about this) do thou Bhagavat explain it to me.'

15. 'He who, after examining all regions, O Sabhiya,' — so said Bhagavat, — 'the divine and the human, and Brahman's region, is delivered from the radical bond of all regions, such a one is called

a Khettagina (he who has conquered the regions) by being so.

16. 'He who, after examining all treasures, the divine and the human, and Brahman's treasure, is delivered from the radical bond of all treasures, such a one is called a Kusala (happy) by being so.

17. 'He who, after examining both kinds of senses, internally and externally, is endowed with a

18. 'He who, having understood the Dhamma of the just and the unjust, internally and externally, in all the world, is to be worshipped by gods and men, he, after breaking through the net of ties, is called a Muni (sage).'

Then Sabhiya, the Paribbâgaka, having approved of and rejoiced at the words of Bhagavat, glad, rejoicing, delighted, highly elated, further asked Bhagavat a question:

19. 'What should one (necessarily) have obtained that people may call him Vedagû?' — so said Sabhiya, — 'and how (may they call him) Anuvidita? and how Viriyavat? How does one become Âgâniya? Asked (about this) do thou, O Bhagavat, explain it to me.'

20. 'He who, having conquered all sensations, O Sabhiya,' — so said Bhagavat, — 'which are (known) to Sama*n*as and to Brâma*n*as, is free from passion for all sensations, he is Vedagû (having passed sensation) after conquering all sensation.

21. 'He who, having seen the delusion of name and form, internally and externally, the root of sickness, and is delivered from the radical bond of all sickness, such a one is called Anuvidita (well-informed) by being so.

22. 'He who is disgusted in this world with all sins, is strong after conquering the pain of hell, is strong and powerful, such a one is called Dhîra (= viriyavat, firm) by being so.

Then Sabhiya, the Paribbâgaka, having approved of and rejoiced at the words of Bhagavat, glad, rejoicing, delighted, highly elated, further asked Bhagavat a question:

24. 'What should a man (necessarily) have obtained that people may call him a Sottiya?' — so said Sabhiya, — 'how (may they call him) an Ariya? and how a Kara*n*avat? how may he become a Paribbâgaka? Asked (about this) do thou, O Bhagavat, explain it

to me.'

25. 'Whosoever, after having heard and understood every Dhamma in the world, O Sabhiya,' — so said Bhagavat, — 'whatsoever is wrong and whatsoever is blameless, is victorious, free from doubt, liberated, free from pain in every respect, him they call a Sottiya (learned in the revelation).

26. 'Whosoever, after having cut off passions and desires, is wise and does not (again) enter the womb, having driven away the threefold sign, the mud (of lust), and who does not (again) enter time (kappa), him they call an Ariya (noble).

27. 'He who in this world, after having attained the (highest) gain in the *Kara*n*as*, is skilful, has always understood the Dhamma, clings to nothing, is liberated, and for whom there are no passions, he is a *Kara*n*avat* (endowed with the obsrvances).

28. 'Whosoever abstains from the action that has a painful result, above and below and across and in

Then Sabhiya, the Paribbâgaka, having approved of and rejoiced at the words of Bhagavat, glad, rejoicing, delighted, highly elated, having risen from his seat, and having put his upper robe upon one shoulder, bending his joined hands towards Bhagavat, praised Bhagavat face to face in appropriate stanzas:

29. 'Having conquered the three and sixty (philosophical) views referring to the disputations of the *Sama*n*as*, thou hast crossed over the darkness of the stream. (?)

30. 'Thou hast passed to the end of and beyond pain, thou art a saint, perfectly enlightened, I consider thee one that has destroyed his passions, thou art glorious, thoughtful, of great understanding, O thou who puts an end to pain, thou hast carried me across.

31. 'Because thou sawest my longing, and carriedst me across my doubt, adoration be to thee, O Muni, who hast attained the (highest) gain in the ways of wisdom; O thou who art a true kinsman of the Âdi*kk*as, thou art compassionate.

32. 'The doubt I had before thou hast cleared away for me, O thou clearly-seeing; surely thou art a Muni, perfectly enlightened, there is no obstacle for thee.

34. 'All gods and both Nârada and Pabbata rejoice at thee, the

chief of the sinless (nâganâga), the great hero, when thou art speaking.

35. 'Adoration be to thee, O noble man, adoration be to thee, O thou best of men; in the world of men and gods there is no man equal to thee.

36. 'Thou art Buddha, thou art the Master, thou art the Muni that conquers Mâra; after having cut off desire thou hast crossed over and hast carried across this generation.

37. 'The elements of existence (upadhi) are overcome by thee, the passions are destroyed by thee, thou art a lion, free from desire, thou hast left behind fear and terror.

38. 'As a beautiful lotus does not adhere to the water, so thou dost not cling to good and evil, to either; stretch forth thy feet, O hero, Sabbiya worships the Master's (feet).'

Then Sabhiya, the Paribbâgaka, stooping with his head to Bhagavat's feet, said this to Bhagavat:

'It is excellent, O venerable! It is excellent, O venerable! As one raises what has been overthrown, or reveals what has been hidden, or tells the way to him who has gone astray, or holds out an oil lamp in the dark that those who have eyes may see the objects, even so by the venerable Gotama in manifold ways the Dhamma has been illustrated; I take refuge in the venerable Gotama, in the Dhamma, and in the Assembly of Bhikkhus; I wish to receive the robe and the orders from the venerable Bhagavat.'

'He who, O Sabhiya, formerly belonging another creed (aññatitthiyapubba), wishes to be adopted into this religion (dhammavinaya), and wishes to receive the robe and the orders, he serves for four months; after the lapse of four months Bhikkhus who have appeased their thoughts will give him the robe and the orders to become a Bhikkhu, (for) I also in this matter acknowledge difference of persons.'

'If, O venerable, those that formerly belonged to another creed and wish to be adopted into this religion and to receive the robe and the orders, serve for four months, and after the lapse of four months Bhikkhus who have appeased their thoughts give them the robe and the orders that they may become Bhikkhus, I will (also) serve for four months, and after the lapse of four months Bhikkhus who have appeased their thoughts shall give (me) the robe and the orders that I may become a Bhikkhu.'

Sabhiya, the Paribbâgaka, received the robe and the orders from Bhagavat, and the venerable Sabhiya, having lately received the upasampadâ, leading a solitary, retired, strenuous, ardent, energetic life, lived after having in a short time in this existence by his own understanding ascertained and possessed himself of that highest perfection of a religious life for the sake of which men of good family rightly wander away from their houses to a houseless state. 'Birth had been destroyed, a religious life had been led, what was to be done had been done, there was nothing else (to be done) for this existence,' so he perceived, and the venerable Sabhiya became one of the saints.

Sabhiyasutta is ended.

7 SELASUTTA

Keniya, the Gatila, invites Buddha with his assembly to take his meals with him on the morrow. Sela, the Brâmana, arrived at that place with his three hundred young men; seeing the preparations he asks what is going on, and is answered that Buddha is expected the next day. On hearing the word 'Buddha,' Sela asks where Buddha lives, goes to him, converses with him, and is converted; so are his followers.

So it was heard by me:
At one time Bhagavat wandering about in Anguttarâpa, with a large assembly of Bhikkhus, with 1250 Bhikkhus, went to Âpana, a town in Anguttarâpa.
And Keniya, the ascetic, with matted hair (gatila) heard the following: 'The Samana, the venerable Gotama, the Sakya son, gone out from the family of the Sakyas, wandering about in Anguttarâpa with a large assembly of Bhikkhus, with 1250 Bhikkhus, has reached Âpana, and the following good praising words met the venerable Gotama: "And so he is Bhagavat, the venerable, the perfectly enlightened, endowed with science and works (viggâkarana), the happy, knowing the world, the incomparable, the charioteer of men that are to be subdued, the master, the enlightened of gods and men, the glorious; he teaches this world and the world of gods, of Mâras, of Brahmans, and beings comprising Samanas and Brâmanas, gods and men, having himself known and seen them face to face; he teaches the Dhamma (which is) good in the beginning, in the middle, and in the end, is full of meaning and rich in words, quite complete; he teaches a religious life, and good is the sight of such saints."'
Then Keniya, the Gatila, went (to the place) where Bhagavat was,

and having gone there he talked pleasantly with him, and after having had some pleasant and remarkable conversation (with him) he sat down apart; and while Keniya, the Gatila, was sitting down apart, Bhagavat, by religious talk, taught, advised, roused, and delighted him. Then Keniya, the Gatila, having been taught, advised, roused, and delighted by Bhagavat through religious talk, said this to Bhagavat:

'Let the venerable Gotama accept my food tomorrow, together with the assembly of Bhikkhus.'

This having been said, Bhagavat answered Keniya, the Gatila: 'Large, O Keniya, is the assembly of Bhikkhus, one thousand two hundred and fifty Bhikkhus, and thou art intimate with the Bramanas.'

A second time Keniya, the Gatila, said this to Bhagavat: 'Although, O venerable Gotama, the assembly of Bhikkhus is large, one thousand two hundred and fifty Bhikkhus, and I am intimate with the Brâmanas, let the venerable Gotama accept my food to-morrow, together with the assembly of Bhikkhus.'

A second time Bhagavat said this to Keniya, the Gatila: 'Large, O Keniya, is the assembly of Bhikkhus, one thousand two hundred and fifty Bhikkhus, and thou art intimate with the Brâmanas.'

A third time Keniya, the Gatila, said this to Bhagavat: 'Although, O venerable Gotama, the assembly of Bhikkhus is large, one thousand two hundred and fifty Bhikkhus, and I am intimate with the Brâhmanas, yet let the venerable Gotama accept my food to-morrow, together with the assembly of Bhikkhus.' Bhagavat assented by being silent. Then Keniya, the Gatila, having learnt the assent of Bhagavat, after rising from his seat went to his hermitage, and having gone there he addressed his friends and servants, his relatives and kinsmen (as follows): 'Let my venerable friends and servants, relatives and kinsmen hear me; — the Samana Gotama has been invited by me to (take his) food (with me) to-morrow, together with the assembly of Bhikkhus; wherefore you must render me bodily service.'

'Surely, O venerable one,' so saying the friends and servants, relatives and kinsmen of Keniya, the Gatila, complying with his request, some of them dug fireplaces, some chopped firewood, some washed the vessels, some placed waterpots, some prepared seats. Keṇiya, the Gaṭila, on the other hand, himself provided a circular pavilion.

At that time the Brâmaṇa Sela lived at Âpaṇa, perfect in the three Vedas, vocabulary, Keṭubha, etymology, Itihâsa as the fifth (Veda), versed in metre, a grammarian, one not deficient in popular controversy and the signs of a great man, he taught three hundred young men the hymns. At that time Keṇiya, the Gaṭila, was intimate with the Brâhmaṇa Sela. Then the Brâmaṇa Sela surrounded by three hundred young men, walking on foot, arrived at the place where the hermitage of Keṇiya, the Gaṭila, was. And the Brâmaṇa Sela saw the Gaṭilas in Keṇiya's hermitage, some of them digging fireplaces, some chopping firewood, some washing the vessels, some placing waterpots, some preparing seats, and Keṇiya, the Gaṭila, on the other hand, himself providing a circular pavilion; seeing Keṇiya, the Gaṭila, he said this: 'Is the venerable Keṇiya to celebrate the marriage of a son or the marriage of a daughter, or is there a great sacrifice at hand, or has Bimbisâra, the king of Magadha, who has a large body of troops, been invited for to-morrow, together with his army?'

'I am not to celebrate the marriage of a son or the marriage of a daughter, nor has Bimbisâra, the king of Magadha, who has a large body of troops, been invited for to-morrow, together with his army, yet a great sacrifice of mine is at hand. The Samaṇa Gotama, the Sakya son, gone out from the Sakya family, wandering about in Aṇguttarâpa with a large assembly of Bhikkhus, one thousand two hundred and fifty Bhikkhus, has reached Âpaṇa, and the following good praising words met the venerable Gotama: "And so he is Bhagavat, the venerable, the perfectly enlightened, endowed with science and works (viggâkaraṇa), the happy, knowing the world, the incomparable, the charioteer of men that are to be subdued, the master, the enlightened of gods and men, the glorious, he has been invited by me for to-morrow, together with the assembly of Bhikkhus."'

'Didst thou say that he is a Buddha, O venerable Keṇiya?'

'Yes, I say, O venerable Sela, that he is a Buddha.'
'Didst thou say that he is a Buddha, O venerable Keniya?',
'Yes, I say, O venerable Sela, that he is a Buddha.'
Then this occurred to the Brâhmana Sela: 'This sound "Buddha" is (indeed) rare, but in our hymns are to be found the thirty-two signs of a great man, and for a great man endowed with these there are two conditions, and no more: if he lives in a house he is a king, a universal (king), a just religious king, a lord of the four-cornered (earth), a conqueror, one who has obtained the security of his people (and) is possessed of the seven gems. These are his seven gems, namely, the wheel gem, the elephant gem, the horse gem, the pearl gem, the woman gem, the householder gem, and the chief gem as the seventh. He has more than a thousand sons, heroes, possessing great bodily strength and crushing foreign armies; he having conquered this ocean-girt earth without a rod and without a weapon, but by justice, lives (in a house). But if, on the other hand, he goes out from (his) house to the houseless state, he becomes a saint, a perfectly enlightened, one who has removed the veil in the world. And where, O venerable Keniya, dwells now that venerable Gotama, the saint and the perfectly enlightened?'
This having been said, Keniya, the Gatila, stretching out his right arm, spoke as follows to the Brâmana Sela: 'There, where yon blue forest line is, O venerable Sela.'
Then the Brâmana Sela together with (his) three hundred young men went to the place where Bhagavat was. Then the Brâmana Sela addressed those young men: 'Come ye, venerable ones, with but little noise, walking step by step, for Bhagavats are difficult of access, walking alone like lions, and when I speak to the venerable Samana Gotama, do ye not utter interrupting words, but wait ye venerable ones, for the end of my speech.'
Then the Brâmana Sela went to the place where Bhagavat was, and having gone there he talked pleasantly with Bhagavat, and after having had some pleasant and remarkable conversation with him he sat down apart, and while sitting down apart Sela, the Brâhmana, looked for the thirty-two signs of a great man on the

body of Bhagavat. And the Brâmaṇa Sela saw the thirty-two signs of a great man on the body of Bhagavat with the exception of two; in respect to two of the signs of a great man he had doubts, he hesitated, he was not satisfied, he was not assured as to the member being enclosed in a membrane and as to his having a large tongue.

Then this occurred to Bhagavat: 'This Brâmaṇa Sela sees in me the thirty-two signs of a great man with the exception of two, in respect to two of the signs of a great man he has doubts, he hesitates, he is not satisfied, he is not assured as to the member being enclosed in a membrane, and as to my having a large tongue.' Then Bhagavat created such a miraculous creature that the Brâmaṇa Sela might see Bhagavat's member enclosed in a membrane. Then Bhagavat having put out his tongue touched and stroked both his ears, touched and stroked both nostrils, and the whole circumference of his forehead he covered with his tongue.

Then this occurred to the Brâhmaṇa Sela: 'The Samaṇa Gotama is endowed with the thirty-two signs of a great man, with them all, not with (only) some of them, and yet I do not know whether he is a Buddha or not; I have heard old and aged Brâhmaṇas, teachers and their previous teachers, say that those who are saints and perfectly enlightened manifest themselves when their praise is uttered. I think I shall praise the Samaṇa Gotama face to face in suitable stanzas.' Then the Brâmaṇa Sela praised Bhagavat face to face in suitable stanzas:

1. 'Thou hast a perfect body, thou art resplendent, well-born, of beautiful aspect, thou hast a golden colour, O Bhagavat, thou hast very white teeth, thou art strong.

2. 'All the signs that are for a well-born man, they are on thy body, the signs of a great man.

3. 'Thou hast a bright eye, a handsome countenance, thou art great, straight, majestic, thou shinest like a sun in the midst of the assembly of the Samaṇas.

4. 'Thou art a Bhikkhu of a lovely appearance, thou hast a skin like gold; what is the use of being a Samaṇa to thee who art possessed of the highest beauty?

5. 'Thou deservest to be a king, a king of universal kings, a ruler of the four-cornered (earth), a conqueror, a lord of the jambu grove (i.e. India).

6. 'Khattiyas and wealthy kings are devoted to thee; rule, O Gotama, as a king of kings, a leader of men.'

7. 'I am a king, O Sela,' — so said Bhagavat, — 'an incomparable, religious king (dhammarâgan), with justice (dhammena) I turn the wheel, a wheel that is irresistible.'

8. 'Thou acknowledgest thyself (to be) perfectly enlightened (sambuddha),' — so said Sela, the Brâhmana, — 'an incomparable, religious king; "with justice I turn the wheel," so thou sayest, O Gotama. '

10. 'The wheel turned by me, O Sela,' — so said Bhagavat, — 'the incomparable wheel of religion, Sâriputta is to turn after (me), he taking after Tathâgata.

11. 'What is to be known is known (by me), what is to be cultivated is cultivated (by me), what is to be left is left by me, therefore I am a Buddha, O Brâmana.

12. 'Subdue thy doubt about me, have faith (in me), O Brâmana, difficult (to obtain) is the sight of Buddhas repeatedly.

13. 'Of those whose manifestation is difficult for you (to obtain) in the world repeatedly, I am, O Brâmana, a perfectly enlightened, an incomparable physician,

14. 'Most eminent, matchless, a crusher of Mâra's army; having subjected all enemies I rejoice secure on every side.'

15. Sela: 'O venerable ones, pay attention to this: as the clearly-seeing (Buddha) says, (so it is): he is a physician, a great hero, and roars like a lion in the forest.

16. 'Who, having seen him, the most eminent, the matchless, the crusher of Mâra's army, is not appeased, even if he be, of black origin (kanhâbhigâtika).

17. 'He who likes me, let him follow after (me), he who does not like me, let him go away; I shall at once take the orders in the presence of him of excellent understanding (i.e. Buddha).'

18. The followers of Sela: 'If this doctrine of the perfectly enlightened pleases thee, we also shall take the orders in the

presence of him of excellent understanding.'

19. These three hundred Brâma*n*as asked with clasped hands (to be admitted into the order): 'We want to cultivate a religious life, O Bhagavat, in thy presence.'

20. 'A religious life is well taught (by me), O Sela,' — so said Bhagavat, — 'an instantaneous, an immediate (life), in which it is not in vain to become an ascetic to one who learns in earnest.'

Then the Brâma*n*a Sela together with his assembly took the robe and the orders in the presence of Bhagavat.

Then Ke*n*iya, the Ga*t*ila, by the expiration of that night, having provided in his hermitage nice hard food and soft food, let Bhagavat know the time (of the meal): 'It is time, O venerable Gotama, the meal is prepared.' Then Bhagavat in the morning, having put on his raiment and taken his bowl and robes, went to the Ga*t*ila Ke*n*iya's hermitage, and having gone there he sat down on the prepared seat, together with the assembly of Bhikkhus. Then Ke*n*iya, the Ga*t*ila, satisfied and served with his own hands the assembly of Bhikkhus, with Buddha at their head, with nice hard food and soft food. Then Ke*n*iya, the Ga*t*ila, having gone up to Bhagavat who had finished eating and had taken his hand out of the bowl, took a low seat and sat down apart, and while Ke*n*iya, the Ga*t*ila, was sitting down apart, Bhagavat delighted him with these stanzas:

21. 'The principal thing in sacrifice is the sacred fire, the principal thing amongst the hymns is the Sâvitti, the king is the principal amongst men, and the sea the principal amongst waters (nadîna*m*).

22. 'Amongst the stars the moon is the principal thing, the sun is the principal thing amongst the burning (objects), amongst those that wish for good works and make offerings the assembly (sa*m*gha) indeed is the principal.'

Then Bhagavat, having delighted Ke*n*iya, the Ga*t*ila, with these stanzas, rose from (his) seat and went away.

Then the venerable Sela together with his assembly leading a solitary, retired, strenuous, ardent, energetic life, lived after having in a short time in this existence by his own understanding ascertained and possessed himself of that highest perfection of a religious life for the sake of which men of good family rightly wander away from their houses to a houseless state; 'birth (had been) destroyed, a religious life (had been) led, what was to be done (had been) done, there was nothing else (to be done) for this existence,' so he perceived, and the venerable Sela together with his assembly became one of the saints.

Then the venerable Sela together with his assembly went to Bhagavat, and having gone (to him) he put his upper robe on one shoulder, and bending his joined hands towards Bhagavat he addressed him in stanzas:

24. 'Thou art Buddha, thou art the Master, thou art the Muni that conquered Mâra, thou hast, after cutting off the affections, crossed over (the stream of existence) and taken over these beings.

25. 'The elements of existence (upadhi) have been overcome by thee, the passions have been destroyed by thee, thou art a lion not seizing on anything, thou hast left behind fear and danger.

26. 'These three hundred Bhikkhus stand here with clasped hands; stretch out thy feet, O hero, let the Nâgas worship the Master's feet.'

Selasutta is ended.

8 SALLASUTTA

Life is short, all mortals are subject to death, but knowing the terms of the world the wise do not grieve, and those who have left sorrow will be blessed. — Text in the Dasaratha-Gâtaka,.

1. Without a cause and unknown is the life of mortals in this world, troubled and brief, and combined with pain.
2. For there is not any means by which those that have been born can avoid dying; after reaching old age there is death, of such a nature are living beings.
3. As ripe fruits are early in danger of falling, so mortals when born are always in danger of death.
4. As all earthen vessels made by the potter end in being broken, so is the life of mortals.
5. Both young and grown-up men, both those who are fools and those who are wise men, all fall into the power of death, all are subject to death.
6. Of those who, overcome by death, go to the other world, a father does not save his son, nor relatives their relations.
7. Mark! while relatives are looking on and lamenting greatly, one by one of the mortals is carried off, like an ox that is going to be killed.
8. So the world is afflicted with death and decay, therefore the wise do not grieve, knowing the terms of the world.
9. For him, whose way thou dost not know, either when he is coming or when he is going, not seeing both ends, thou grievest in vain.
10. If he who grieves gains anything, (although he is only) a fool hurting himself, let the wise man do the same.
11. Not from weeping nor from grieving will any one obtain

peace of mind; (on the contrary), the greater his pain will be, and his body will suffer.

12. He will be lean and pale, hurting himself by himself, (and yet) the dead are not saved, lamentation (therefore) is of no avail.

13. He who does not leave grief behind, goes (only) deeper into pain; bewailing the dead he falls into the power of grief.

14. Look at others passing away, men that go (to what they deserve) according to their deeds, beings trembling already here, after falling into the power of death.

15. In whatever manner people think (it will come to pass), different from that it becomes, so great is the disappointment (in this world); see, (such are) the terms of the world.

16. Even if a man lives a hundred years or even more, he is at last separated from the company of his relatives, and leaves life in this world.

17. Therefore let one, hearing (the words of) the saint, subdue his lamentation; seeing the one that has passed away and is dead, (let him say): 'He will not be found by me (any more).'

18. As a house on fire is extinguished by water, so also the wise, sensible, learned, clever man rapidly drives away sorrow that has arisen, as the wind a tuft of cotton.

19. He who seeks his own happiness should draw out his arrow (which is) his lamentation, and complaint, and grief.

20. He who has drawn out the arrow and is not dependent (on anything) will obtain peace of mind; he who has overcome all sorrow will become free from sorrow, and blessed (nibbuta).

Sallasutta is ended.

9 VÂSE*TTH*ASUTTA

A dispute arose between two young men, Bhâradvâga and Vâse*tth*a, the former contending man to be a Brâma*n*a by birth, the latter by deeds. They agreed to go and ask Sama*n*a Gotama, and he answered that man is a Brâma*n*a by his work only. The two young men are converted. — Text (from Ma*gghi*manikâya) and translation in Alwis's Buddhist Nirvâna,.

So it was heard by me:
At one time Bhagavat dwelt at I*kkh*âna*m*kala, in the I*kkh*âna*m*kala forest. At that time many distinguished, wealthy Brâma*n*as lived at I*kkh*âna*m*kala, as the Brâma*n*a *Kam*kin, the Brâma*n*a Târukkha, the Brâma*n*a Pokkharasâti, the Brâhmana *G*ânusso*n*i, the Brâma*n*a Todeyya, and other distinguished, wealthy Brâma*n*as.
Then this dialogue arose between the young men Vâsettha and Bhâradvâga while walking about:
'How does one become a Brâma*n*a?'
The young man Bhâradvâga said: 'When one is noble by birth on both sides, on the mother's and on the father's side, of pure conception up to the seventh generation of ancestors, not discarded and not reproached in point of birth, in this way one is a Brâma*n*a.'
The young man Vâse*tth*a said: 'When one is virtuous and endowed with (holy) works, in this way he is a Brâma*n*a.'
Neither could the young man Bhâradvâga convince the young man Vâse*tth*a, nor could the young man Vâse*tth*a convince the young man Bhâradvâga. Then the young man Vâse*tth*a addressed the young man Bhâradvâga: 'O Bhâradvâga, this Sama*n*a Gotama, the Sakya son, gone out from the Sakya family, dwells at

I*kkh*âna*m*kala, in the forest of I*kkh*âna*m*kala, and the following good praising words met the venerable Gotama: "And so he is Bhagavat, the venerable, the enlightened, the glorious, let us go, O venerable Bhâradvâ*g*a, let us go (to the place) where the Sama*n*a Gotama is, and having gone there let us ask the Sama*n*a Gotama about this matter, and as the Sama*n*a Gotama replies so will we understand it.'"

'Very well, O venerable one;' so the young man Bhâradvâ*g*a answered the young man Vâse*tth*a. Then the young men Vâse*tth*a and Bhâradvâ*g*a went (to the place) where Bhagavat was, and having gone, they talked pleasantly with Bhagavat, and after having had some pleasant and remarkable conversation (with him) they sat down apart. Sitting down apart the young man Vâse*tth*a addressed Bhagavat in stanzas:

1. 'We are accepted and acknowledged masters of the three Vedas, I am (a pupil) of Pokkharasâti, and this young man is (the pupil) of Târukkha.

2. 'We are accomplished in all the knowledge propounded by those who are acquainted with the three Vedas, we are padakas (versed in the metre), veyyâkara*n*as (grammarians?), and equal to our teachers in recitation (*g*appa).

3. 'We have a controversy regarding (the distinctions of) birth, O Gotama! Bhâradvâ*g*a says, one is a Brâma*n*a by birth, and I say, by deeds; know this, O thou clearly-seeing!

4. 'We are both unable to convince each other, (therefore) we have come to ask thee (who art) celebrated as perfectly enlightened.

5. 'As people adoring the full moon worship (her) with uplifted clasped hands, so (they worship) Gotama in the world.

6. 'We ask Gotama who has come as an eye to the world: Is a man a Brâhma*n*a by birth, or is he so by deeds? Tell us who do not know, that we may know a Brâma*n*a.'

7. 'I will explain to you, O Vâse*tth*a,' — so said Bhagavat, — 'in due order the exact distinction of living beings according to species, for their species are manifold.

8. 'Know ye the grass and the trees, although they do not exhibit

(it), the marks that constitute species are for them, and (their) species are manifold.

9. 'Then (know ye) the worms, and the moths, and the different sorts of ants, the marks that constitute species are for them, and (their) species are manifold.

10. 'Know ye also the four-footed (animals), small and great, the marks that constitute species are for them, and (their) species are manifold.

11. 'Know ye also the serpents, the long-backed snakes, the marks that constitute species are for them, and (their) species are manifold.

12. 'Then know ye also the fish which range in the water, the marks that constitute species are for them, and (their) species are manifold.

13. 'Then know ye also the birds that are borne along on wings and move through the air, the marks that constitute species are for them, and (their) species are manifold.

14. 'As in these species the marks that constitute species are abundant, so in men the marks that constitute species are not abundant.

15. 'Not as regards their hair, head, ears, eyes, mouth, nose, lips, or brows,

16. 'Nor as regards their neck, shoulders, belly, back, hip, breast, female organ, sexual intercourse,

17. 'Nor as regards their hands, feet, palms, nails, calves, thighs, colour, or voice are there marks that constitute species as in other species.

18. 'Difference there is in beings endowed with bodies, but amongst men this is not the case, the difference amongst men is nominal (only).

19. 'For whoever amongst men lives by cowkeeping, — know this, O Vâse*ttha*, — he is a husbandman, not a Brâma*n*a.'

20. 'And whoever amongst men lives by different mechanical arts, — know this, O Vâse*ttha*, — he is an artisan, not a Brâma*n*a.

21. 'And whoever amongst men lives by trade, — know this, O Vâse*ttha*, — he is a merchant, not a Brâma*n*a.

22. And whoever amongst men lives by serving others, — know this, O Vâse*ttha*, — he is a servant, not a Brâhma*na*.

23. 'And whoever amongst men lives by theft, — know this, O Vâse*ttha*, — he is a thief, not a Brâhma*na*.

24. 'And whoever amongst men lives by archery, — know this, O Vâse*ttha*, — he is a soldier, not a Brâma*na*.

25. 'And whoever amongst men lives by performing household ceremonials, — know this, O Vâse*ttha*, — he is a sacrificer, not a Brâma*na*.

26. 'And whoever amongst men possesses villages and countries, — know this, O Vâse*ttha*, — he is a king, not a Brâma*na*.

27. 'And I do not call one a Brâma*na* on account of his birth or of his origin from (a particular) mother; he may be called bhovâdi, and he may be wealthy, (but) the one who is possessed of nothing and seizes upon nothing, him I call a Brâhma*na*.

28. 'Whosoever, after cutting all bonds, does not tremble, has shaken off (all) ties and is liberated, him I call a Brâma*na*.

29. 'The man who, after cutting the strap (i.e. enmity), the thong (i.e. attachment), and the rope (i.e. scepticism) with all that pertains to it, has destroyed (all) obstacles (i.e. ignorance), the enlightened (buddha), him I call a Brâma*na*.

30. 'Whosoever, being innocent, endures reproach, blows, and bonds, the man who is strong in (his) endurance and has for his army this strength, him I call a Brâma*na*.

31. 'The man who is free from anger, endowed with (holy) works, virtuous, without desire, subdued, and wearing the last body, him I call a Brâhma*na*.

32. 'The man who, like water on a lotus leaf, or a mustard seed on the point of a needle, does not cling to sensual pleasures, him I call a Brâhma*na*.

33. 'The man who knows in this world the destruction of his pain, who has laid aside (his) burden, and is liberated, him I call a Brâma*na*.

34. 'The man who has a profound understanding, who is wise, who knows the true way and the wrong way, who has attained the highest good, him I call a Brâma*na*.

35. 'The man who does not mix with householders nor with the houseless, who wanders about without a house, and who has few wants, him I call a Brâhmana.

36. 'Whosoever, after refraining from hurting (living) creatures, (both) those that tremble and those that are strong, does not kill or cause to be killed, him I call a Brâmana.

37. 'The man who is not hostile amongst the hostile, who is peaceful amongst the violent, not seizing (upon anything) amongst those that seize (upon everything), him I call a Brâmana.

38. 'The man whose passion and hatred, arrogance and hypocrisy have dropt like a mustard seed from the point of a needle, him I call a Brâmana.

39. 'The man that utters true speech, instructive and free from harshness, by which he does not offend any one, him I call a Brâmana.

40. 'Whosoever in the world does not take what has not been given (to him), be it long or short, small or large, good or bad, him I call a Brâhmana.

41. 'The man who has no desire for this world or the next, who is desireless and liberated, him I call a Brâmana.

42. 'The man who has no desire, who knowingly is free from doubt; and has attained the depth of immortality, him I call a Brâmana.

43. 'Whosoever in this world has overcome good and evil, both ties, who is free from grief and defilement, and is pure, him I call a Brâmana.

44. 'The man that is stainless like the moon, pure, serene, and undisturbed, who has destroyed joy, him I call a Brâmana.

45. 'Whosoever has passed over this quagmire difficult to pass, (who has passed over) revolution (samsâra) and folly, who has crossed over, who has reached the other shore, who is meditative, free from desire and doubt, calm without seizing (upon anything), him I call a Brâmana.

46. 'Whosoever in this world, after abandoning sensual pleasures, wanders about houseless, and has destroyed the existence of sensual pleasures (kâmabhava), him I call a Brâmana.

47. 'Whosoever in this world, after abandoning desire, wanders about houseless, and has destroyed the existence of desire (ta*nh*âbhava), him I call a Brâma*n*a.

48. 'Whosoever, after leaving human attachment (yoga), has overcome divine attachment, and is liberated from all attachment, him I call a Brâhma*n*a.

49. 'The man that, after leaving pleasure and disgust, is calm and free from the elements of existence (nirupadhi), who is a hero, and has conquered all the world, him I call a Brâma*n*a.

50. 'Whosoever knows wholly the vanishing and reappearance of beings, does not cling to (anything); is happy (sugata), and enlightened, him I call a Brâma*n*a.

51. 'The man whose way neither gods nor Gandhabbas nbr men know, and whose passions are destroyed, who is a saint, him I call a Brâma*n*a.

52. 'The man for whom there is nothing, neither before nor after nor in the middle, who possesses nothing, and does not seize (upon anything), him I call a Brâma*n*a.

53. 'The (man that is undaunted like a) bull, who is eminent, a hero, a great sage (mahesi), victorious, free from desire, purified, enlightened, him I call a Brâma*n*a.

54. 'The man who knows his former dwellings, who sees both heaven and hell, and has reached the destruction of births, him I call a Brâma*n*a.

55. 'For what has been designated as "name" and "family" in the world is only a term, what has been designated here and there is understood by common consent.

56. 'Adhered to for a long time are the views of the ignorant, the ignorant tell us, one is a Brâma*n*a by birth.

57. 'Not by birth is one a Brâma*n*a, nor is one by birth no Brâma*n*a; by work (kammanâ) one is a Brâma*n*a, by work one is no Brâma*n*a.

58. 'By work one is a husbandman, by work one is an artisan, by work one is a merchant, by work one is a servant.

59. 'By work one is a thief, by work one is a soldier, by work one is a sacrificer, by work one is a king.

60. 'So the wise, who see the cause of things and understand the result of work, know this work as it really is.

61. 'By work the world exists, by work mankind exists, beings are bound by work as the linch-pin of the rolling cart (keeps the wheel on).

62. 'By penance, by a religious life, by self-restraint, and by temperance, by this one is a Brâmana, such a one (they call) the best Brâmana.

63. 'He who is endowed with the threefold knowledge, is calm, and has destroyed regeneration, — know this, O Vâsettha, — he is to the wise Brahman and Sakka.'

This having been said, the young men Vâsettha and Bhâradvâga spoke to Bhagavat as follows:

'It is excellent, O venerable Gotama! It is excellent, O venerable Gotama! As one raises what has been overthrown, or reveals what has been hidden, or tells the way to him who has gone astray, or holds out an oil lamp in the dark that those who have eyes may see the objects, even so by the venerable Gotama in manifold ways the Dhamma has been illustrated; we take refuge in the venerable Gotama, in the Dhamma, and in the Assembly of Bhikkhus; may the venerable Gotama receive us as followers (upâsaka), who from this day for life have taken refuge (in him).'

Vâsetthasutta is ended.

10 KOKÂLIYASUTTA

Kokâliya abuses Sâriputta and Moggallâna to Buddha; therefore as soon as he has left Buddha, he is struck with boils, dies and goes to the Paduma hell, whereupon Buddha describes to the Bhikkhus the punishment of backbiters in hell.

So it was heard by me:
At one time Bhagavat dwelt at Sâvatthî, in Getavana, in the park of Anâthapindika. Then the Bhikkhu Kokâliya approached Bhagavat, and after having approached and saluted Bhagavat he sat down apart; sitting down apart the Bhikkhu Kokâliya said this to Bhagavat: "O thou venerable one, Sâriputta and Moggallâna have evil desires, they have fallen into the power of evil desires.'
When this had been said, Bhagavat spoke to the Bhikkhu Kokâliya as follows: '(Do) not (say) so, Kokâliya; (do) not (say) so, Kokâliya; appease, O Kokâliya, (thy) mind in regard to Sâriputta and Moggallâna: Sâriputta and Moggallâna are amiable.'
A second time the Bhikkhu Kokâliya said this to Bhagavat: 'Although thou, O venerable Bhagavat, (appearest) to me (to be) faithful and trustworthy, yet Sâriputta and Moggallâna have evil desires, they have fallen into the power of evil desires.'
A second time Bhagavat said this to the Bhikkhu Kokâliya: '(Do) not (say) so, Kokâliya; (do) not (say) so, Kokâliya; appease, O Kokâliya, (thy) mind in regard to Sâriputta and Moggallâna: Sâriputta and Moggallâna are amiable.'
A third time the Bhikkhu Kokâliya said this to Bhagavat: 'Although thou, O venerable Bhagavat, (appearest) to me (to be) faithful and trustworthy, yet Sâriputta and Moggallâna have evil desires, Sâriputta and Moggallâna have fallen into the power of evil desires.'

A third time Bhagavat said this to the Bhikkhu Kokâliya: '(Do) not (say) so, Kokâliya; (do) not (say) so, Kokâliya; appease, O Kokâliya, (thy) mind in regard to Sâriputta and Moggallâna: Sâriputta and Moggallâna are amiable.'

Then the Bhikkhu Kokâliya, after having risen from his seat and saluted Bhagavat and walked round him towards the right, went away; and when he had been gone a short time, all his body was struck with boils as large as mustard seeds; after being only as large as mustard seeds, they became as large as kidney beans; after being only as large as kidney beans, they became as large as chick peas; after being only as large as chick peas, they became as large as a Kola*tthi* egg (?); after being only as large as a Kola*tthi* egg, they became as large as the jujube fruit; after being only as large as the jujube fruit, they became as large as the fruit of the emblic myrobalan; after being only as large as the fruit of the emblic myrobalan, they became as large as the unripe beluva fruit; after being only as large as the unripe beluva fruit, they became as large as a billi fruit (?); after being as large as a billi fruit, they broke, and matter and blood flowed out. Then the Bhikkhu Kokâliya died of that disease, and when he had died the Bhikkhu Kokâliya went to the Paduma hell, having shown a hostile mind against Sâriputta and Moggallâna. Then when the night had passed Brahman Sahampati of a beautiful appearance, having lit up all *G*etavana, approached Bhagavat, and having approached and saluted Bhagavat, he stood apart, and standing apart Brahman Sahampati said this to Bhagavat: 'O thou venerable one, Kokâliya, the Bhikkhu, is dead and after death, O thou venerable one, the Bhikkhu Kokâliya is gone to the Paduma hell, having shown a hostile mind against Sâriputta and Moggallâna.'

This said Brahman Sahampati, and after saying this and saluting Bhagavat, and walking round him towards the right, he disappeared there.

Then Bhagavat, after the expiration of that night, addressed the Bhikkhus thus: 'Last night, O Bhikkhus, when the night had (nearly) passed, Brahman Sahampati of a beautiful appearance, having lit up all *G*etavana, approached Bhagavat, and having approached and saluted Bhagavat, he stood apart, and standing apart Brahman Sahampati said this to Bhagavat: "O thou venerable one, Kokâliya, the Bhikkhu, is dead; and after death, O thou venerable one, the Bhikkhu Kokâliya is gone to the Paduma hell, having shown a hostile mind against Sâriputta and Moggallâna." This said Brahman Sahampati, O Bhikkhus, and having said this and saluted me, and walked round me towards the right, he disappeared there.'

When this had been said, a Bhikkhu asked Bhagavat: 'How long is the rate of life, O venerable one, in the Paduma hell?'

'Long, O Bhikkhu, is the rate of life in the Paduma hell, it is not easy to calculate either (by saying) so many years or so many hundreds of years or so many thousands of years or so many hundred thousands of years.'

'But it is possible, I suppose, to make a comparison, O thou venerable one?' 'It is possible, O Bhikkhu;' so saying, Bhagavat spoke (as follows): 'Even as, O Bhikkhu, (if there were) a Kosala load of sesamum seed containing twenty khâris, and a man after the lapse of every hundred years were to take from it one sesamum seed at a time, then that Kosala load of sesamum seed, containing twenty khâris, would, O Bhikkhu, sooner by this means dwindle away and be used up than one Abbuda hell; and even as are twenty Abbuda hells, O Bhikkhu, so is one Nirabbuda hell; and even as are twenty Nirabbuda hells, O Bhikkhu, so is one Ababa hell; and even as are twenty Ababa hells, O Bhikkhu, so is one Ahaha hell; and even as are twenty Ahaha hells, O Bhikkhu, so is one A*ta*ta hell; and even as are twenty A*ta*ta hells, O Bhikkhu, so is one Kumuda hell; and even as are twenty Kumuda hells, O Bhikkhu, so is one Sogandhika hell; and even as are twenty Sogandhika hells, O Bhikkhu, so is one Uppalaka hell; and even as are twenty Uppalaka hells, O Bhikkhu, so is one Pu*nd*arîka hell; and even as are twenty Pu*nd*arîka hells, O Bhikkhu, so is one Paduma hell; and to the Paduma hell, O Bhikkhu, the Bhikkhu Kokâliya is gone, having shown a hostile mind against Sâriputta and Moggallâna.' This said Bhagavat, and having said this Sugata, the Master, furthermore spoke as follows:

1. 'To (every) man that is born, an axe is born in his mouth, by which the fool cuts himself, when speaking bad language.
2. 'He who praises him who is to be blamed or blames him who as to be praised, gathers up sin in his mouth, and through that (sin) he will not find any joy.
3. 'Trifling is the sin that (consists in) losing riches by dice; this is a greater sin that corrupts the mind against Sugatas.
4. 'Out of the one hundred thousand Nirabbudas (he goes) to thirty-six, and to five Abbudas; because he blames an Ariya he goes to hell, having employed his speech and mind badly.
5. 'He who speaks falsely goes to hell, or he who having done something says, "I have not done it;" both these after death become equal, in another world (they are both) men guilty of a mean deed.
6. 'He who offends an offenceless man, a pure man, free from sin, such a fool the evil (deed) reverts against, like fine dust thrown against the wind.
7. 'He who is given to the quality of covetousness, such a one censures others in his speech, (being himself) unbelieving, stingy, wanting in affability, niggardly, given to backbiting.
8. 'O thou foul-mouthed, false, ignoble, blasting, wicked, evil-doing, low, sinful, base-born man, do not be garrulous in this world, (else) thou wilt be an inhabitant of hell.
9. 'Thou spreadest pollution to the misfortune (of others), thou revilest the just, committing sin (yourself), and having done many evil deeds thou wilt go to the pool (of hell) for a long time.
10. 'For one's deeds are not lost, they will surely come (back to you), (their) master will meet with them, the fool who commits sin will feel the pain in himself in the other world.
11. 'To the place where one is struck with iron rods, to the iron stake with sharp edges he goes; then there is (for him) food as appropriate, resembling a red-hot ball of iron.
12. 'For those who have anything to say (there) do not say fine things, they do not approach (with pleasing faces); they do not find refuge (from their sufferings), they lie on spread embers, they enter a blazing pyre.

13. 'Covering (them) with a net they kill (them) there with iron hammers; they go to dense darkness, for that is spread out like the body of the earth.

14. 'Then (they enter) an iron pot, they enter a blazing pyre, for they are boiled in those (iron pots) for a long time, jumping up and down in the pyre.

15. 'Then he who commits sin is surely boiled in a mixture of matter and blood; whatever quarter he inhabits, he becomes rotten there from coming in contact (with matter and blood).

16. 'He who commits sin will surely be boiled in the water, the dwelling-place of worms; there it is not (possible) to get to the shore, for the jars (are) exactly alike. (?)

17. 'Again they enter the sharp Asipattavana with mangled limbs; having seized the tongue with a hook, the different watchmen (of hell) kill (them).

18. 'Then they enter Vetaraṁ, that is difficult to cross and has got streams of razors with sharp edges; there the fools fall in, the evil-doers after having done evil.

19. 'There black, mottled flocks of ravens eat them who are weeping, and dogs, jackals, great vultures, falcons, crows tear (them).

20. 'Miserable indeed is the life here (in hell) which the man sees that commits sin. Therefore should a man in this world for the rest of his life be strenuous, and not indolent.

21. 'Those loads of sesamum seed which are carried in Paduma hell have been counted by the wise, they are (several) nahutas and five koṭis, and twelve hundred koṭis besides.

22. 'As long as hells are called painful in this world, so long people will have to live there for a long time; therefore amongst those who have pure, amiable, and good qualities one should always guard speech and mind.'

Kokâliyasutta is ended.

II NÂLAKASUTTA

The Isi Asita, also called Ka*n*hasiri, on seeing the gods rejoicing, asks the cause of it, and having heard that Buddha has been born, he descends from Tusita heaven. When the Sakyas showed the child to him, he received it joyfully and prophesied about it. Buddha explains to Nâlaka, the sister's son of Asita, the highest state of wisdom Vatthugâthâ.

1. The Isi Asita saw in (their) resting-places during the day the joyful, delighted flocks of the Tidasa gods, and the gods in bright clothes, always highly praising Inda, after taking their clothes and waving them.
2. Seeing the gods with pleased minds, delighted, and showing his respect, he said this on that occasion: 'Why is the assembly of the gods so exceedingly pleased, why do they take their clothes and wave them?
3. 'When there was an encounter with the Asuras, a victory for the gods, and the Asuras were defeated, then there was not such a rejoicing. What wonderful (thing) have the gods seen that they are so delighted?
4. 'They shout and sing and make music, they throw (about their) arms and dance; I ask you, the inhabitants of the tops of (mount) Meru, remove my doubt quickly, O venerable ones!'
5. 'The Bodhisatta, the excellent pearl, the incomparable, is born for the good and for a blessing in the world of men, in the town of the Sakyas, in the country of Lumbinî. Therefore we are glad and exceedingly pleased.
6. 'He, the most excellent of all beings, the preeminent man, the bull of men, the most excellent of all creatures will turn the wheel (of the Dhamma) in the forest called after the Isis, (he who is)

like the roaring lion, the strong lord of beasts.'

7. Having heard that noise he descended from (the heaven of) Tusita. Then he went to Suddhodana's palace, and having sat down there he said this to the Sakyas: 'Where is the prince? I wish to see (him).'

8. Then the Sakyas showed to (the Isi), called Asita, the child, the prince who was like shining gold, manufactured by a very skilful (smith) in the mouth of a forge, and beaming in glory and having a beautiful appearance.

9. Seeing the prince shining like fire, bright like the bull of stars wandering in the sky, like the burning sun in autumn, free from clouds, he joyfully obtained great delight.

10. The gods held in the sky a parasol with a thousand circles and numerous branches, yaks' tails with golden sticks were fanned, but those who held the yaks' tails and the parasol were not seen.

11. The Isi with the matted hair, by name Kaṇhasiri, on seeing the yellow blankets (shining) like a golden coin, and the white parasol held over his head, received him delighted and happy.

12. And having received the bull of the Sakyas, he who was wishing to receive him and knew the signs and the hymns, with pleased thoughts raised his voice, saying: 'Without superior is this, the most excellent of men.'

13. Then remembering his own migration he was displeased and shed tears; seeing this the Sakyas asked the weeping Isi, whether there would be any obstacle in the prince's path.

14. Seeing the Sakyas displeased the Isi said: 'I do not remember anything (that will be) unlucky for the prince, there will be no obstacles at all for him, for this is no inferior (person). Be without anxiety.

15. ' This prince will reach the summit of perfect enlightenment, he will turn the wheel of the Dhamma, he who sees what is exceedingly pure (i.e. Nibbâna), this (prince) feels for the welfare of the multitude, and his religion will be widely spread.

16. 'My life here will shortly be at an end, in the middle (of his life) there will be death for me; I shall not hear the Dhamma of the incomparable one; therefore I am afflicted, unfortunate, and

suffering.'

17. Having afforded the Sakyas great joy he went out from the interior of the town to lead a religious life; but taking pity on his sister's son, he induced him to embrace the Dhamma of the incomparable one.

18. 'When thou hearest from others the sound "Buddha," (or) "he who has acquired perfect enlightenment walks the way of the Dhamma," then going there and enquiring about the particulars, lead a religious life with that Bhagavat.'

19. Instructed by him, the friendly-minded, by one who saw in the future what is exceedingly pure (i.e. Nibbâna), he, Nâlaka, with a heap of gathered-up good works, and with guarded senses dwelt (with him), looking forward to Gina (i.e. Buddha).

20. Hearing the noise, while the excellent Gina turned the wheel (of the Dhamma), and going and seeing the bull of the Isis, he, after being converted, asked the eminent Muni about the best wisdom, when the time of Asita's order had come.

The Vatthugâthâs are ended.

21. 'These words of Asita are acknowledged true (by me), therefore we ask thee, O Gotama, who art perfect in all things (dhamma).

22. 'O Muni, to me who am houseless, and who wish to embrace a Bhikkhu's life, explain when asked the highest state, the state of wisdom (moneyya).'

23. 'I will declare to thee the state of wisdom,' — so said Bhagavat, — 'difficult to carry out, and difficult to obtain; come, I will explain it to thee, stand fast, be firm.

24. 'Let a man cultivate equanimity: which is (both) reviled and praised in the village, let him take care not to corrupt his mind, let him live calm, and without pride.

25. 'Various (objects) disappear, like a flame of fire in the wood; women tempt the Muni, let them not tempt him.

26. 'Let him be disgusted with sexual intercourse, having left behind sensual pleasures of all kinds, being inoffensive and dispassionate towards living creatures, towards anything that is feeble or strong.

27. 'As I am so are these, as these are so am I, identifying himself with others, let him not kill nor cause (any one) to kill.
28. 'Having abdoned desire and covetousness let him act as one that sees clearly where a common man sticks, let him cross over this hell.
29. 'Let him be with an empty stomach, taking little food, let him have few wants and not be covetous; not being consumed by desire he will without desire be happy.
30. 'Let the Muni, after going about for alms, repair to the outskirts of the wood, let him go and sit down near the root of a tree.
31. 'Applying himself to meditation, and being wise, let him find his pleasure in the outskirts of the wood, let him meditate at the root of a tree enjoying himself.
32. 'Then when night is passing away let him repair to the outskirts of the village, let him not delight in being invited nor in what is brought away from the village.
33. 'Let not the Muni, after going to the village, walk about to the houses in haste; cutting off (all) talk while seeking food, let him not utter any coherent speech.
34. '"What I have obtained that is good," "I did not get (anything that is) good," so thinking in both cases he returns to the tree unchanged.
35. "Wandering about with his alms-bowl in his hand, considered dumb without being dumb, let him not blush at a little gift, let him not despise the giver.
36. 'Various are the practices illustrated by the Samaṇa, they do not go twice to the other shore, this (is) not once thought. (?)
37. 'For whom there is no desire, for the Bhikkhu who has cut off the stream (of existence) and abandoned all kinds of work, there is no pain.
38. 'I will declare to thee the state of wisdom,' — so said Bhagavat, — 'let one be like the edge of a razor, having struck his palate with his tongue, let him be restrained in (regard to his) stomach.
39. 'Let his mind be free from attachment, let him not think

much (about worldly affairs), let him be without defilement, independent, and devoted to a religious life.

40. 'For the sake of a solitary life and for the sake of the service that is to be carried out by Samaṇas, let him learn, solitariness is called wisdom; alone indeed he will find pleasure.

41. 'Then he will shine through the ten regions, having heard the voice of the wise, of the meditating, of those that have abandoned sensual pleasures, let my adherent then still more devote himself to modesty and belief.

42. 'Understand this from the waters in chasms and cracks: noisy go the small waters, silent goes the vast ocean.

43. 'What is deficient that makes a noise, what is full that is calm; the fool is like a half-(filled) water-pot, the wise is like a full pool.

44. 'When the Samaṇa speaks much that is possessed of good sense, he teaches the Dhamma while knowing it, while knowing it he speaks much.

45. 'But he who while knowing it is self-restrained, and while knowing it does not speak much, such a Muni deserves wisdom (mona), such a Muni has attained to wisdom (mona).'

Nâlakasutta is ended.

12 DVAYATÂNUPASSANÂSUTTA

All pain in the world arises from upadhi, avig͟gâ, sam̐khârâ viññâṇa, phassa, vedanâ, taṇhâ, upâdâna, ârambha, âhâra, iñgita, nissaya, rûpa, mosadhamma, sukha.

So it was heard by me:
At one time Bhagavat dwelt at Sâvatthî in Pubbârâma, Migâramâtar's mansion. At that time Bhagavat on the Uposatha day, on the fifteenth, it being full moon, in the evening was sitting in the open air, surrounded by the assembly of Bhikkhus. Then Bhagavat surveying the silent assembly of Bhikkhus addressed them (as follows):
'Whichever Dhammas there are, O Bhikkhus, good, noble, liberating, leading to perfect enlightenment, — what is the use to you of listening to these good, noble, liberating Dhammas, leading to perfect enlightenment? If, O Bhikkhus, there should be people that ask so, they shall be answered thus: "Yes, for the right understanding of the two Dhammas." "Which two do you mean?" "(I mean), this is pain, this is the origin of pain," this is one consideration, "this is the destruction of pain, this is the way leading to the destruction of pain," this is the second consideration; thus, O Bhikkhus, by the Bhikkhu that considers the Dyad duly, is strenuous, ardent, resolute, of two fruits one fruit is to be expected: in this world perfect knowledge, or, if any of the (five) attributes still remain, the state of an Anâgâmin (one that does not return).' This said Bhagavat, (and) when Sugata had said this, the Master further spoke:
1. 'Those who do not understand pain and the origin of pain, and where pain wholly and totally is stopped, and do not know the way that leads to the cessation of pain,

2. 'They, deprived of the emancipation of thought and the emancipation of knowledge, are unable to put an end (to samsâra), they will verily continue to undergo birth and decay.
3. 'And those who understand pain and the origin of pain, and where pain wholly and totally is stopped, and who know the way that leads to the cessation of pain,
4. 'They, endowed with the emancipation of thought and the emancipation of knowledge, are able to put an end (to samsâra), they will not undergo birth and decay.
'"Should there be a perfect consideration of the Dyad in another way," if, O Bhikkhus, there are people that ask so, they shall be told, there is, and how there is: "Whatever pain arises is all in consequence of the upadhis (elements of existence)," this is one consideration, "but from the complete destruction of the upadhis, through absence of passion, there is no origin of pain," this is the second consideration; thus, O Bhikkhus, by the Bhikkhu that considers the Dyad duly, that is strenuous, ardent, resolute, of two fruits one fruit is to be expected: in this world perfect knowledge, or, if any of the (five) attributes still remain, the state of an Anâgâmin (one that does not return).' This said Bhagavat, (and) when Sugata had said this, the Master further spoke:
5. 'Whatever pains there are in the world, of many kinds, they arise having their cause in the upadhis; he who being ignorant creates upadhi, that fool again undergoes pain; therefore being wise do not create upadhi, considering what is the birth and origin of pain.
'"Should there be a perfect consideration of the Dyad in another way," if, O Bhikkhus, there are people that ask so, they shall be told, there is, and how there is: "Whatever pain arises is all in consequence of aviggâ (ignorance)," this is one consideration, "but from the complete destruction of aviggâ, through absence of passion, there is no origin of pain," this is the second consideration; thus, O Bhikkhus, by the Bhikkhu that considers the Dyad duly, that is strenuous, ardent, resolute, of two fruits one fruit is to be expected: in this world perfect knowledge, or, if any of the (five) attributes still remain, the state of an Anâgâmin

(one that does not return).' This said Bhagavat, (and) when Sugata had said this, the Master further spoke:

6. 'Those who again and again go to sa*m*sâra with birth and death, to existence in this way or in that way, — that is the state of avi*gg*â.

7. 'For this avi*gg*â is the great folly by which this (existence) has been traversed long, but those beings who resort to knowledge do not go to rebirth.

'"Should there be a perfect consideration of the Dyad in another way," if, O Bhikkhus, there are people that ask so, they shall be told, there is, and how there is: "Whatever pain arises is all in consequence of the sa*m*khâras (matter)," this is one consideration, "but from the complete destruction of the sa*m*khâras, through absence of passion, there is no origin of pain," this is the second consideration; thus, O Bhikkhus, by the Bhikkhu that considers the Dyad duly, that is strenuous, ardent, resolute, of two fruits one fruit is to be expected: in this world perfect knowledge, or, if any of the (five) attributes still remain, the state of an Anâgâmin (one that does not return).' This said Bhagavat; (and) when Sugata had said this, the Master further spoke:

8. 'Whatever pain arises is all in consequence of the sa*m*khâras, by the destruction of the sa*m*khâras there will be no origin of pain.

9. 'Looking upon this pain that springs from the sa*m*khâras as misery, from the cessation of all the sa*m*khâras, and from the destruction of consciousness will arise the destruction of pain, having understood this exactly,

10. 'The wise who have true views and are accomplished, having understood (all things) completely, and having conquered all association with Mâra, do not go to re-birth.

'"Should there be a perfect consideration of the Dyad in another way," if, O Bhikkhus, there are people that ask so, they shall be told, there is, and how there is: "Whatever pain arises is all in consequence of viññâ*n*a (consciousness)," this is one consideration, "but from the complete destruction of viññâ*n*ana, through absence of passion, there is no origin of pain," this is the second consideration; thus, O Bhikkhus, by the Bhikkhu that considers the Dyad duly, that is strenuous, ardent, resolute, of two fruits one fruit is to be expected: in this world perfect knowledge, or, if any of the (five) attributes still remain, the state of an Anâgâmin (one that does not return).' This said Bhagavat, (and) when Sugata had said this, the Master further spoke:

11. 'Whatever pain arises is all in consequence of viññāna, by the destruction of viññāna there is no origin of pain.

12. 'Looking upon this pain that springs from viññāna as misery, from the cessation of viññāna a Bhikkhu free from desire (will be) perfectly happy (parinibbuta).

'"Should there be a perfect consideration of the Dyad in another way," if, O Bhikkhus, there are people that ask so, they shall be told, there is, and how there is: "Whatever pain arises is all in consequence of phassa (touch)," this is one consideration, "but from the complete destruction of phassa, through absence of passion, there is no origin of pain," this is the second consideration; thus, O Bhikkhus, by the Bhikkhu that considers the Dyad duly, that is strenuous, ardent, resolute, of two fruits one fruit is to be expected: in this world perfect knowledge, or, if any of the (five) attributes still remain, the state of an Anâgâmin (one that does not return).' This said Bhagavat, (and) when Sugata had said this, the Master further spoke:

13. 'For those who are ruined by phassa, who follow the stream of existence, who have entered a bad way, the destruction of bonds is far off.

14. 'But those who, having fully understood phassa, knowingly have taken delight in cessation, they verily from the comprehension of phassa, and being free from desire, are perfectly happy.

'"Should there be a perfect consideration of the Dyad in another way," if, O Bhikkhus, there are people that ask so, they shall be told, there is, and how there is: "Whatever pain arises is all in consequence of the vedanâs (sensations)," this is one consideration, "but from the complete destruction of the vedanâs, through absence of passion, there no origin of pain," this is the second consideration; thus, O Bhikkhus, by the Bhikkhu that considers the Dyad duly, that is strenuous, ardent, resolute, of two fruits one fruit is to be expected: in this world perfect knowledge, or, if any of the (five) attributes still remain, the state of an Anâgâmin (one that does not return).' This said Bhagavat, (and) when Sugata had said this, the Master further spoke:

15. 'Pleasure or pain, together with want of pleasure and want of pain, whatever is perceived internally and externally,

16. 'Looking upon this as pain, having touched what is perishable and fragile, seeing the decay (of everything), the Bhikkhu is disgusted, having from the perishing of the vedanâs become free from desire, and perfectly happy.

'"Should there be a perfect consideration of the Dyad in another way," if, O Bhikkhus, there are people that ask so, they shall be told, there is, and how there is: "Whatever pain arises is all in consequence of tanhâ (desire)," this is one consideration, "but from the complete destruction of tanhâ, through absence of passion, there is no origin of pain," this is the second consideration; thus, O Bhikkhus, by the Bhikkhu that considers the Dyad duly, that is strenuous, ardent, resolute, of two fruits one fruit is to be expected: in this world perfect knowledge, or, if any of the (five) attributes still remain, the state of an Anâgâmin (one that does not return).' This said Bhagavat, (and) when Sugata had said this, the Master further spoke:

17. 'A man accompanied by tanhâ, for a long time transmigrating into existence in this way or that way, does not overcome transmigration (samsâra).

18. 'Looking upon this as misery, this origin of the pain of tanhâ, let the Bhikkhu free from tanhâ, not seizing (upon anything), thoughtful, wander about.

'"Should there be a perfect consideration of the Dyad in another way," if, O Bhikkhus, there are people that ask so, they shall be told, there is, and how there is: "Whatever pain arises is all in consequence of the upâdânas (the seizures)," this is one consideration, "but from the complete destruction of the upâdânas, through absence of passion, there is no origin of pain," this is the second consideration; thus, O Bhikkhus, by the

Bhikkhu that considers the Dyad duly, that is strenuous, ardent, resolute, of two fruits one fruit is to be expected: in this world perfect knowledge, or, if any of the (five) attributes still remain, the state of an Anâgâmin (one that does not return).' This said Bhagavat, (and) when Sugata had said this, the Master further spoke:

19. 'The existence is in consequence of the upâdânas; he who has come into existence goes to pain, he who has been born is to die, this is the origin of pain.

20. 'Therefore from the destruction of the upâdânas the wise with perfect knowledge, having seen (what causes) the destruction of birth, do not go to re-birth.

'"Should there be a perfect consideration of the Dyad in another way," if, O Bhikkhus, there are people that ask so, they shall be told, there is, and how there is: "Whatever pain arises is all in consequence of the ârambhas (exertions)," this is one consideration, "but from the complete destruction of the ârambhas, through absence of passion, there is no origin of pain," this is the second consideration; thus, O Bhikkhus, by the Bhikkhu that considers the Dyad duly, that is strenuous, ardent, resolute, of two fruits one fruit is to be expected: in this world perfect knowledge, or, if any of the (five) attributes still remain, the state of an Anâgâmin (one that does not return).' This said Bhagavat, (and) when Sugata had said this, the Master further spoke:

21. 'Whatever pain arises is all in consequence of the ârambhas, by the destruction of the ârambhas there is no origin of pain.

22, 23. 'Looking upon this pain that springs from the ârambhas as misery, having abandoned all the ârambhas, birth and transmigration have been crossed over by the Bhikkhu who is liberated in non-exertion, who has cut off the desire for existence, and whose mind is calm; there is for him no re-birth. , 74

'"Should there be a perfect consideration of the Dyad in another way," if, O Bhikkhus, there are people that ask so, they shall be told, there is, and how there is: "Whatever pain arises is all in consequence of the âhâras (food?)," this is one consideration, "but from the complete destruction of the âhâras, through absence of passion, there is no origin of pain," this is the second consideration; thus, O Bhikkhus, by the Bhikkhu that considers the Dyad duly, that is strenuous, ardent, resolute, of two fruits one fruit is to be expected: in this world perfect knowledge, or, if any of the (five) attributes still remain, the state of an Anâgâmin (one that does not return).' This said Bhagavat, (and) when Sugata had said this, the Master further spoke:

24. 'Whatever pain arises is all in consequence of the âhâras, by the destruction of the âhâras there is no origin of pain.

25. 'Looking upon this pain that springs from the âhâras as misery, having seen the result of all âhâras, not resorting to all âhâras,

26. 'Having seen that health is from the destruction of desire, he that serves discriminatingly and stands fast in the Dhamma cannot be reckoned as existing, being accomplished.

"'Should there be a perfect consideration of the Dyad in another way," if, O Bhikkhus, there are people that ask so, they shall be told, there is, and how there is: "Whatever pain arises is all in consequence of the iñgitas (commotions)," this is one consideration, "but from the complete destruction of the iñgitas, through absence of passion, there is no origin of pain," this is the second consideration; thus, O Bhikkhus, by the Bhikkhu that considers the Dyad duly, that is strenuous, ardent, resolute, of two fruits one fruit is to be expected: in this world perfect knowledge, or, if any of the (five) attributes still remain, the state of an Anâgâmin (one that does not return).' This said Bhagavat, (and) when Sugata had said this, the Master further spoke:

27. 'Whatever pain arises is all in consequence of the iñgitas, by the destruction of the iñgitas there is no origin of pain.

28. 'Looking upon this pain that springs from the iñgitas as misery, and therefore having abandoned the iñgitas and having stopped the samkhâras; let the Bhikkhu free from desire and not seizing (upon anything), thoughtful, wander about.

"'Should there be a perfect consideration of the Dyad in another way," if, O Bhikkhus, there are people that ask so, they shall be told, there is, and how there is: "For the nissita (dependent) there is vacillation," this is one consideration, "the independent (man) does not vacillate," this is the second consideration; thus, O Bhikkhus, by the Bhikkhu that considers the Dyad duly, that is strenuous, ardent, resolute, of two fruits one fruit is to be expected: in this world perfect knowledge, or, if any of the (five) attributes still remain, the state of an Anâgâmin (one that does not return).' This said Bhagavat, (and) when Sugata had said this, the Master further spoke:

29. 'The independent (man) does not vacillate, and the dependent (man) seizing upon existence in one way or in another, does not overcome samsâra. .

30. 'Looking upon this as misery (and seeing) great danger in things you depend upon, let a Bhikkhu wander about independent, not seizing (upon anything), thoughtful.

'"Should there be a perfect consideration of the Dyad in another way," if, O Bhikkhus, there are people that ask so, they shall be told, there is, and how there is: "The formless (beings), O Bhikkhus, are calmer than the rûpas (for ruppa, i.e. form-possessing)," this is one consideration, "cessation is calmer than the formless," this is another consideration, "thus, O Bhikkhus, by the Bhikkhu that considers the Dyad duly, that is strenuous, ardent, resolute, of two fruits one fruit is to be expected: in this world perfect knowledge, or, if any of the (five) attributes still remain, the state of an Anâgâmin (one that does not return).' This said Bhagavat, (and) when Sugata had said this, the Master further spoke:

31. 'Those beings who are possessed of form, and those who dwell in the formless (world), not knowing cessation, have to go to re-birth.

32. 'But those who, having fully comprehended the forms, stand fast in the formless (worlds), those who are liberated in the cessation, such beings leave death behind.

'"Should there be a perfect consideration of the Dyad in another way," if, O Bhikkhus, there are people that ask so, they shall be told, there is, and how there is: "What has been considered true by the world of men, together with the gods, Mâra, Brahman, and amongst the Samaṇas, Brâmaṇas, gods, and men, that has by the noble through their perfect knowledge been well seen to be really false," this is one consideration; "what, O Bhikkhus, has been considered false by the world of men, together with the gods, Mâra, Brahman, and amongst the Samaṇas, Brâmaṇas, gods, and men, that has by the noble through their perfect knowledge been well seen to be really true," this is another consideration. Thus, O Bhikkhus, by the Bhikkhu that considers the Dyad duly, that is strenuous, ardent, resolute, of two fruits one fruit is to be expected: in this world perfect knowledge, or, if any of the (five) attributes still remain, the state of an Anâgâmin (one that does not return).' This said Bhagavat, (and) when Sugata had said this, the Master further spoke:

33. 'Seeing the real in the unreal, the world of men and gods dwelling in name and form, he thinks: "This is true."

34. 'Whichever way they think (it), it becomes otherwise, for it is false to him, and what is false is perishable. (?)

35. 'What is not false, the Nibbâna, that the noble conceive as true, they verily from the comprehension of truth are free from desire (and) perfectly happy.

"'Should there be a perfect consideration of the Dyad in another way," if, O Bhikkhus, there are people that ask so, they shall be told, there is, and how there is: "What, O Bhikkhus, has been considered pleasure by the world of men, gods, Mâra, Brahman, and amongst the Samaṇas, Brâmaṇas, gods, and men, that has by the noble by (their) perfect knowledge been well seen to be really pain," this is one consideration; "what, O Bhikkhus, has been considered pain by the world of men, gods, Mâra, Brahman, and amongst the Samaṇas, Brâhmaṇas, gods, and men, that has by the noble by their perfect knowledge been well seen to be really pleasure," this is the second consideration. Thus, O Bhikkhus, by the Bhikkhu who considers the Dyad duly, who is strenuous, ardent, resolute, of two fruits one fruit is to be expected: in this world perfect knowledge, or, if any of the (five) attributes still remain, the state of an Anâgâmin (one who does not return).'

This said Bhagavat, (and) when Sugata had said so, the Master further spoke:

36. 'Form, sound, taste, smell, and touch are all wished for, pleasing and charming (things) as long as they last, so it is said.

37. 'By you, by the world of men and gods these (things) are deemed a pleasure, but when they cease it is deemed pain by them.

38. 'By the noble the cessation of the existing body is regarded as pleasure; this is the opposite of (what) the wise in all the world (hold).

39. 'What fools say is pleasure that the noble say is pain, what fools say is pain that the noble know as pleasure: — see here is a thing difficult to understand, here the ignorant are confounded.

40. 'For those that are enveloped there is gloom, for those that do not see there is darkness, and for the good it is manifest, for those that see there is light; (even being) near, those that are ignorant of the way and the Dhamma, do not discern (anything).

41. 'By those that are overcome by the passions of existence, by those that follow the stream of existence, by those that have entered the realm of Mâra, this Dhamma is not perfectly understood.

42. 'Who except the noble deserve the well-understood state (of Nibbâna)? Having perfectly conceived this state, those free from passion are completely extinguished.'

This spoke Bhagavat. Glad those Bhikkhus rejoiced at the words of Bhagavat. While this explanation was being given, the minds of sixty Bhikkhus, not seizing (upon anything), were liberated.

IV ATTHAKAVAGGA

I KÂMASUTTA

Sensual pleasures are to be avoided.

1. If he who desires sensual pleasures is successful, he certainly becomes glad-minded, having obtained what a mortal wishes for.
2. But if those sensual pleasures fail the person who desires and wishes (for them), he will suffer, pierced by the arrow (of pain).
3. He who avoids sensual pleasures as (he would avoid treading upon) the head of a snake with his foot, such a one, being thoughtful (sato), will conquer this desire.
4. He who covets extensively (such) pleasures (as these), fields, goods, or gold, cows and horses, servants, women, relations,
5. Sins will overpower him, dangers will crush him, and pain will follow him as water (pours into) a broken ship.
6. Therefore let one always be thoughtful, and avoid pleasures; having abandoned them, let him cross the stream, after baling out the ship, and go to the other shore.

Kâmasutta is ended.

2 GUHA*TTH*AKASUTTA

Let no one cling to existence and sensual pleasures.

1. A man that lives adhering to the cave (i.e. the body), who is covered with much (sin), and sunk into delusion, such a one is far from seclusion, for the sensual pleasures in the world are not easy to abandon.
2. Those whose wishes are their motives, those who are linked to the pleasures of the world, they are difficult to liberate, for they cannot be liberated by others, looking for what is after or what is before, coveting these and former sensual pleasures.
3. Those who are greedy of, given to, and infatuated by sensual pleasures, those who are niggardly, they, having entered upon what is wicked, wail when they are subjected to pain, saying: 'What will become of us, when we die away from here?'
4. Therefore let a man here learn, whatever he knows as wicked in the world, let him not for the sake of that (?) practise (what is) wicked; for short is this life, say the wise.
5. I see in the world this trembling race given to desire for existences; they are wretched men who lament in the mouth of death, not being free from the desire for reiterated existences.
6. Look upon those men trembling in selfishness, like fish in a stream nearly dried up, with little water; seeing this, let one wander about unselfish, without forming any attachment to existences.
7. Having subdued his wish for both ends, having fully understood touch without being greedy, not doing what he has himself blamed, the wise (man) does not cling to what is seen and heard.
8. Having understood name, let the Muni cross over the stream,

not defiled by any grasping; having pulled out the arrow (of passion), wandering about strenuous, he does not wish for this world or the other.
Guha*tth*akasutta is ended.

3 DU*TTHA TTHA*KASUTTA

The Muni undergoes no censure, for he has shaken off all systems of philosophy, and is therefore independent.

1. Verily, some wicked-minded people censure, and also just-minded people censure, but the Muni does not undergo the censure that has arisen; therefore there is not a discontented (khila) Muni anywhere.
2. How can he who is led by his wishes and possessed by his inclinations overcome his own (false) view? Doing his own doings let him talk according to his understanding.
3. The person who, without being asked, praises his own virtue and (holy) works to others, him the good call ignoble, one who praises himself.
4. But the Bhikkhu who is calm and of a happy mind, thus not praising himself for his virtues, him the good call noble, one for whom there are no desires anywhere in the world.
5. He whose Dhammas are (arbitrarily) formed and fabricated, placed in front, and confused, because he sees in himself a good result, is therefore given to (the view which is called) kuppa-pa*tikk*a-santi. (?)
6. For the dogmas of philosophy are not easy to overcome, amongst the Dhammas (now this and now that) is adopted after consideration; therefore a man rejects and adopts (now this and now that) Dhamma amongst the dogmas.
7. For him who has shaken off (sin) there is nowhere in the world any prejudiced view of the different existences; he who has shaken off (sin), after leaving deceit and arrogance behind, which (way) should he go, he (is) independent.
8. But he who is dependent undergoes censure amongst the

Dhammas; with what (name) and how should one name him who is independent? For by him there is nothing grasped or rejected, he has in this world shaken off every (philosophical) view.
Du*ttha*tt*h*akasutta is ended.

4 SUDDHA*TTHA*KASUTTA

No one is purified by philosophy, those devoted to philosophy run from one teacher to another, but the wise are not led by passion, and do not embrace anything in the world as the highest.

1. I see a pure, most excellent, sound man, by his views a man's purification takes place, holding this opinion, and having seen this view to be the highest he goes back to knowledge, thinking to see what is pure.
2. If a man's purification takes place by (his philosophical) views, or he by knowledge leaves pain behind, then he is purified by another (way than the ariyamagga, i.e. the noble way), together with his upadhis, on account of his views he tells him to say so.
3. But the Brâhma*n*a who does not cling to what has been seen, or heard, to virtue and (holy) works, or to what has been thought, to what is good and to what is evil, and who leaves behind what has been grasped, without doing anything in this world, he does not acknowledge that purification cornes from another.
4. Having left (their) former (teacher) they go to another, following their desires they do not break asunder their ties; they grasp, they let go like a monkey letting go the branch (just) after having caught (hold of it).
5. Having himself undertaken some (holy) works he goes to various (things) led by his senses, but a man of great understanding, a wise man who by his wisdom has understood the Dhamma, does not go to various (occupations).
6. He being secluded amongst all the Dhammas, whatever has been seen, heard, or thought — how should any one in this world be able to alter him, the seeing one, who wanders openly?
7. They do not form (any view), they do not prefer (anything),

they do not say, 'I am infinitely pure;' having cut the tied knot of attachment, they do not long for (anything) anywhere in the world.

8. He is a Brâhmana that has conquered (sin); by him there is nothing embraced after knowing and seeing it; he is not affected by any kind of passion; there is nothing grasped by him as the highest in this world.

Suddhatthakasutta is ended.

5 PARAMA*TTH*AKASUTTA

One should not give oneself to philosophical disputations; a Brâhma*n*a who does not adopt any system of philosophy, is unchangeable, has reached Nibbâna.

1. What one person, abiding by the (philosophical) views, saying, 'This is the most excellent,' considers the highest in the world, everything different from that he says is wretched, therefore he has not overcome dispute.

2. Because he sees in himself a good result, with regard to what has been seen (or) heard, virtue and (holy) works, or what has been thought, therefore, having embraced that, he looks upon everything else as bad.

3. The expert call just that a tie dependent upon which one looks upon anything else as bad. Therefore let a Bhikkhu not depend upon what is seen, heard, or thought, or upon virtue and (holy) works.

4. Let him not form any (philosophical) view in this world, either by knowledge or by virtue and (holy) works, let him not represent himself equal (to others), nor think himself either low or distinguished.

5. Having left what has been grasped, not seizing upon anything he does not depend even on knowledge. He does not associate with those that are taken up by different things, he does not return to any (philosophical) view.

6. For whom there is here no desire for both ends, for reiterated existence either here or in another world, for him there are no resting-places (of the mind) embraced after investigation amongst the doctrines (dhammesu).

7. In him there is not the least prejudiced idea with regard to what has been seen, heard, or thought; how could any one in this world alter such a Brâhma*n*a who does not adopt any view?

8. They do not form (any view), they do not prefer (anything), the Dhammas are not chosen by them, a Brâhmaṇa is not dependent upon virtue and (holy) works; having gone to the other shore, such a one does not return.

Paramaṭṭhakasutta is ended.

6 GARÂSUTTA

From selfishness come grief and avarice; The Bhikkhu who has turned away from the world and wanders about houseless, is independent, and does not wish for purification through another.

1. Short indeed is this life, within a hundred years one dies, and if any one lives longer, then he dies of old age.
2. People grieve from selfishness, perpetual cares kill them, this (world) is full of disappointment; seeing this, let one not live in a house.
3. That even of which a man thinks 'this is mine' is left behind by death: knowing this, let not the wise (man) turn himself to worldliness (while being my) follower.
4. As a man awakened does not see what he has met with in his sleep, so also he does not see the beloved person that has passed away and is dead.
5. Both seen and heard are the persons whose particular name is mentioned, but only the name remains undecayed of the person that has passed away.
6. The greedy in their selfishness do not leave sorrow, lamentation, and avarice; therefore the Munis leaving greediness wandered about seeing security (i.e. Nibbâna).
7. For a Bhikkhu, who wanders about unattached and cultivates the mind of a recluse, they say it is proper that he does not show himself (again) in existence.
8. Under all circumstances the independent Muni does not please nor displease (any one); sorrow and avarice do not stick to him (as little) as water to a leaf.
9. As a drop of water does not stick to a lotus, as water does not stick to a lotus, so a Muni does not cling to anything, namely, to what is seen or heard or thought.
10. He who has shaken off (sin) does not therefore think (much

of anything) because it has been seen or heard or thought; he does not wish for purification through another, for he is not pleased nor displeased (with anything).
Garâsutta is ended.

7 TISSAMETTEYYASUTTA

Sexual intercourse should be avoided.

1. 'Tell me, O venerable one,' — so said the venerable Tissa Metteyya, — 'the defeat of him who is given to sexual intercourse; hearing thy precepts we will learn in seclusion.'
2. 'The precepts of him who is given to sexual intercourse, O Metteyya,' — so said Bhagavat, — 'are lost, and he employs himself wrongly, this is what is ignoble in him.
3. 'He who, having formerly wandered alone, gives himself up to sexual intercourse, him they call in the world a low, common fellow, like a rolling chariot.
4. 'What honour and renown he had before, that is lost for him; having seen this let him learn to give up sexual intercourse.
5. 'He who overcome by his thoughts meditates like a miser, such a one, having heard the (blaming) voice of others, becomes discontented.
6. 'Then he makes weapons (i.e. commits evil deeds) urged by the doctrines of others, he is very greedy, and sinks into falsehood.
7. 'Designated "wise" he has entered upon a solitary life, then having given himself up to sexual intercourse, he (being) a fool suffers pain.
8. 'Looking upon this as misery let the Muni from first to last in the world firmly keep to his solitary life, let him not give himself up to sexual intercourse.
9. 'Let him learn seclusion, this is the highest for noble men, but let him not therefore think himself the best, although he is verily near Nibbâna.
10. 'The Muni who wanders void (of desire), not coveting sensual pleasures, and who has crossed the stream, him the creatures that

are tied in sensual pleasures envy.'
Tissametteyyasutta is ended.

8 PASŪRASUTTA

Disputants brand each other as fools, they wish for praise, but being repulsed they become discontented; one is not purified by dispute, but by keeping to Buddha, who has shaken off all sin.

1. Here they maintain 'purity,' in other doctrines (dhamma) they do not allow purity; what they have devoted themselves to, that they call good, and they enter extensively upon the single truths.
2. Those wishing for dispute, having plunged into the assembly, brand each other as fools mutually, they go to others and pick a quarrel, wishing for praise and calling themselves (the only) expert.
3. Engaged in dispute in the middle of the assembly, wishing for praise he lays about on all sides; but when his dispute has been repulsed he becomes discontented, at the blame he gets angry he who sought for the faults (of others).
4. Because those who have tested his questions say that his dispute is lost and repulsed, he laments and grieves having lost his disputes; 'he has conquered me,' so saying he wails.
5. These disputes have arisen amongst the Samaṇas, in these (disputes) there is (dealt) blow (and) stroke; having seen this, let him leave off disputing, for there is no other advantage in trying to get praise.
6. Or he is praised there, having cleared up the dispute in the middle of the assembly; therefore he will laugh and be elated, having won that case as he had a mind to.
7. That which is his exaltation will also be the field of his defeat, still he talks proudly and arrogantly; seeing this, let no one dispute, for the expert do not say that purification (takes place) by that.

8. As a hero nourished by kingly food goes about roaring, wishing for an adversary — where he (i.e. the philosopher, Di*tth*igatika) is, go thou there, O hero; formerly there was nothing like this to fight against.

9. Those who, having embraced a (certain philosophical) view, dispute and maintain 'this only (is) true,' to them say thou when a dispute has arisen, 'Here is no opponent for thee.'

10. Those who wander about after having secluded themselves, without opposing view to view — what (opposition) wilt thou meet with amongst those, O Pasûra, by whom nothing in this world is grasped as the best?

11. Then thou wentest to reflection thinking in thy mind over the (different philosophical) views; thou hast gone into the yoke with him who has shaken off (all sin), but thou wilt not be able to proceed together (with him).

Pasûrasutta is ended.

9 MÂGANDIYASUTTA

A dialogue between Mâgandiya and Buddha. The former offers Buddha his daughter for a wife, but Buddha refuses her. Mâgandiya says that purity cornes from philosophy, Buddha from 'inward peace.' The Muni is a confessor of peace, he does not dispute, he is free from marks.

1. Buddha: 'Even seeing Ta*n*hâ, Arati, and Ragâ (the daughters of Mâra), there was not the least wish (in me) for sexual intercourse. What is this (thy daughter's body but a thing) full of water and excrement? I do not even want to touch it with my foot.'
2. Mâgandiya: 'If thou dost not want such a pearl, a woman desired by many kings, what view, virtue, and (holy) works, (mode of) life, re-birth dost thou profess?'
3. '"This I say," so (I do now declare), after investigation there is nothing amongst the doctrines which such a one (as I would) embrace, O Mâgandiya,' — so said Bhagavat, — 'and seeing (misery) in the (philosophical) views, without adopting (any of them), searching (for truth) I saw "inward peace."'
4. 'All the (philosophical) resolutions that have been formed,' — so said Mâgandiya, — 'those indeed thou explainest without adopting (any of them); the notion "inward peace" which (thou mentionest), how is this explained by the wise?'
5. 'Not by (any philosophical) opinion, not by tradition, not by knowledge, O Mâgandiya,' — so said Bhagavat, — 'not by virtue and (holy) works can any one say that purity exists; nor by absence of (philosophical) opinion, by absence of tradition, by absence of knowledge, by absence of virtue and (holy) works either; having abandoned these without adopting (anything else), let him, calm and independent, not desire existence.

6. 'If one cannot say by (any philosophical) opinion, or by tradition, or by knowledge,' — so said Mâgandiya, — 'or by virtue and (holy) works that purity exists, nor by absence of (philosophical) opinion, by absence of tradition, by absence of knowledge, by absence of virtue and (holy) works, then I consider the doctrine foolish, for by (philosophical) opinions some return to purity.'

7. 'And asking on account of (thy philosophical) opinion, O Mâgandiya,' — so said Bhagavat, — 'thou hast gone to infatuation in what thou hast embraced, and of this (inward peace) thou hast not the least idea, therefore thou holdest it foolish.

8. 'He who thinks himself equal (to others), or distinguished, or low, he for that very reason disputes; but he who is unmoved under those three conditions, for him (the notions) "equal" and "distinguished" do not exist.

9. 'The Brâhma*n*a for whom (the notions) "equal" and "unequal" do not exist, would he say, "This is true?" Or with whom should he dispute, saying, "This is false?" With whom should he enter into dispute?

10. 'Having left his house, wandering about houseless, not making acquaintances in the village, free from lust, not desiring (any future existence), let the Muni not get into quarrelsome talk with people.

11. 'Let not an eminent man (nâga) dispute after having embraced those (views) separated from which he (formerly) wandered in the world; as the thorny lotus elambu*g*a is undefiled by water and mud, so the Muni, the confessor of peace, free from greed, does not cling to sensual pleasures and the world.

12. 'An accomplished man does not by (a philosophical) view, or by thinking become arrogant, for he is not of that sort; not by (holy) works, nor by tradition is he to be led, he is not led into any of the resting-places (of the mind).

13. 'For him who is free from marks there are no ties, to him who is delivered by understanding there are no follies; (but those) who grasped after marks and (philosophical) views, they wander about

in the world annoying (people).'
Mâgandiyasutta is ended.

10 PURÂBHEDASUTTA

Definition of a calm Muni.

1. 'With what view and with what virtue is one called calm, tell me that, O Gotama, (when) asked about the best man?'
2. 'He whose desire is departed before the dissolution (of his body),' — so said Bhagavat, — 'who does not depend upon beginning and end, nor reckons upon the middle, by him there is nothing preferred.
3. 'He who is free from anger, free from trembling, free from boasting, free from misbehaviour, he who speaks wisely, he who is not elated, he is indeed a Muni who has restrained his speech.
4. 'Without desire for the future he does not grieve for the past, he sees seclusion in the phassas (touch), and he is not led by (any philosophical) views.
5. 'He is unattached, not deceitful, not covetous, not envious, not impudent, not contemptuous, and not given to slander.
6. 'Without desire for pleasant things and not given to conceit, and being gentle, intelligent, not credulous, he is not displeased (with anything).
7. 'Not from love of gain does he learn, and he does not get angry on account of loss, and untroubled by desire he has no greed for sweet things.
8. 'Equable (upekhaka), always thoughtful, he does not think himself equal (to others) in the world, nor distinguished, nor low: for him there are no desires (ussada).
9. 'The man for whom there is nothing upon which he depends, who is independent, having understood the Dhamma, for whom there is no desire for coming into existence or leaving existence,
10. 'Him I call calm, not looking for sensual pleasures; for him

there are no ties, he has overcome desire.

11. 'For him there are no sons, cattle, fields, wealth, nothing grasped or rejected is to be found in him,

12. 'That fault of which common people and Samanas and Brâhmanas say that he is possessed, is not possessed by him, therefore he is not moved by their talk.

13. 'Free from covetousness, without avarice, the Muni does not reckon himself amongst the distinguished, nor amongst the plain, nor amongst the low, he does not enter time, being delivered from time.

14. 'He for whom there is nothing in the world (which he may call) his own, who does not grieve over what is no more, and does not walk amongst the Dhammas (after his wish), he is called calm.'

Purâbhedasutta is ended.

II KALAHAVIVÂDASUTTA

The origin of contentions, disputes, &c. &c.

1. 'Whence (do spring up) contentions and disputes, lamentation and sorrow together with envy; and arrogance and conceit together with slander, whence do these spring up? pray, tell me this.'
2. 'From dear (objects) spring up contentions and disputes, lamentation and sorrow together with envy; arrogance and conceit together with slander; contentions and disputes are joined with envy, and there is slander in the disputes arisen.'
3. 'The dear (objects) in the world whence do they originate, and (whence) the covetousness that prevails in the world, and desire and fulfilment whence do they originate, which are (of consequence) for the future state of a man?'
4. 'From wish originate the dear (objects) in the world, and the covetousness that prevails in the world, and desire and fulfilment originate from it, which are (of consequence) for the future state of a man.'
5. 'From what has wish in the world its origin, and resolutions whence do they spring, anger and falsehood and doubt, and the Dhammas which are made known by the Samana (Gotama)?'
6. 'What they call pleasure and displeasure in the world, by that wish springs up; having seen decay and origin in (all) bodies, a person forms (his) resolutions in the world.
7. 'Anger and falsehood and doubt, these Dhammas are a couple; let the doubtful learn in the way of knowledge, knowingly the Dhammas have been proclaimed by the Samana.'
8. 'Pleasure and displeasure, whence have they their origin, for want of what do these not arise? This notion which (thou

mentionest), viz. "decay and origin," tell me from what does this arise.'

9. 'Pleasure and displeasure have their origin from phassa (touch), when there is no touch they do not arise. This notion which (thou mentionest), viz. "decay and origin," this I tell thee has its origin from this.'

10. 'From what has phassa its origin in the world and from what does grasping spring up? For want of what is there no egotism, by the cessation of what do the touches not touch? '

11. 'On account of name and form the touches (exist), grasping has its origin in wish; by the cessation of wishes there is no egotism, by the cessation of form the touches do not touch.'

12. 'How is one to be constituted that (his) form may cease to exist, and how do joy and pain cease to exist? Tell me this, how it ceases, that we should like to know, such was my mind?'

13. 'Let one not be with a natural consciousness, nor with a mad consciousness, nor without consciousness, nor with (his) consciousness gone; for him who is thus constituted form ceases to exist, for what is called delusion has its origin in consciousness.' (?)

14. 'What we have asked thee thou hast explained unto us; we will ask thee another question, answer us that: Do not some (who are considered) wise in this world tell us that the principal (thing) is the purification of the yakkha, or do they say something different from this?'

15. 'Thus some (who are considered) wise in this world say that the principal (thing) is the purification of the yakkha; but some of them say samaya (annihilation), the expert say (that the highest purity lies) in anupâdisesa (none of the five attributes remaining).

16. 'And having known these to be dependent, the investigating Muni, having known the things we depend upon, and after knowing them being liberated, does not enter into dispute, the wise (man) does not go to reiterated existence.'

Kalahavivâdasutta is ended.

12 KŪLAVIYŪHASUTTA

A description of disputing philosophers. The different schools of philosophy contradict each other, they proclaim different truths, but the truth is only one. As long as the disputations are going on, so long will there be strife in the world.

1. Abiding by their own views, some (people), having got into contest, assert themselves to be the (only) expert (saying), '(He) who understands this, he knows the Dhamma; he who reviles this, he is not perfect.'
2. So having got into contest they dispute: 'The opponent (is) a fool, an ignorant (person),' so they say. Which one of these, pray, is the true doctrine (vâda)? for all these assert themselves (to be the only) expert.
3. He who does not acknowledge an opponent's doctrine (dhamma), he is a fool, a beast, one of poor understanding, all are fools with a very poor understanding; all these abide by their (own) views.
4. They are surely purified by their own view, they are of a pure understanding, expert, thoughtful, amongst them there is no one of poor understanding, their view is quite perfect!
5. I do not say, 'This is the reality,' which fools say mutually to each other; they made their own views the truth, therefore they hold others to be fools.
6. What some say is the truth, the reality, that others say is void, false, so having disagreed they dispute. Why do not the Samaṇas say one (and the same thing)?
7. For the truth is one, there is not a second, about which one intelligent man might dispute with another intelligent man; (but) they themselves praise different truths, therefore the Samaṇas do

not say one and the same thing).
8. Why do the disputants that assert themselves (to be the only) expert, proclaim different truths? Have many different truths been heard of, or do they (only) follow (their own) reasoning?
9. There are not many different truths in the world, no eternal ones except consciousness; but having reasoned on the (philosophical) views they proclaim a double Dhamma, truth and falsehood.
10. In regard to what has been seen, or heard, virtue and (holy) works, or what has been thought, and on account of these (views) looking (upon others) with contempt, standing in (their) resolutions joyful, they say that the opponent is a fool and an ignorant person (?)
11. Because he holds another (to be) a fool, therefore he calls himself expert, in his own opinion he is one that tells what is propitious, others he blames, so he said. (?)
12. He is full of his overbearing (philosophical) view, mad with pride, thinking himself perfect, he is in his own opinion anointed with the spirit (of genius), for his (philosopbical) view is quite complete.
13. If he according to another's report is low, then (he says) the other is also of a low understanding, and if he himself is accomplished and wise, there is not any fool amongst the Samanas.
14. 'Those who preach a doctrine (dhamma) different from this, fall short of purity and are imperfect,' so the Titthiyas say repeatedly, for they are inflamed by passion for their own (philosophical) views.
15. Here they maintain purity, in other doctrines (dhamma) they do not allow purity; so the Titthiyas, entering extensively (upon details), say that in their own way there is something firm.
16. And saying that there is something firm in his own way he holds his opponent to be a fool; thus he himself brings on strife, calling his opponent a fool and impure (asuddhadhamma).
17. Standing in (his) resolution, having himself measured (teachers, &c.), he still more enters into dispute in the world; but

having left all resolutions nobody will excite strife in the world.
Kûlaviyûhasutta is ended.

13 MAHÂVIYÛHASUTTA

Philosophers cannot lead to purity, they only praise themselves and stigmatise others. But a Brâhmana has overcome all dispute, he is indifferent to learning, he is appeased.

1. Those who abiding in the (philosophical) views dispute, saying, 'This is the truth,' they all incur blame, and they also obtain praise in this matter.
2. This is little, not enough to (bring about) tranquillity, I say there are two fruits of dispute; having seen this let no one dispute, understanding Khema (i.e. Nibbâna) to be the place where there is no dispute.
3. The opinions that have arisen amongst people, all these the wise man does not embrace; he is independent. Should he who is not pleased with what has been seen and heard resort to dependency? (?)
4. Those who consider virtue the highest of all, say that purity is associated with restraint; having taken upon themselves a (holy) work they serve. Let us learn in this (view), then, his (the Master's) purity; wishing for existence they assert themselves to be the only expert.
5. If he falls off from virtue and (holy) works, he trembles, having missed (his) work; he laments, he prays for purity in this world, as one who has lost his caravan or wandered away from his house.
6. Having left virtue and (holy) works altogether, and both wrong and blameless work, not praying for purity or impurity, he wanders abstaining (from both purity and impurity), without having embraced peace.
7. By means of penance, or anything disliked, or what has been seen, or heard, or thought, going upwards they wail for what is

pure, without being free from desire for reiterated existence.

8. For him who wishes (for something there always are) desires, and trembling in (the midst of his) plans; he for whom there is no death and no re-birth, how can he tremble or desire anything?

9. What some call the highest Dhamma, that others again call wretched; which one of these, pray, is the true doctrine (vâda)? for all these assert themselves (to be the only) expert.

10. Their own Dhamma they say is perfect, another's Dhamma again they say is wretched; so having disagreed they dispute, they each say their own opinions (are) the truth.

11. If one (becomes) low by another's censure, then there will be no one distinguished amongst the Dhammas; for they all say another's Dhamma (is) low, in their own they say there is something firm.

12. The worshipping of their own Dhamma is as great as their praise of their own ways; all schools would be in the same case, for their purity is individual.

13. There is nothing about a Brâhmana dependent upon others, nothing amongst the Dhammas which he would embrace after investigation; therefore he has overcome the disputes, for he does not regard any other Dhamma as the best.

14. 'I understand, I see likewise this,' so saying, some by (their philosophical) views return to purity. If he saw purity, what then (has been effected) by another's view? Having conquered they say that purity exists by another. (?)

15. A seeing man will see name and form, and having seen he will understand those (things); let him at pleasure see much or little, for the expert do not say that purity exists by that.

16. A dogmatist is no leader to purity, being guided by prejudiced views, saying that good consists in what he is given to, and saying that purity is there, he saw the thing so.

17. A Brâhmana does not enter time, (or) the number (of living beings), (he is) no follower of (philosophical) views, nor a friend of knowledge; and having penetrated the opinions that have arisen amongst people, he is indifferent to learning, while others acquire it.

18. The Muni, having done away with ties here in the world, is no partisan in the disputes that have arisen; appeased amongst the unappeased he is indifferent, not embracing learning, while others acquire it.

19. Having abandoned his former passions, not contracting new ones, not wandering according to his wishes, being no dogmatist, he is delivered from the (philosophical) views, being wise, and he does not cling to the world, neither does he blame himself.

20. Being secluded amongst all the doctrines (dhamma), whatever has been seen, heard, or thought, he is a Muni who has laid down his burden and is liberated, not belonging to time (na kappiyo), not dead, not wishing for anything. So said Bhagavat.

Mahâviyûhasutta is ended.

14 TUVA*T*AKASUTTA

How a Bhikkhu attains bliss, what his duties are, and what he is to avoid.

1. 'I ask thee, who art a kinsman of the Âdi*kk*as and a great Isi, about seclusion (viveka) and the state of peace. How is a Bhikkhu, after having seen it, extinguished, not grasping at anything in the world?'

2. 'Let him completely cut off the root of what is called papañ*k*a (delusion), thinking "I am wisdom;"' — so said Bhagavat, — 'all the desires that arise inwardly, let him learn to subdue them, always being thoughtful.

3. 'Let him learn every Dhamma inwardly or outwardly; let him not therefore be proud, for that is not called bliss by the good.

4. 'Let him not therefore think himself better (than others or) low or equal (to others); questioned by different people, let him not adorn himself.

5. 'Let the Bhikkhu be appeased inwardly, let him not seek peace from any other (quarter); for him who is inwardly appeased there is nothing grasped or rejected.

6. 'As in the middle (i.e. depth) of the sea no wave is born, (but as it) remains still, so let the Bhikkhu be still, without desire, let him not desire anything whatever.'

7. He with open eyes expounded clearly the Dhamma that removes (all) dangers; tell (now) the religious practices; the precepts or contemplation.

8. Bhagavat: 'Let him not be greedy with his eyes, let him keep his ears from the talk of the town, let him not be greedy after sweet things, and let him not desire anything in the world.

9. 'When he is touched by the touch (of illness), let the Bhikkhu

not lament, and let him not wish for existence anywhere, and let him not tremble at dangers.

10. 'Having obtained boiled rice and drink, solid food and clothes, let him not store up (these things), and let him not be anxious, if he does not get them.

11. 'Let him be meditative, not prying, let him abstain from misbehaviour, let him not be indolent, let the Bhikkhu live in his quiet dwelling.

12. 'Let him not sleep too much, let him apply himself ardently to watching, let him abandon sloth, deceit, laughter, sport, sexual intercourse, and adornment.

13. 'Let him not apply himself to practising (the hymns of) the Âthabba*n*a(-veda), to (the interpretation of) sleep and signs, nor to astrology; let not (my) follower (mâmaka) devote himself to (interpreting) the cry of birds, to causing impregnation, nor to (the art of) medicine.

14. 'Let the Bhikkhu not tremble at blame, nor puff himself up when praised; let him drive off covetousness together with avarice, anger, and slander.

15. 'Let the Bhikkhu not be engaged in purchase and sale, let him not blame others in anything, let him not scold in the village, let him not from love of gain speak to people.

16. 'Let not the Bhikkhu be a boaster, and let him not speak coherent language; let him not learn pride, let him not speak quarrelsome language.

17. 'Let him not be led into falsehood, let him not consciously do wicked things; and with respect to livelihood, understanding, virtue, and (holy) works let him not despise others.

18. 'Having heard much talk from much-talking Sama*n*as let him not irritated answer them with harsh language; for the good do not thwart others.

19. 'Having understood this Dhamma, let the investigating and always thoughtful Bhikkhu learn; having conceived bliss to consist in peace, let him not be indolent in Gotama's commandments.

20. 'For he a conqueror unconquered saw the Dhamma visibly, without any traditional instruction; therefore let him learn,

heedful in his, Bhagavat's, commandments, and always worshipping.'
Tuvaṭakasutta is ended.

15 ATTADA*ND*ASUTTA

Description of an accomplished Muni.

1. From him who has seized a stick fear arises. Look at people killing (each other); I will tell of grief as it is known to me.
2. Seeing people struggling like fish in (a pond with) little water, seeing them obstructed by each other, a fear came over me.
3. The world is completely unsubstantial, all quarters are shaken; wishing for a house for myself I did not see (one) uninhabited.
4. But having seen (all beings) in the end obstructed, discontent arose in me; then I saw in this world an arrow, difficult to see, stuck in the heart.
5. He who has been pierced by this arrow runs through all quarters; but having drawn out that arrow, he will not run, he will sit down (quietly).
6. There (many) studies are gone through; what is tied in the world let him not apply himself to (untie) it; having wholly transfixed desire, let him learn his own extinction (nibbâna).
7. Let the Muni be truthful, without arrogance, undeceitful, free from slander, not angry, let him overcome avarice.
8. Let the man who has turned his mind to Nibbâna conquer sleepiness, drowsiness, and sloth; let him not live together with indolence, let him not indulge in conceit.
9. Let him not be led into falsehood, let him not turn his affection to form; let him penetrate arrogance, let him wander abstaining from violence.
10. Let him not delight in what is old, let him not bear with what is new, let him not grieve for what is lost, let him not give himself up to desire.
11. (This desire) I call greed, the great stream, I call (it)

precipitation, craving, a trouble, a bog of lust difficult to cross.

12. The Muni who without deviating from truth stands fast on the firm ground (of Nibbâna, being) a Brâhma*n*a, he, having forsaken everything, is indeed called calm.

13. He indeed is wise, he is accomplished, having understood the Dhamma independent (of everything); wandering rightly in the world he does not envy any one here.

14. Whosoever has here overcome lust, a tie difficult to do away with in the world, he does not grieve, he does not covet, having cut off the stream, and being without bonds.

15. What is before (thee), lay that aside; let there be nothing behind thee; if thou wilt not grasp after what is in the middle, thou wilt wander calm.

16. The man who has no desire at all for name and form (individuality) and who does not grieve over what is no more, he indeed does not decay in the world.

17. He who does not think, 'this is mine' and 'for others there is also something,' he, not having egotism, does not grieve at having nothing.

18. Not being harsh, not greedy, being without desire, and being the same under all circumstances (samo), — that I call a good result, when asked about an undaunted man.

19. For him who is free from desire, for the discerning (man) there is no Sa*m*khâra; abstaining from every sort of effort he sees happiness everywhere.

20. The Muni does not reckon himself amongst the plain, nor amongst the low, nor amongst the distinguished; being calm and free from avarice, he does not grasp after nor reject anything.

Attada*nd*asutta is ended.

16 SÂRIPUTTASUTTA

On Sâriputta asking what a Bhikkhu is to devote himself to, Buddha shows what life he is to lead.

1. 'Neither has before been seen by me,' — so said the venerable Sâriputta, — 'nor has any one heard of such a beautifully-speaking master, a teacher arrived from the Tusita heaven.
2. 'As he, the clearly-seeing, appears to the world of men and gods, after having dispelled all darkness, so he wanders alone in the midst (of people).
3. 'To this Buddha, who is independent, unchanged, a guileless teacher, who has arrived (in the world), I have come supplicatingly with a question from many who are bound in this world.
4. 'To a Bhikkhu who is loath (of the world) and affects an isolated seat, the root of a tree or a cemetery, or (who lives) in the caves of the mountains,
5. 'How many dangers (are there not) in these various dwelling-places at which the Bhikkhu does not tremble in his quiet dwelling!
6. 'How many dangers (are there not) in the world for him who goes to the immortal region, (dangers) which the Bhikkhu overcomes in his distant dwelling!
7. 'Which are his words, which are his objects in this world, which are the virtue and (holy) works of the energetic Bhikkhu?
8. 'What study having devoted himself to, intent on one object, wise and thoughtful, can he blow off his own filth as the smith (blows off) that of the silver?'
9. 'What is pleasant for him who is disgusted (with birth, &c.), O Sâriputta,' — so said Bhagavat, — 'if he cultivates a lonely

dwelling-place, and loves perfect enlightenment in accordance with the Dhamma, that I will tell thee as I understand it.

10. 'Let not the wise and thoughtful Bhikkhu wandering on the borders be afraid of the five dangers: gad-flies and (all other) flies, snakes, contact with (evil) men, and quadrupeds.

11. 'Let him not be afraid of adversaries, even having seen many dangers from them; further he will overcome other dangers while seeking what is good.

12. 'Touched by sickness and hunger let him endure cold and excessive heat, let him, touched by them in many ways, and being houseless, make strong exertions.

13. 'Let him not commit theft, let him not speak falsely, let him touch friendly what is feeble or strong, what he acknowledges to be the agitation of the mind, let him drive that off as a partisan of Kanha (i.e. Mâra).

14. 'Let him not fall into the power of anger and arrogance; having dug up the root of these, let him live, and let him overcome both what is pleasant and what is unpleasant.

15. 'Guided by wisdom, taking delight in what is good, let him scatter those dangers, let him overcome discontent in his distant dwelling, let him overcome the four causes of lamentation.

16. 'What shall I eat, or where shall I eat? — he lay indeed uncomfortably (last night) — where shall I lie this night? let the Sekha who wanders about houseless subdue these lamentable doubts.

17. 'Having had in (due) time both food and clothes, let him know moderation in this world for the sake of happiness; guarded in these (things) and wandering restrained in the village let him, even (if he be) irritated, not speak harsh words.

18. 'Let him be with down-cast eyes, and not prying, devoted to meditation, very watchful; having acquired equanimity let him with a composed mind cut off the seat of doubt, and misbehaviour.

19. 'Urged on by words (of his teachers) let him be thoughtful and rejoice (at this urging), let him break stubbornness in his fellow-students, let him utter propitious words and not

unseasonable, let him not think detractingly of others.

20. 'And then the five impurities in the world, the subjection of which he must learn thoughtfully, — let him overcome passion for form, sound and taste, smell and touch.

21. 'Let the Bhikkhu subdue his wish for these Dhammas and be thoughtful, and with his mind well liberated, then in time he will, reflecting upon Dhamma, and having become intent upon one object, destroy darkness.' So said Bhagavat.

V PÂRÂYANAVAGGA

I VATTHUGÂTHÂ

To the Brâhmaṇa Bâvarî, living on the banks of the Godhâvarî, in Assaka's territory, comes another Brâhmaṇa and asks for five hundred pieces of money, but not getting them he curses Bâvarî, saying, 'May thy head on the seventh day hence cleave into seven.' A deity comforts Bâvarî by referring him to Buddha. Then Bâvarî sends his sixteen disciples to Buddha, and each of them asks Buddha a question.

1. From the beautiful city of the Kosalas (Sâvatthî) a Brâhmaṇa, well versed in the hymns, went to the South (Dakkhiṇâpatha) wishing for nothingness.
2. In Assaka's territory, in the neighbourhood of Aḷaka, he dwelt on the banks of the Godhâvarî, (living) on gleanings and fruit.
3. And close by the bank there was a large village, with the income of which he prepared a great sacrifice.
4. Having offered the great sacrifice, he again entered the hermitage. Upon his re-entering, another Brâhmaṇa arrived,
5. With swollen feet, trembling, covered with mud, with dust on his head. And he going up to him (i.e. the first Brâhmaṇa) demanded five hundred (pieces of money).
6. Bâvarî, seeing him, bade him be seated, asked him whether he was happy and well, and spoke as follows:
7. 'What gifts I had are all given away by me; pardon me, O Brâhmaṇa, I have no five hundred.'
8. 'If thou wilt not give to me who asks, may thy head on the seventh clay cleave into seven.'
9. So after the usual ceremonies this impostor made known his

fearful (curse). On hearing these his words Bâvarî became sorrowful.

10. He wasted away taking no food, transfixed by the arrow of grief, but yet his mind delighted in meditation.

11. Seeing Bâvarî struck with horror and sorrowful, the benevolent deity (of that place) approached him and said as follows:

12. 'He does not know (anything about) the head; he is a hypocrite coveting riches; knowledge of the head and head-splitting is not found in him.'

13. 'If the venerable (deity) knows it, then tell me, when asked, all about the head and head-splitting; let us hear thy words.'

14. 'I do not know this; knowledge of it is not found in me; as to the head and head-splitting, this is to be seen by Buddhas (only).'

15. 'Who then, say, in the circumference of the earth knows the head and head-splitting, tell me that, O deity?'

16. 'Formerly went out from Kapilavatthu a ruler of the world, an offspring of the Okkâka king, the Sakya son, the light-giving;

17. 'He is, O Brâhma*n*a, the perfectly Enlightened (Sambuddha); perfect in all things, he has attained the power of all knowledge, sees clearly in everything; he has arrived at the destruction of all things, and is liberated in the destruction of the upadhis.

18. 'He is Buddha, he is Bhagavat in the world, he, the clearly-seeing, teaches the Dhamma; go thou to him and ask, he will explain it to thee.'

19. Having heard the word 'Sambuddha,' Bâvarî rejoiced, his grief became little, and he was filled with great delight.

20. Bâvarî glad, rejoicing, and eager asked the deity: 'In what village or in what town or in what province dwells the chief of the world, that going there we may adore the perfectly Enlightened, the first of men?'

21. 'In Sâvatthî, the town of the Kosalas, dwells *G*ina (the Victorious), of great understanding and excellent wide knowledge, he the Sakya son, unyoked, free from passion, skilled in head-splitting, the bull of men.'

22. Then (Bâvarî) addressed his disciples, Brâhma*n*as, perfect in

the hymns: 'Come, youths, I will tell (you something), listen to my words:

23. 'He whose appearance in the world is difficult to be met with often, he is at the present time born in the world and widely renowned as Sambuddha (the perfectly Enlightened); go quickly to Sâvatthî and behold the best of men.'

24. 'How then can we know, on seeing him, that he is Buddha, O Brâhmaṇa? Tell us who do not know him, by what may we recognise him?

25. 'For in the hymns are to be found the marks of a great man, and thirty-two are disclosed altogether, one by one.'

26. 'For him on whose limbs these marks of a great man are to be found, there are two ways left, a third does not exist.

27. 'If he abides in a dwelling, he will subdue this earth without rod (or) sword, he will rule with justice.

28. 'And if he departs from his dwelling for the wilderness, he becomes the saint, incomparable Sambuddha, who has removed the veil (from the world).

29. 'Ask in your mind about my birth and family, my marks, hymns, and my other disciples, the head and head-splitting.

30. 'If he is Buddha, the clear-sighted, then he will answer by word of mouth the questions you have asked in your mind.'

31, 32, 33. Having heard Bâvarî's words his disciples, sixteen Brâhmaṇas, Agita, Tissametteyya, Puṇṇaka, further Mettagû, Dhotaka and Upasîva, and Nanda, further Hemaka, the two Todeyya and Kappa, and the wise Gatukaṇṇî, Bhadrâvudha and Udaya, and also the Brâhmaṇa Posâla, and the wise Mogharâgan, and the great Isi Piṅgiya, 6-100

34. All of them, having each their host (of pupils), and being themselves widely renowned throughout the world, thinkers delighting in meditation, wise, scented with the perfume of former (good deeds),

35. Having saluted Bâvarî and gone round him towards the right, all with matted hair and bearing hides, departed with their faces turned to the north.

36. To Patiṭṭhâna of Aḷaka first, then to Mâhissatî, and also to

Uggenî, Gonaddha, Vedisâ, Vanasavhaya,

37. And also to Kosambî, Sâketa, and Sâvatthî, the most excellent of cities, to Setavya, Kapilavatthu, and the city of Kusinâra,

38. And to Pâva, the city of wealth, to Vesâlî, the city of Magadha, to Pâsânaka Ketiya (the Rock Temple), the lovely, the charming.

39. As he who is athirst (longs for) the cold water, as the merchant (longs for) gain, as he who is plagued by heat (longs for) shade, so in haste they ascended the mountain.

40. And Bhagavat at that time attended by the assembly of the Bhikkhus taught the Dhamma to the Bhikkhus, and roared like a lion in the forest.

41. Agita beheld Sambuddha as the shining (sun) without (burning) rays, as the moon on the fifteenth, having reached her plenitude.

42. Then observing his limbs and all the marks in their fulness, standing apart, rejoiced, he asked the questions of his mind: —

43. 'Tell me about (my master's) birth, tell me about his family together with the marks, tell me about his perfection in the hymns, how many (hymns) does the Brâhmana recite?'

44. Bhagavat said: 'One hundred and twenty years (is his) age, and by family he is a Bâvarî; three are his marks on the limbs, and in the three Vedas he is perfect.

45. 'In the marks and in the Itihâsa together with Nighandu and Ketubha — he recites five hundred — and in his own Dhamma he has reached perfection.'

46. Agita thought: 'Explain fully the marks of Bâvarî, O thou best of men, who cuts off desire; let there be no doubt left for us.'

47. Bhagavat said: 'He covers his face with his tongue, he has a circle of hair between the eye-brows, (his) privy member (is) hidden in a sheath, know this, O young man.'

48. Not hearing him ask anything, but hearing the questions answered, the multitude reflected overjoyed and with joined hands: —

49. 'Who, be he a god, or Brahman, or Inda, the husband of Sugâ, asked in his mind those questions, and to whom did that (speech)

reply?'

50. Agita said: 'The head and head-splitting Bâvarî asked about; explain that, O Bhagavat, remove our doubt, O Isi.'

51. Bhagavat said: 'Ignorance is the head, know this; knowledge cleaves the head, together with belief, thoughtfulness, meditation, determination, and strength.'

52. Then with great joy having composed himself the young man put his hide on one shoulder fell at (Bhagavat's) feet (and saluted him) with his head, (saying):

53. 'Bâvarî, the Brâhmana, together with his disciples, O thou venerable man, delighted and glad, does homage to thy feet, O thou clearly-seeing.'

54. Bhagavat said: 'Let Bâvarî, the Brâhmana, be glad together with his disciples! Be thou also glad, live long, O young man!

55. 'For Bâvarî and for thee, for all there are all (kinds of) doubt; having got an opportunity, ask ye whatever you wish.'

56. After getting permission from Sambuddha, Agita sitting there with folded hands asked Tathâgata the first question.

The Vatthugâthâs are ended.

2 AGITAMÂNAVAPUKKHÂ

1. 'By what is the world shrouded,' — so said the venerable Agita, — 'by what does it not shine? What callest thou its pollution, what is its great danger?'
2. 'With ignorance is the world shrouded, O Agita,' — so said Bhagavat, — 'by reason of avarice it does not shine; desire I call its pollution, pain is its great danger.'
3. 'The streams of desire flow in every direction,' — so said the venerable Agita; — 'what dams the streams, say what restrains the streams, by what may the streams be shut off?'
4. 'Whatever streams there are in the world, O Agita,' — so said Bhagavat, — 'thoughtfulness is their dam, thoughtfulness I call the restraint of the streams, by understanding they are shut off.'
5. 'Both understanding and thoughtfulness,' — so said the venerable Agita, — 'and name and shape, O venerable man, — asked about this by me, declare by what is this stopped?'
6. Buddha: 'This question which thou hast asked, O Agita, that I will explain to thee; (I will explain to thee) by what name and shape are totally stopped; by the cessation of consciousness this is stopped here.'
7. Agita: 'Those who have examined (all) Dhammas (i.e. the saints), and those who are disciples, (and those who are) common men here, — when thou art asked about their mode of life, declare it unto me, thou who art wise, O venerable man.'
8. Buddha: 'Let the Bhikkhu not crave for sensual pleasures, let him be calm in mind, let him wander about skilful in all Dhammas, and thoughtful.'

Agitamânavapukkhâ is ended.

3 TISSAMETTEYYAMÂNAVAPUKKHÂ

1. 'Who is contented in the world,' — so said the venerable Tissametteyya, — 'who is without commotions? Who after knowing both ends does not stick in the middle, as far as his understanding is concerned? Whom dost thou call a great man? Who has overcome desire in this world?'

2. 'The Bhikkhu who abstains from sensual pleasures, O Metteyya,' — so said Bhagavat, — 'who is free from desire, always thoughtful, happy by reflection, he is without commotions, he after knowing both ends does not stick in the middle, as far as his understanding is concerned; him I call a great man; he has overcame desire in this world.'

Tissametteyyamânavapukkhâ is ended.

4 PU*NN*AKAMÂ*NA*VAPU*KKH*Â

1. 'To him who is without desire, who has seen the root (of sin),' — so said the venerable Pu*nn*aka, — 'I have come supplicatingly with a question: on account of what did the Isis and men, Khattiyas and Brâhma*n*as, offer sacrifices to the gods abundantly in this world? (about this) I ask thee, O Bhagavat, tell me this.'
2. 'All these Isis and men, Khattiyas and Brâhma*n*as, O Pu*nn*aka,' — so said Bhagavat, — 'who offered sacrifices to the gods abundantly in this world, offered sacrifices, O Pu*nn*aka, after reaching old age, wishing for their present condition.'
3. 'All these Isis and men, Khattiyas and Brâhma*n*as,' — so said the venerable Pu*nn*aka, — 'who offered sacrifices to the gods abundantly in this world, did they, O Bhagavat, indefatigable in the way of offering, cross over both birth and old age, O venerable man? I ask thee, O Bhagavat, tell me this.'
4. 'They wished for, praised, desired, abandoned (sensual pleasures), O Pu*nn*aka,' — so said Bhagavat, — 'they desired sensual pleasures on account of what they reached by them; they, devoted to offering, dyed with the passions of existence, did not cross over birth and old age, so I say.'
5. 'If they, devoted to offering,' — so said the venerable Pu*nn*aka, — 'did not by offering cross over birth and old age, O venerable man, who then in the world of gods and men crossed over birth and old age, O venerable man, I ask thee, O Bhagavat, tell me this?'
6. 'Having considered everything in the world, O Pu*nn*aka,' — so said Bhagavat, — 'he who is not defeated anywhere in the world, who is calm without the smoke of passions, free from woe, free from desire, he crossed over birth and old age, so I say.'
Pu*nn*akamâ*n*avapu*kkh*â is ended.

5 METTAGÛMÂNAVAPU*KKH*Â

1. 'I ask thee, O Bhagavat, tell me this,' — so said the venerable Mettagû, — 'I consider thee accomplished and of a cultivated mind, why are these (creatures), whatsoever they are of many kinds in the world, always subject to pain?

2. 'Thou mayest well ask me concerning the origin of pain, O Mettagû,' — so said Bhagavat, — 'I will explain that to thee in the way I myself know it: originating in the upadhis pains arise, whatsoever they are, of many kinds in the world.

3. 'He who being ignorant creates upadhi, that fool again undergoes pain; therefore let not the wise man create upadhi, considering (that this is) the birth and origin of pain.'

4. Mettagû: 'What we have asked thee thou hast explained to us; another (question) I ask thee, answer that, pray: How do the wise cross the stream, birth and old age, and sorrow and lamentation? Explain that thoroughly to me, O Muni, for this thing (dhamma) is well known to thee.'

5. 'I will explain the Dhamma to thee, O Mettagû,' — so said Bhagavat, — 'if a man in the visible world, without any traditional instruction, has understood it, and wanders about thoughtful, he may overcome desire in the world.'

6. Mettagû: 'And I take a delight in that, in the most excellent Dhamma, O great Isi, which if a man has understood, and he wanders about thoughtful, he may overcome desire in the world.'

7. 'Whatsoever thou knowest, O Mettagû,' — so said Bhagavat, — '(of what is) above, below, across, and in the middle, taking no delight and no rest in these things, let thy mind not dwell on existence.

8. 'Living so, thoughtful, strenuous, let the Bhikkhu wandering about, after abandoning selfishness, birth, and old age, and

sorrow, and lamentation, being a wise man, leave pain in this world.'

9. Mettagû: 'I delight in these words of the great Isi; well expounded, O Gotama, is (by thee) freedom from upadhi (i.e. Nibbâna). Bhagavat in truth has left pain, for this Dhamma is well known to thee.

10. 'And those also will certainly leave pain whom thou, O Muni, constantly mayest admonish; therefore I bow down to thee, having come hither, O chief (nâga), may Bhagavat also admonish me constantly.'

11. Buddha: 'The Brâhmana whom I may acknowledge as accomplished, possessing nothing, not cleaving to the world of lust, he surely has crossed this stream, and he has crossed over to the other shore, free from harshness (akhila), (and) free from doubt.

12. 'And he is a wise and accomplished man in this world; having abandoned this cleaving to reiterated existence he is without desire, free from woe, free from longing, he has crossed over birth and old age, so I say.'

Mettagûmânavapukkhâ is ended.

6 DHOTAKAMÂNAVAPUKKHÂ

1. 'I ask thee, O Bhagavat, tell me this,' — so said the venerable Dhotaka, — 'I long for thy word, O great Isi; let one, having listened to thy utterance, learn his own extinction.'

2. 'Exert thyself then, O Dhotaka,' — so said Bhagavat, — 'being wise and thoughtful in this world, let one, having listened to my utterance, learn his own extinction.'

3. Dhotaka: 'I see in the world of gods and men a Brâhmana wandering about, possessing nothing; therefore I bow down to thee, O thou all-seeing one, free me, O Sakka, from doubts.'

4. Buddha: 'I shall not go to free any one in the world who is doubtful, O Dhotaka; when thou hast learned the best Dhamma, then thou shalt cross this stream.'

5. Dhotaka: 'Teach (me), O Brâhmana, having compassion (on me), the Dhamma of seclusion (i.e. Nibbâna), that I may understand (it and) that I, without falling into many shapes like the air, may wander calm and independent in this world.' (?)

6. 'I will explain to thee peace, O Dhotaka,' — so said Bhagavat; — 'if a man in the visible world, without any traditional instruction, has understood it, and wanders about thoughtful, he may overcome desire in the world.'

7. Dhotaka: 'And I take delight in that, the highest peace, O great Isi, which if a man has understood, and he wanders about thoughtful, he may overcome desire in the world.'

8. 'Whatsoever thou knowest, O Dhotaka,' — so said Bhagavat, — '(of what is) above, below, across, and in the middle, knowing this to be a tie in the world, thou must not thirst for reiterated existence.'

Dhotakamânavapukkhâ is ended.

7 UPASÎVAMÂNAVAPU*KKHÂ*

1. 'Alone, O Sakka; and without assistance I shall not be able to cross the great stream,' — so said the venerable Upasîva; — 'tell me an object, O thou all-seeing one, by means of which one may cross this stream.'

2. 'Having in view nothingness, being thoughtful, O Upasîva,' — so said Bhagavat, — 'by the reflection of nothing existing shalt thou cross the stream; having abandoned sensual pleasures, being loath of doubts, thou shalt regard the extinction of desire (i.e. Nibbâna), both day and night.'

3. Upasîva: 'He whose passion for all sensual pleasures has departed, having resorted to nothingness, after leaving everything else, and being delivered in the highest deliverance by knowledge, will he remain there without proceeding further?'

4. 'He whose passion for all sensual pleasures has departed, O Upasîva,' — so said Bhagavat, — 'having resorted to nothingness after leaving everything else, and being delivered in the highest deliverance by knowledge, he will remain there without proceeding further.'

5. Upasîva: 'If he remains there without proceeding further for a multitude of years, O thou all-seeing one, (and if) he becomes there tranquil and delivered, will there be consciousness for such a one?'

6. 'As a flame blown about by the violence of the wind, O Upasîva,' — so said Bhagavat, — 'goes out, cannot be reckoned (as existing), even so a Muni, delivered from name and body, disappears, and cannot be reckoned (as existing).'

7. Upasîva: 'Has he (only) disappeared, or does he not exist (any longer), or is he for ever free from sickness? Explain that thoroughly to me, O Muni, for this Dhamma is well known to

thee.'

8. 'For him who has disappeared there is no form, O Upasîva,' — so said Bhagavat, — 'that by which they say he is, exists for him no longer, when all things (dhamma) have been cut off, all (kinds of) dispute are also cut off.'

Upasîvamâ*n*avapu*kkh*â is ended.

8 NANDAMĀNAVAPUKKHĀ

1. 'There are Munis in the world,' — so said the venerable Nanda, — 'so people say. How is this (understood) by thee? Do they call him a Muni who is possessed of knowledge or him who is possessed of life?'

2. Buddha: 'Not because of (any philosophical) view, nor of tradition, nor of knowledge, O Nanda, do the expert call (any one) a Muni; (but) such as wander free from woe, free from desire, after having secluded themselves, those I call Munis.'

3. 'All these Samanas and Brâhmanas,' — so said the venerable Nanda, — 'say that purity comes from (philosophical) views, and from tradition, and from virtue and (holy) works, and in many (other) ways. Did they, in the way in which they lived in the world, cross over birth and old age, O venerable man? I ask thee, O Bhagavat, tell me this.'

4. 'All these Samanas and Brâhmanas, O Nanda,' — so said Bhagavat, — 'say that purity comes from (philosophical) views, and from tradition, and from virtue and (holy) works, and in many (other) ways; still they did not, in the way in which they lived in the world, cross over birth and old age, so I say.'

5. 'All these Samanas and Brâhmanas,' — so said the venerable Nanda, — 'say that purity comes from (philosophical) views, and from tradition, and from virtue and (holy) works, and in many (other) ways; if thou, O Muni, sayest that such have not crossed the stream, who then in the world of gods and men crossed over birth and old age, O venerable man? I ask thee, O Bhagavat, tell me this.'

6. 'I do not say that all Samanas and Brâhmanas, O Nanda,' — so said Bhagavat, — 'are shrouded by birth and old age; those who, after leaving in this world what has been seen or heard or thought,

and all virtue and (holy) works, after leaving everything of various kinds, after penetrating desire, are free from passion, such indeed I call men that have crossed the stream.'

7. Nanda: 'I delight in these words of the great Isi; well expounded (by thee), O Gotama, is freedom from upadhi (i.e. Nibbâna); those who, after leaving in this world what has been seen or heard or thought, and all virtue and (holy) works, after leaving everything of various kinds, after penetrating desire, are free from passion, such I call men that have crossed the stream.'

Nandamâ*n*avapu*kkh*â is ended.

9 HEMAKAMÂNAVAPUKKHA

1. 'Those who before in another world,' — so said the venerable Hemaka, — 'explained to me the doctrine of Gotama, saying, "So it was, so it will be," all that (was only) oral tradition, all that (was only) something that increased (my) doubts.

2. 'I took no pleasure in that, but tell thou me the Dhamma that destroys desire, O Muni, which if a man has understood, and he wanders about thoughtful, he may cross desire in the world.'

3. Buddha: 'In this world (much) has been seen, heard, and thought; the destruction of passion and of wish for the dear objects that have been perceived, O Hemaka, is the imperishable state of Nibbâna.

4. 'Those who, having understood this, are thoughtful, calm, because they have seen the Dhamma, tranquil and divine, such have crossed desire in this world.'

Hemakamânavapukkhâ is ended.

10 TODEYYAMÂNAVAPUKKHÂ

1. 'He in whom there live no lusts,' — so said the venerable Todeyya, — 'to whom there is no desire, and who has overcome doubt, what sort of deliverance is there for him?'

2. 'He in whom there live no lusts, O Todeyya,' — so said Bhagavat, — 'to whom there is no desire, and who has overcome doubt, for him there is no other deliverance.'

3. Todeyya: 'Is he without breathing or is he breathing, is he possessed of understanding or is he forming himself an understanding? Explain this to me, O thou all-seeing one, that I may know a Muni, O Sakka.'

4. Buddha: 'He is without breathing, he is not breathing, he is possessed of understanding, and he is not forming himself an understanding; know, O Todeyya, that such is the Muni, not possessing anything, not cleaving to lust and existence.'

Todeyyamânavapukkhâ is ended.

11 KAPPAMĀNAVAPUKKHĀ

1. 'For those who stand in the middle of the water,' — so said the venerable Kappa, — 'in the formidable stream that has set in, for those who are overcome by decay and death, tell me of an island, O venerable man, and tell thou me of an island that this (pain) may not again come on.'
2. 'For those who stand in the middle of the water, O Kappa,' — so said Bhagavat, — 'in the formidable stream that has set in, for those overcome by decay and death, I will tell thee of an island, O Kappa.'
3. 'This matchless island, possessing nothing (and) grasping after nothing, I call Nibbāna, the destruction of decay and death.
4. 'Those who, having understood this, are thoughtful (and) calm, because they have seen the Dhamma, do not fall into the power of Māra, and are not the companions of Māra.'

Kappamānavapukkhā is ended.

12 GATUKAṆṆIMÂṆAVAPUKKHÂ

1. 'Having heard of a hero free from lust,' — so said the venerable Gatukaṇṇin, — 'who has crossed the stream, I have come to ask him who is free from lust; tell me the seat of peace, O thou with the born eye (of wisdom), tell me this truly, O Bhagavat.

2. 'For Bhagavat wanders about after having conquered lust as the hot sun (conquers) the earth by its heat; tell the Dhamma to me who has (only) little understanding, O thou of great understanding, that I may ascertain how to leave in this world birth and decay.'

3. 'Subdue thy greediness for sensual pleasures, O Gatukaṇṇin,' — so said Bhagavat, — 'having considered the forsaking of the world as happiness, let there not be anything either grasped after or rejected by thee.

4. 'What is before thee, lay that aside; let there be nothing behind thee; if thou wilt not grasp after what is in the middle, thou wilt wander calm.

5. 'For him whose greediness for name and form is wholly gone, O Brâhmaṇa, for him there are no passions by which he might fall into the power of death.'

Gatukaṇṇimâṇavapukkhâ is ended.

13 BHADRÂVUDHAMÂNAVAPU*KKH*Â

1. 'I entreat the wise (Buddha), the houseless, who cuts off desire,' — so (said) the venerable Bhadrâvudha, — 'who is free from commotion, forsakes joy, has crossed the stream, is liberated, and who leaves time behind; having heard the chief's (word), they will go away from here.
2. 'Different people have come together from the provinces, longing (to hear) thy speech, O hero; do thou expound it thoroughly to them, for this Dhamma is well known to thee.'
3. 'Let one wholly subdue the desire of grasping (after everything), O Bhadrâvudha,' — so said Bhagavat, — 'above, below, across, and in the middle; for whatever they grasp after in the world, just by that Mâra follows the man.
4. 'Therefore, knowing this, let not the thoughtful Bhikkhu grasp after anything in all the world, considering as creatures of desire this generation, sticking fast in the realm of death.'

Bhadrâvudhamâ*n*avapu*kkh*â is ended.

14 UDAYAMÂNAVAPU*KKH*Â

1. 'To Buddha who is sitting meditating, free from pollution,' — so said the venerable Udaya, — 'having performed his duty, who is without passion, accomplished in all things (dhamma), I have come with a question; tell me the deliverance by knowledge, the splitting up of ignorance.'
2. '(It consists in) leaving lust and desire, O Udaya,' — so said Bhagavat, — 'and both (kinds of) grief, and driving away sloth, and warding off misbehaviour.
3. 'The deliverance by knowledge which is purified by equanimity and thoughtfulness and preceded by reasoning on Dhamma I will tell thee, the splitting up of ignorance.'
4. Udaya: 'What is the bond of the world, what is its practice? By the leaving of what is Nibbâna said to be?'
5. Buddha: 'The world is bound by pleasure, reasoning is its practice; by the leaving of desire Nibbâna is said to be.'
6. Udaya: 'How does consciousness cease in him that wanders thoughtful? Having come to ask thee, let us hear thy words.'
7. Buddha: 'For him who both inwardly and outwardly does not delight in sensation, for him who thus wanders thoughtful, consciousness ceases.'

Udayamâ*n*avapu*kkh*â is ended.

15 POSÂLAMÂNAVAPUKKHÂ

1. 'He who shows the past (births, &c.),' — so said the venerable Posâla, — 'who is without desire and has cut off doubt, to him who is accomplished in all things (dhamma), I have come supplicatingly with a question.

2. 'O Sakka, I ask about his knowledge who is aware of past shapes, who casts off every corporeal form, and who sees that there exists nothing either internally or externally; how can such a one be led (by anybody)?

3. 'Tathâgata, knowing all the faces of consciousness, O Posâla,' — so said Bhagavat, — 'knows (also) him who stands delivered, devoted to that (object).

4. 'Having understood that the bonds of pleasure do not originate in nothingness (?), he sees clearly in this (matter), this (is) the knowledge of a perfect, accomplished Brâhmana.'

Posâlamânavapukkhâ is ended.

16 MOGHARÂGAMÂNAVAPUKKHÂ

1. 'Twice have I asked Sakka,' — so said the venerable Mogharâgan, — 'but the clearly-seeing has not explained it to me; if the divine Isi is asked for the third time, he will explain it, so I have heard.
2. 'There is this world, the other world, Brahman's world together with the world of the gods; I do not know thy view, the famous Gotama's (view).
3. 'To this man who sees what is good I have come supplicatingly with a question: How is any one to look upon the world that the king of death may not see him?'
4. 'Look upon the world as void, O Mogharâgan, being always thoughtful; having destroyed the view of oneself (as really existing), so one may overcome death; the king of death will not see him who thus regards the world.'

Mogharâgamânavapukkhâ is ended.

17 PIṄGIYAMÂNAVAPUKKHÂ

1. 'I am old, feeble, colourless,' — so said the venerable Piṅgiya, — 'my eyes are not clear, my hearing is not good; lest I should perish a fool on the way, tell me the Dhamma, that I may know how to leave birth and decay in this world.'

2. 'Seeing others afflicted by the body, O Piṅgiya,' — so said Bhagavat, — '(seeing) heedless people suffer in their bodies; — therefore, O Piṅgiya, shalt thou be heedful, and leave the body behind, that thou mayest never come to exist again.'

3. Piṅgiya: 'Four regions, four intermediate regions, above and below, these are the ten regions; there is nothing which has not been seen, heard, or thought by thee, and (is there) anything in the world not understood (by thee)? Tell (me) the Dhamma, that I may know how to leave birth and decay in this world'

4. 'Seeing men seized with desire, O Piṅgiya,' — so said Bhagavat, — 'tormented and overcome by decay, — therefore thou, O Piṅgiya, shalt be heedful, and leave desire behind, that thou mayest never come to exist again.'

Piṅgiyamânavapukkhâ is ended.

This said Bhagavat, living in Magadha at Pâsâṇaka Ketiya (the Rock Temple). Sought by sixteen Brâhmaṇas, the followers (of Bavarî, and) questioned by each of them in turn, he responded to the questions. If a man, having understood the meaning and tenor of each question, lives according to the Dhamma, then he will go to the further shore of decay and death, for these Dhammas lead to the further shore, and therefore this order of Dhamma was called 'the way to the other shore.'

1, 2. Agita, Tissametteyya, Puṇṇaka and Mettagû, Dhotaka and Upasîva, Nanda and Hemaka, the two Todeyya and Kappa, and the wise Gatukaṇṇin, Bhadrâvudha and Udaya, and also the

Brâhma*n*a Posâla, and the wise Mogharâgan, and Pi̱ngiya the great Isi, 3, 112

3. These went up to Buddha, the Isi of exemplary conduct; asking subtle questions they went up to the supreme Buddha.

4. Buddha, being asked, responded to their questions truly, and in responding to the questions the Muni delighted the Brâhma*n*as.

5. They, having been delighted by the clearly-seeing Buddha, the kinsman of the Âdi*kk*as, devoted themselves to a religious life near the man of excellent understanding.

6. He who lived according to what had been taught by Buddha (in answer) to each single question, went from this shore to the other shore.

7. From this shore he went to the other shore entering upon the most excellent way; this way is to lead to the other shore, therefore it is called 'the way to the other shore.'

8. 'I will proclaim accordingly the way to the further shore,' — so said the venerable Pi̱ngiya; — 'as he saw it, so he told it; the spotless, the very wise, the passionless, the desireless lord, for what reason should he speak falsely?

9. 'Well! I will praise the beautiful voice of (Buddha), who is without stain and folly, and who has left behind arrogance and hypocrisy.

10. 'The darkness-dispelling Buddha, the all-seeing, who thoroughly understands the world, has overcome all existences, is free from passion, has left behind all pain, is rightly called (Buddha), he, O Brâhma*n*a, has come to me.

11. 'As the bird, having left the bush, takes up his abode in the fruitful forest, even so I, having left men of narrow views, have reached the great sea, like the ha*m*sa.

12. 'Those who before in another world explained the doctrine of Gotama, saying, "So it was, so it will be," all that was only oral tradition, all that was only something that increased my doubts.

13. 'There is only one abiding dispelling darkness, that is the high-born, the luminous, Gotama of great understanding, Gotama of great wisdom,

14. 'Who taught me the Dhamma, the instantaneous, the

immediate, the destruction of desire, freedom from distress, whose likeness is nowhere.'

15. Bâvarî: 'Canst thou stay away from him even for a moment, O Piṅgiya, from Gotama of great understanding, from Gotama of great wisdom,

16. 'Who taught thee the Dhamma, the instantaneous, the immediate, the destruction of desire, freedom from distress, whose likeness is nowhere?'

17. Piṅgiya: 'I do not stay away from him even for a moment, O Brâhmaṇa, from Gotama of great understanding, from Gotama of great wisdom,

18. 'Who taught me the Dhamma, the instantaneous, the immediate, the destruction of desire, freedom from distress, whose likeness is nowhere.

19. 'I see him in my mind and with my eye, vigilant, O Brâhmaṇa, night and day; worshipping I spend the night, therefore I think I do not stay away from him.

20. 'Belief and joy, mind and thought incline me towards the doctrine of Gotama; whichever way the very wise man goes, the very same I am inclined to. (?)

21. 'Therefore, as I am worn out and feeble, my body does not go there, but in my thoughts I always go there, for my mind, O Brâhmaṇa, is joined to him.

22. 'Lying in the mud (of lusts) wriggling, I jumped from island to island; then I saw the perfectly Enlightened, who has crossed the stream, and is free from passion.'

23. Bhagavat: 'As Vakkali was delivered by faith, (as well as) Bhadrâvudha and Âḷavi-Gotama, so thou shalt let faith deliver thee, and thou shalt go, O Piṅgiya, to the further shore of the realm of death.'

24. Piṅgiya: 'I am highly pleased at hearing the Muni's words; Sambuddha has removed the veil, he is free from harshness, and wise.

25. 'Having penetrated (all things) concerning the gods, he knows everything of every description; the Master will put an end to all questions of the doubtful that (will) admit (him).

26. 'To the insuperable, the unchangeable (Nibbâna), whose likeness is nowhere, I shall certainly go; in this (Nibbâna) there will be no doubt (left) for me, so know (me to be) of a dispossessed mind.'

www.ingramcontent.com/pod-product-compliance
Lightning Source LLC
Chambersburg PA
CBHW071435300426
44114CB00013B/1438